McGlathery School C

02, 1926.

Alcorn County, Mississippi

1870 - 2002

TURNER PUBLISHING COMPANY

Saw mill crew Alcorn County, MS. Front: 4th from right is Will Whitttemore. Back row 2nd from right is Calvin Carl Hearn.

© Copyright 2002 Alcorn County Genealogical Society
All rights reserved.
Publishing Rights: Turner Publishing Company

Publishing Consultant: Keith R. Steele
Project Editor: Charlotte Harris
Designer: Susan L. Harwood

Library of Congress Control Number: 2002109641

ISBN: 978-1-68162-513-3

Limited Edition

John Franklin Byrd was a flagman on a train when he met and married Annie Woollard. She died at the age of 33. He married Elizabeth Peters Stone Bastrome. John was a carpenter and built the house at 1017 E. 5th Street. John Franklin is the son of John H. and Nancy (Lewallen) Byrd. Picture taken ca. 1880.

Mary Frances "Fannie" Surratt

TABLE OF CONTENTS

Hallie(Burrow) Harbin, Rosa (Dixon) Burrow, unidentified man, Tom Dixon, little girl is probably Ruby (Dixon) Osborne. Taken around 1916/1917.

Clarence Lamberth hauling logs to yard near railroad in West Cornith ca. 1925. Note rail care to right of horses. A farmer in the Pleasant Hill Community, Mr. Lamberth made extra money by logging in "off season."

BOOK COMMITTEE MESSAGE

At right, pictured from left: Betty Robertson, Pres.; Bonitha Rast, Vicki Roach, Sam Jones, Betty Forman, Kenneth Roaten, Editor and Keith Steele.

At left, pictured from left: Fredra Wilbanks, Doug Durm and Lila B. Voyles.

When the Alcorn County Genealogical Society was formed in 1992, we had four main goals in mind:

1. to personally gain knowledge of family histories.
2. to become familiar with our local community history
3. to develop resources to be used for public research
4. to preserve history

For these reasons we give you this Pictorial History of Alcorn County, Mississippi.

Our heritage here in Alcorn County is one in which we can be proud. Through pictures we have tried to capture it from its beginning in 1870 to the present. We wish we could have used every single picture turned in but due to space we simply could not. We are, however, very pleased with the results and overwhelmed by the generosity of those of you who have furnished us with your precious memories. Also a special thank you goes to those of you who provided the sponsored pages. Without your support and encouragement this project would not have become a reality.

The book committee, pictured above, has worked tirelessly and devoted many hours to compile all the pictures and materials turned in. I, personally, want to congratulate them on a job well done. And lastly, a thank you goes to you, who purchased a copy of this book. We hope you enjoy your stroll through the past.

Betty King Robertson, President
Alcorn County Genealogical Society

Back: Mary Ann (Allen) Abel, Usley Jane Flanagan, Mary Elizabeth Abel (Jess Abel's daughter by first marriage to Adaline Brown). Front: Jessie M. Abel, Charlie, Thomas, John. Front: Nancy, Elizabeth Ann (Betsy) Flanagan Abel, Amanda.

Herman Abel and William Floyd McLemore. Herman's grandmother, Betsy Flanagan (Mrs. Jessie) Abel and Floyd's mother, Willie Rebecca (Mrs. Whit) McLemore were sisters.

Lula Bell Stone Abel and husband Thomas Abel, son of Jessie M. Abel and Elizabeth Ann (Betsy) Flanagan Abel.

Modena Talley Aldridge made baskets with honeysuckle vines.

Rufus LaFayette Allen (b. 1862, d. 1931), youngest son of Andrew and Mary Allen, pioneer settlers of Wheeler Grove Community. Picture from late 1800s.

Sarah Bobo "Sallie" Whitlow Allen (b. 1864, d.1941) wife of Rufus Lafayette Allen. She lived in the Wheeler Grove Community, ca. 1940.

The family of Rufus and Sallie Allen, ca. 1902. Back row: Fred Allen, Tom Allen, Wallace Allen, Andy Allen. Front row: Will Allen, Rufus Allen, Harry Allen, Sallie Whitlow Allen, Mary Allen.

Will Allen, Wheeler Grove Road, preparing to hitch up his team for another work day on the farm early 1940s.

The Will Allen Family, ca. 1912. Back row: R.C. Allen, Will Allen, Florence Latch Allen, Shirley Allen, Frank Allen, Dennis Allen, Raymond Allen, Elsie Wilson Allen (wife of Raymond Allen). Front row: Grady Allen, Don Allen, Bobby Allen, Helen Allen, Mark Allen (not shown is Mary Lou Allen Wilson).

Four generations: Judy (Allen) Crum, Daisy (Forman) Allen, Tiffany (Crum) Gifford and Kylie Gifford.

Frank, Charles and Daisy (Forman) Allen, 1951-52.

Fred and Sudie Burns Allen, ca. 1960. They lived in the Wheeler Grove Community.

Willie Charles Allen, son of Frank and Daisy (Forman) Allen, 1961-62.

Dana LeAnn Allen, daughter of Wanda Allen, 1999.

Dana LeAnn Allen and Wanda Allen in 1999. Dana's Junior Prom.

Daisy (Forman) Allen and her first great-grandchild, Kylie Gifford, who was born on Daisy's birthday.

Back row: Newman Allen, Rhonda (Allen) Devers, Wanda Allen and David Allen. Front row: Daisy (Forman) Allen and Judy (Allen) Crum (five of Daisy's six children), Easter April 12, 1998.

Dana LeAnn (Allen) Jones and Kylie Gifford, 2001.

L-R: Blake Allen, Faye Allen, David Allen, November 25, 2001.

Blake Allen, son of David Allen and Vickie (Gann) Allen, 1996.

Kelly Allen, daughter of Newman and Linda (Dees) Allen.

L-R: Rickey Allen (son of Charles), Charles Allen Sr., Billy Dale Crum, Charles Allen Jr., Billy Joe Crum. Taken in 1995, both Charles Sr. and Billy Dale died in 1996.

Linda (Dees) Allen, Kelly Allen, Newman Allen and Andy Allen, Easter April 12, 1998.

Front row, L-R: James Reed Allen, Mable (Forman) Allen, Brice Wilbanks. Second row, L-R: Tommy Bonds, Sandra (Allen) Bonds, Sarah (Allen) Wilbanks, Rickey Wilbanks. Third row, L-R: Beth Wilbanks, Brian Bonds, Brent Wilbanks, Brad Bonds, Byron Bonds, 1996.

Front row: Mable (Forman) Allen, James Reid Allen. Back row: Sarah (Allen) Wilbanks and Sandra (Allen) Bonds, 1991.

James Reid Allen and Mable (Forman) Allen, 1993.

Andy Lee Allen, age 10 , son of Newman and Linda (Dees) Allen.

William Anderson Calvery, wife Arminie Byrd, daughter of John Howard and Nancy Byrd, (unknown lady on right), 1919 in Chilton, TX.

"Cope" Anderson (center with white shirt), son of William Wallace Anderson and Nancy (Byrd) Anderson, 1913.

Covus and Anderson's children, R-L: Brewer Franklin Anderson (age 24), Jewel (age 21), Crystal (age 15), Opal (age 12), Mabel (age 10) and Grace (age 6).

Armstrong Family with relatives from California. First row: Ila Wade, Iness Williams (CA), Archie, Mary Ruth, Glen Armstrong, Dalton Williams (CA). Second row: Artie Lambert, Dora Armstrong, Jessie Armstrong and Nancy Rinehart.

L-R: Elvie Byron Austin and unidentified person, taken before 1917.

L-R: James Byron Austin, Elvie Charles Austin, Robert Smith Austin, ca. 1936.

Grace Lee Austin, 1946-47. "Old Grant House," Jackson Street, Corinth, MS.

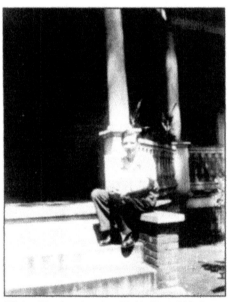

Elvie Charles Austin, 1946-47. "Old Grant House," Jackson Street, Corinth, MS.

Women in front, L-R: Grace (Smith) Austin, Anne Smith, Henda Ledbetter. Men, top to bottom: Green Lee Smith, Elvie Byron Austin. Boys pictured: (unsure of which one is which) Thomas Lee Ledbetter, Grady Joe Ledbetter, ? Jasper, ca. 1926.

Matthew Jefferson Babb (b. 1918, d.1874), father of Mary Elizabeth Babb Jones. He and his mother, Catherine Babb homesteaded land in old Tishomingo County which was later divided forming Alcorn County.

"Babbs, I took this picture after we had on our overcoats ready to start on our trip home. Leaving was the only thing unpleasant on our trip; goodbye is a hard word to say. God grant that we may be permitted to see all these loved ones again in the flesh, if not we will meet them in the 'Better Land.' This December 26, 1915. Dan W. Babb Jr."

Daniel Wesley Babb, oldest son of Matthew Jefferson Babb. He fought in the Civil War as captain, commanding Co. B of the 6th Jr. Mississippi Cav. under Bedford Forrest. He became a Methodist minister and married Sam B. Jones Sr. and Lily Ophelia Parks, parents of Sam Jr.

John W. and Frances Louisa when they were older with their daughter Fala Richardson Bailey between 1910-16.

George Barnett, Denise Sanders, (back) Sherry Crum, Jeff Bingham, Kathy (Jones) McCalister and Jerry Malone. They were in the 2nd grade at Farmington School. Mrs. Windsor had taken them all to the zoo, 1970.

Lona Bain (b. 1893, d. 1989)

Emily Ballard and Kenneth Render

Barnes and Bray Family Reunion

Mrs. Ellen Barnes, 85 years old, Dairy Queen for Day, milking cow at courthouse.

Five generations: Ellen Barnes, Gaston Rodgers, Doris Cummings, Barbara Randolph, Terry Randolph.

Arnet, Glennis "Shorty", J.B., Grady, Melzar and Cedailua Barnes, children of Clifford and Lola (Dixon) Barnes.

Lola (Dixon) Barnes, 1944.

Joyce Cedailua Barnes, Lola (Dixon) Barnes, Doris Wallace, 1944.

Doris (Wallace) Barnes and Johnny Barnes

Doris and Johnny Barnes

Grady and Doris (Wallace) Barnes

Johnny Barnes, son of Grady and Doris (Wallace) Barnes.

Maxine (Wallace) Barnes, Glennis "Shorty" Barnes, Diane Barnes, October 13, 1956.

Diane (Barnes) Copeland, Jill (Copeland) Pate, Maxine (Wallace) Barnes, May 1996.

Vera and Ben Barnes, parents of Clifford Barnes.

J.B. and Dorothy (Martin) Barnes, December 1984.

James Clifford Barnes

J.R. Barnes, first child of Clifford and Lola (Dixon) Barnes.

Leon Samuel Barnes and Jewell (Butler) Barnes, parents of Christine (Barnes) Latch, Juanita (Barnes) Robbins, Tommy Leon Barnes and James Larry Barnes.

Harold and Carol Barnes, Christmas 1985. Twin son of Melzar and Gloria Barnes.

Robert "Bob" Barnes and Belle (Peters) Barnes parents of Leon Samuel, Lee Dee Barnes and Orina (Barnes) Derrick, ca. 1915.

L-R: Ezralee (Maddox) Barringer, Bob Mays, Minnie Reece Maddox, Duell (Maddox) Reece, Walter Reece.

Dr. Joseph A. Beavo and wife, the former Kay Hudson and children, Anders and Marie Beavo, 1989.

Casey Wayne Bearden, age 15, son of Kenneth "Shorty" and Janet (Forman) Bearden.

Randi Dawn Bearden, age 14, daughter of Kenneth "Shorty" and Janet (Forman) Bearden.

Lecy Alene Bell, daughter of John Edmond and Emma Latisha (Thomason) Bell is shown here in her wedding dress. Lecy was born December 16, 1902, Houston County, TN. Lecy married David Allen "Dave" Parker, son of John Thomas and Sarah Elizabeth (Morris/Morrison) Parker on September 7, 1919 in Tennessee. They had 12 children.

July 4, 1916. Lillian Beeding, Oda Beeding, Dewey Surratt, Raymond Beeding, Joe Surratt, Laura Surratt, Martha June Crabtree, Denner Beeding, Bertha Beeding, Maudi Faye Surratt, Mattie Mae Surratt, Josephine Surratt, Verdel Beeding, Fred Beeding, Earl Surratt.

Holmes and Kate Moreland Bennett at their home, 203 Second Street, Corinth, MS.

L-R: Lloyd E. Bennett and John Peeler. This picture was made at the William Bennett home near Chalybeate, MS where Lloyd was born and reared. Lloyd lived in Corinth in the 1920s when he was a waiter at Lloyd's Café, owned by Lloyd Gann and when he operated a café for Union News at the depot. He, also, owned and operated a café in Corinth.

Families of James Francis and Priscilla (Odle) Bell and James and Roxie (Bell) Moore. L-R: Waymon Moore, son of James and Roxie (Bell) Moore; Anderson Moore, son of James and Roxie (Bell) Moore; Nell Blythe Moore, daughter of James and Roxie (Bell) Moore and the mother of Jerry B. Jones; Roxie (Bell) Moore, daughter of James F. and Priscilla (Odle) Bell; James Francis Bell, husband of Priscilla Odle; Priscilla (Odle) Bell, wife of James Francis Bell. Her name is also spelled Priscella on the census records. Priscilla is the daughter of William A. and Nancy Odle and is a half-sister to John Ransom Odle and full sister to James O'Riley and Andrew J. Odle; Mitte Bell, daughter of James F. and Priscilla Bell; Joe Bell, son of James and Priscilla Bell; John Ransom Odle, half-brother to Priscilla Odle and son of William A. Odle and Susie Wilson Odle. He was also known as Frank Odle. Front row, L-R: Hester Moore, son of James and Roxie (Bell) Moore; Alice Moore, daughter of James and Roxie (Bell) Moore; Luther Lindsey Moore, son of James and Roxie (Bell) Moore. Photo was taken in Lawrence County, AL about 1897-98. This is known because Mr. Jones' mother, Nell Blythe Moore is approximately 1 year old in the photo and she was born April 10, 1897. Since the children are not wearing any shoes, this has to be in fall months of 1897 or summer of 1898.

The driver is Robert Allen Bennett of Kossuth, MS. The man in the back seat is William Bennett, Robert's brother of Chalybeate, MS. The child is Roy Bennett, their great-nephew who is the son of Homer Bennett of Corinth. Picture taken at Shiloh National Park.

The Preston Biggers Family, taken in 2000. Front row, L-R: Beth Thomas, Betty Knight. Middle row: Elisha Knight, Emma Kate Knight, Jimmy Lee Biggers, Preston Biggers, Jerry Bigger. Back row: Preston Knight, David Thomas, Peggy Thomas, Dr. Edward Knight, Stafford Knight.

Nancy L. Berryman Jones, 1875-1900. First wife of J.A. "Jim" Jones, mother of Lottie Jones Brooks and grandmother of Fredra Brooks Wilbanks.

James Bingham, Leon Bingham, Leslie Bingham, early 1900s

James Charlie and Julia Bingham and first child, Thelma Inez Bingham, April 1918

J.B. and Gladys Bingham Potts, September 1963

L-R: Billy Bingham, Roy Bingham, Willie Max South, James Everett Bingham, Ronnie South, Linda Fay Hammock,(two women) Margaret Adkins South, Nora Smith Bingham about 1953, girl at porch, Ella Mae Bingham.

Leslie Bingham (son), Charlie Bingham (father), Hazel Bingham (daughter), Ida Reynolds Bingham (mother), Lima Bingham (daughter), Leon Bingham (son.

Cousins: Janie Bingham Arnold, Cleo Bingham Lancaster, Gladys Bingham Potts, July 1988

John L. Bivens and Mary (Harvey) Bivens, taken July 11, 1858 on their wedding day.

Brian Jay Bonds, son of Tommy and Sandra (Allen) Bonds, 1991.

Front row, L-R: Luther Bonds, Clara Bonds, Goldie Hearn Bonds holding Martha Bonds. Back row: Eunice Bonds, Oscar Bonds, R.C. Bonds, Lee Bonds and Sallie Bonds.

James Byron Bonds, son of Tommy and Sandra (Allen) Bonds, 1998.

John Braden Bonds, son of Tommy and Sandra (Allen) Bonds, 2000.

Martha "Mat" (McAfee) Booker, Daisy Booker, Thomas Daniel Booker

Standing L-R: Delbert C. Bowen, James H. Bowen. Seated: Ernest Darris Bowen, Bonitha Bowen

Charlie Martin Bowen, Lina Jane North Bowen, late 1930s

L-R: Ted Bowen, Eser D. Bowen, Pauline Bowen Rast

L-R: Robert North, Fauls North, Lina North Bowen

17

L-R: Betty Bowen Callis, Brenda Bowen Browning, Bonitha Bowen Rast

Charlie Eser D. Bowen, Zelma Crow(e) Bowen

L-R: Dr. Leroy Brackstone, Dr. Tommy Sweat and Dr. Frank Davis. Photo taken at Country Club to celebrate Dr. Brackstone and Dr. Davis having practiced medicine for 50 years.

John and Beatrice Bowers, Geraldine, Margaret Ann Bowers and Ralph Coleman, 1942 Ford car and 1946 Ford truck.

Brothers L-R: Tommy Bradley, R.E. "Rady" Bradley, John Robert "Rob" Bradley, James K. "Jake" Bradley, Maurice Catlet "Mutt" Bradley, Amos Bradley.

Back row, L-R: Jake Bradley, Gene Howell, Syble Howell, Mary Eve Bradley, Rob Bradley, Mary Ellen Bradley (child in arms), Amos Bradley, Maurice (Mutt) Bradley, (child) Maurice, Sue Lee Scott, Jimmy Scott. Middle row: Rose Emma Bradley, Mary Bradley. Front row: Edna Earl Bradley, Tommy A. Bradley, Edith Bradley, (child) Edward, Rosie Graham Bradley, (child) Rose Mary Scott, Earl Carter Bradley (holding two children), Sue Bradley, Martha Helen Bradley, Charlie Graham.

Benjamin Harrison and Elizabeth (Langston) Bragg Family. Photo taken on the Benjamin Bragg homeplace on Bragg Mountain, Alcorn County, MS. L-R: William Bragg, son of Benjamin and Elizabeth Bragg; Thomas Bragg, son of Benjamin and Elizabeth Bragg and husband of Tillie (Dees) Bragg (not shown) and father of Virginia Bragg (young child in front row between grandparents); Willis Wingo, husband of Alice (Bragg) Wingo; Alice (Bragg) Wingo, daughter of Benjamin and Elizabeth and wife of Willis Wingo; Virginia D. Bragg, daughter of Benjamin and Elizabeth Bragg; Susan Bragg, daughter of Benjamin and Elizabeth Bragg. Seated L-R: Benjamin Harrison Bragg, husband to Elizabeth (Langston) Bragg; Virginia Bragg, daughter of Thomas and Tillie (Dees) Brag; Elizabeth (Langston) Bragg, second wife of Benjamin and the mother and grandmother of the children in this photo.

Top row, L-R: Minnie O. (Bray) Wadsworth, Robert Dow Bray, William J. Bray and wife, Mary C. (Borden) Bray. Front row, L-R: Gertrude, daughter of Minnie, Nancy Jane (Streetman) Bray, John Henry Bray and wife, Paralee (Burks) Bray. Picture was sent on a postcard to Ms. Lula M. Chaney Gann (daughter of Nancy Jane from first marriage) in Burnsville, MS August 8, 1910. The picture was taken on Spruce Pine Mountain, Franklin County, AL. Nancy Jane (Streetman) Bray moved her family from the Crossroads area in Burnsville, MS after her husband, Jessie G. Bray died around 1880 (buried somewhere in Wennasoga, MS). Nancy Jane is buried in the Shady Grove Cemetery, north of Burnsville.

Bray Family Reunion (c. 1910). The Bray families would gather across the street from the Shady Grove Missionary Church every year. Many of the Bray's are buried in the Shady Grove Cemetery. The first man on the left in the overalls is John Henry Bray. The Bray's arrived into Tishmingo County in 1861 and many descendants still live in the area today. One of the original families was 2nd Lt. (CSA) William Henry Bray, buried in the New Salem Baptist Church Cemetery.

Nancy Jane (Streetman) Bray (b. 1850, d. 1927), daughter of John R. Streetman and Elizabeth J. Clay and Jessie G. Bray (b. 1852, d. 1880), son of William H. and Nancy Ann Bray. Nancy Jane is buried in Shady Grove Cemetery, Burnsville and Jessie is buried somewhere in Wennasoga, MS.

Billy J. Brooks (b. 1929), Truit A. Brooks (b. 1916, d. 1978), Vernell Brooks Killough (b. 1922), Fredra Brooks Wilbanks (b. 1917); siblings of Howard and Lottie Jones Brooks.

Margie Bradley Brooks, Billy Brooks, Joy Dale Wilbanks Rhodes, Fredra Brooks Wilbanks, Vernell Brooks Killough, May 23, 2001 at Pigeon Forge, TN.

Clara (Bridges) McCord (b. 1912, d.2000) and Franklin A. McCord (b. 1915, d. 1967). Parents were Andrew and Effie (Green) McCord.

Howard Ernest holding Nellie Vernell, Ruby Ione (Rorie) Brown holding Helen Juanita with Gilbert Earl standing in back and Mildred Ellen standing in front, ca. 1936.

Brown sisters: Lizzie Poindexter, Ann Strachan South, Ida Roye, Willie Brown, Ella Strachan and Josie Voyles

Mike and Debra Brown with her grandmother Vadeen Wilbanks, 1999.

Lois Rorie and Ione (Rorie) Brown, daughters of Eugene and Lena Rorie with their cousin Walter Lee Rorie, son of James Frederick Wither Rorie and Sarah Elizabeth Rorie. Picture taken in 1986 at the Eugene Rorie home.

John Edgar Brown, Annie Mattie Bell Singley and Eller Fay Brown. Father, mother and sister of Eller Drew (Brown) Cox.

Mike and Debra Brown

The Bumpass Family, ca. 1940. L-R: Rufus Malcolm, Minnie Ethel Mattox (wife of Rufus), Mary Eva (wife of James Ward Rogers), Madgie Beatrice and husband Marcus Homer Fryar, Anna Priscilla (wife of James Monroe Roaten), Margaret Catherine and husband Will F. Marecle.

Early 1950s photo of some of the Bumpass clan. L-R: Margaret Catherine, Rufus Malcolm, Golda (wife of Arthur Criswell Bumpass), Arthur Criswell, Minnie Ethel Mattox, Mary Bumpass Rogers, Madgie Beatrice (wife of Homer Fryar).

Troy Bumpass and daughter Dimple Bumpass Yarber standing beside the newly set tombstone for Dr. Gabriel Bumpass founder of Waterloo, AL in Lauderdale County during a dedication ceremony in honor of Dr. Bumpass, great-great-grandfather of Troy. Troy served as an alderman for Corinth in the mid 1950s. He now serves as chairman in three positions: the Urban Renewal Commission, TVA Regional Housing Authority and the Jury Commission. Troy donated the property for the now existing City Park and has operated a Hosiery Mill located on South Parkway since 1954.

Kenneth R. Roaten and cousin Dimple Bumpass Yarber beside their great-great-great-grandfather Dr. Gabriel Bumpass's newly dedicated tombstone (founder of Waterloo, AL). Dr. Gabriel Bumpass created the "Bumpass Trail" from the Carolinas down into Tennessee and Alabama. A number of the doctor's descendants settled in what is now Alcorn County around Corinth and Kossuth areas.

James Robert Bumpass (b. Jan. 2, 1954, d. Nov. 11, 1936) and wife Cleopatra "Cosey" Whittle Bumpass (b. Jan. 7, 1854, d. Feb. 19, 1936).

Ruby Bumpass and Velma Lancaster

C.T. and Ruth Bullard

The Burcham twins, left Middleton (b. 1889, d. 1977) and right Winston (b. 1889, d. 1972).

Family of William S. (b. 1838, d. 1922) and Nancy Ann Palmer Burcham (b. 1835, d. 1911). William served in Co. C, Moreland's Regt., Alabama Cav., CSA. L-R: Tommy Burcham (d. 1940), Frank Burcham, John Henry Burcham (b. 1863, d. 1949), Hezicar Burcham (b. 1866, d. 1957), Levi Burcham (b. 1889, d. 1961), Eligah Hensley Burcham (b. 1873, d. 1950), Annie Burcham Stricklin (b. 1877, d. 1996) ca. 1940.

Elmer Burress and Jewel Horn Burress, owners of Burress Generator & Starter Shop, formerly located on Tate Street.

The Burns Family of Tuscumbia, Alcorn County, MS. Top row, left: Bruce Butler, Effie Dunn, Martin Butler, Leonard Nichols, Elbie/Velma Mathis, Beatrice Coleman, Lola Mathis, Elbie Coleman, (back of Beatrice and Lola) Will and Sally Reardon, Nonie Coleman, Jewel Coleman, Ruby Odle, J.V. Odle, Martin Dixon, Stella Dixon, (behind Elbie and Nonie) Clovis Carper. Row 2: Chester Burns, Corbitt Whitted, Everett Butler, Duke Mathis, Erby Butler. Row 3: Gladys Bass and little dog, Johnnie Bass, Leonard Ingram, Clye Burns, Velma Burns, Feak Rogers holding son Curtis, Bid Mathis holding Betty Sue Burns, Mary Mathis, Tynce Hopper, Opal Bell, (above Opal) J.B. Butler holding Willie D. Butler. In front: T. Baby Butler, Nancy Butler, Maude Butler, Myrtle Nichols, Bruce Nichols, Ethel Ingram holding baby Frank. Row 4: Boy Coleman, Lillian Coleman holding Hugh baby, Mary Rogers holding Sybil, Olen Coleman, Shorty Coleman, Audrey Coleman, S.M. Coleman, Estil Coleman.

Rev. Bobby Neal Burress, son of James Elmer Burress and Jewel Cecil Horn Burress. Retired school teacher and former principal of Corinth Junior High School, former superintendent of education of Iuka Public Schools, former vice-president of Blue Mountain College and retired Baptist minister. Pastored over 45 years and preached in most Baptist churches in northeast Mississippi. Married Quida Faye Smith and is father of Vicki Lynn Burress Roach, Cindy Neal Burress Leatherwood, David Randal Burress and Judy Ann Burress Whitehead; grandfather of Bobby and Amy Roach, Jennafer Leatherwood and Bryson Duncan.

Rubin Elbert Burress (b. 1876, d. 1922) son of Reubin Burress and Samantha Emaline Taylor Ozella Viola Tittle (b. 1880, d. 1962), daughter of James C. "Jim" Tittle and Julia Adeline Hopkins.

William "Bill" Burrow and Rosa (Dixon) Burrow. Taken before they married.

Bill Burrow, Robert Burrow, Billy Burrow, Rosa (Dixon) Burrow, Nell (Burrow) Butler and Connie Butler, early 1950s.

Billy Norris Burrow and daughter Ginger Leigh Burrow. Taken in Indian Creek Cemetery, Chewalla, TN in 1988.

Around 1942 this photo was taken of Newton Gilbert "Boss" Butler and his wife Armedia Millie Smith Butler. The children, back left: Burnis Gilbert Tyson and Mattie Jo Osborn. The youngest was Archie Noel Tyson, brother of Gilbert.

Newton Gilbert "Boss" Butler (b. February 2, 1873, d. May 29, 1960) and wife Armedia Millie Smith Butler (b. August 10, 1879, d. Jan. 21, 1966) ca. early 1950s.

Connie (Butler) Rowsey, Audrey Butler, Nell (Burrow) Butler and Jimmy Butler, ca. 1964.

Connie Butler, Robert Burrow, Mattie Bell (Henson) Burrow, Jimmy Butler and Nell Butler. Taken November 1960 on top of Backbone at the Burrow's Place.

23

Rufus Turner Bynum and Kate Jones Bynum, 1881.

Bynum Family Ancestors. Laura Alice Jones married George W. Bynum, 1909.

Bynum Family Ancestors. Laura Alice Jones married George W. Bynum, 1909.

John H. Byrd was Grace Pundt's great-grandfather and Nancy (Lewallen) was her great-grandmother. These are their first six children. Back row: Rev. John H. Byrd, the first pastor at Union Baptist Church; Monroe Washington Byrd, William H. died in the Civil War, Matthew Byrd in white dress. Front row: Eli Byrd, Nancy (Lewallen) Byrd holding Mary Byrd, Armenia Byrd standing. As far as they know John H. had 18 children. There were more children with Nancy Gann.

Aunt Lettie, brother and sisters. Lettie was the wife of Andrew Jackson Byrd.

Chris and Cleo Byrd with daughter.

James Christopher Columbus Byrd

Goddard Callahan and Ora Lee (Jobe) Callahan

Spring 1908, Samuel Stevens Calvary (b. 1877, d. 1920), Eddie Belle Scott Calvary (b. 1891, d. 1978), Lona Susan Calvary (b. 1908, d. 1989).

Children of Samuel Stevens and Eddie Belle Scott Calvary. L-R: Lona Susan (b. 1908, d. 1989), J.B. Randolph (b. 1912, d. 1995), Jewell Eddie (b. 1910, d. 1998) and baby John Hillie (b. 1915, d. 1991).

Lily Pearl Putt Carter (b. 1895, d. 1955) and husband George Ezekiel "Zeke" Carter (b. 1894, d. 1949).

Lily Pearl Putt Carter (b. 1895, d. 1955)

Back row, L-R: Edith Carter, Lola Carter, Macile Carter, Estelle Carter Stewart. Seated: Lily Pearl Putt Carter (mother of Edith, Lola, Macile and Estell) holding Marilyn Lynette Stewart, daughter of Estell in 1943.

Winfred and Virginia Doles Carter, Marilyn Stewart and Mike Jones in 1951.

Mike and Penny Chambers, twins Shea and Tyler, August 1989

George Cheek, son of Silas and Edith (Phillips) Cheek, brother of Sarah (Cheek) Rorie.

Charles Chastain and Henry Lee Hardin at Hardin Grocery across from Green Laundry.

Rev. Robert Greenberry Childers (b. 1853, MS, d. 1917 (MS). A Free Will Baptist minister, son of John E. and Mary Bonds Childers.

Katie McElyea Childers (b. 1856, MS, d. 1939, TN). Wife of Rev. R.G. Childers, daughter of Elias C. and Nancy McElyea.

Irene Clark (b. 1894, d. 1920) and Byrl Clark (b. 1893, d. 1918). Parents Emma (Suitor) and T. Albert Clark.

The Alvin and Dora Childers Family. Back row: Odis, Georgia, Roy V., Altha, Alvin, Alford and Dora Mae. Front row: Dorothy, James, Sarah and Milton, Thanksgiving 1953.

Daughters of Emma E. (Suitor) and Albert Clark. L-R: Irene (b. 1894, d. 1920), Alice (b. 1895, d. 1969), Lillian (b. 1896, 1985), Mamie (b. 1899, d. 1974).

Twins Calvin (b. 1899, MS, d. 1975, MS) and Alvin Childers (b. 1899, MS, d. 1971, TN), sons of Rev. R.G. and Katie Childers.

John W. Clements, Emmaline LuEllen Clements. From Pontotock, MS to Alcorn County, MS.

John Walter Clements, father of Oswald Clements and grandfather of Edna Shipman.

Tom McKinney Coleman Family, ca. 1920. Maude Modina Hancock Coleman. Boys in back, L-R: Aaron Bilbo Coleman, Ronel Lonzo Coleman, boy standing in front is Steve Clayton Coleman and the boy in Maude's lap is Thomas Hill Coleman.

Children and wives of Tom and Maude Hancock Coleman: Ronel, Thomas Hill, Aaron and Steve Clayton Coleman.

Thomas McKenny Coleman holding Larry Coleman, Mike Coleman and Frazier Coleman.

Thomas Hill Coleman and Larry Coleman

Evelyn Coleman, Ethelyn Barlow, Claude Walter Stoop, Willie Lou Stoop

Travis Len Coleman Sr., Debra Jean (Robbins) Coleman (daughter of Shirley Butler), Michael Scott Coleman and Travis Len "T.C." Coleman Jr.

Jennifer Lyn, Jessica Lee and Walter Hill Coleman

Jennifer Lyn Coleman, Walter Hill Coleman and Jessica Lee Coleman

James Bertram Combs and Delia Combs. James Bertram Combs was born in 1865 in Augusta, GA. He came to Corinth in 1889 to become principal of the Corinth Colored School, a position he held for 27 years. In recognition of his service, the city of Corinth named a housing development, Combs Court in his honor. James Combs died in 1946 at the age of 81. He and his wife Delia are buried in Forest Hill Cemetery.

Ronel "Babe" Lonzo Coleman

Ronel "Babe" Coleman with wife Dimple Dilworth Coleman and children, Ralph Dilworth standing and Dennis in Dimple's lap.

Grace and Ruth Cornelius

Mark M. Cornelius family and friends at Liddon Lake Sunday afternoon in 1945.

Mark M. Cornelius Family

Christine Cornelius grinding sorghum cane getting ready to make molasses.

Christine and Elizabeth Cornelius cooking molasses on family farm near Oakland School.

Audie Cornelius at old homeplace.

Mark M. Cornelius and family Easter Sunday, 1960.

Sally Narmore Cosby and her grandchildren; Annie Meyers' children, 1920s.

Mark M. Cornelius Family

Mark. M. Cornelius Family

Cox Family, ca. 1930. Sitting is Emily Keslar Cox (mother, b. 1847, d. 1934.). Standing: Ella Cox Rinehart (b. 1868, d. 1949), Willie Idella Cox Rinehart Rorie (b. 1874, d. 1944), Nannie Belle Cox Richardson (b. 1872, d. 1966).

L-R: Mary Glenn Cox (b. 1929, d. 1960), Eddie Belle Scott Calvary Cox (b. 1891, d. 1978) holding Loyd David "Bud" Cox (b. 1932), Jerry David Cox (b. 1863, d. 1943). Spring 1933.

Charles Burton Cox of Rienzi served in the U.S. Army between May 1956 and March 1958. SP3(T) Cox was stationed at Fort Jackson, SC when discharged in March 1958.

L-R: Zelma Mae Crowe Bowen, Alma M.T. Crowe Hesler, 1912.

Julia Thigpen Crowe

Isaac Calwell Crowe

Crow Family Home. Dolphus Crow and J.C. Crow, 1957.

Crowe and Smith Reunion, 1929, Hwy. 45 North at George Smiths. Back row, L-R: Tommy Smith, John Crowe, Isaac Crowe, George Washington Smith, Arthur McCarter, Willie Bea McAnally, Ilene Dodd, Ethel Morgan, Delbert Forsyth, Allen Smith, Eser D. Bowen, baby James Bowen. Seated, L-R: Nora Smith Dodd, Leona Crowe, Julia Thigpen Crowe, Rebecca Crowe Smith, Lillie Smith McCarter, baby Ethleen McCarter. Bottom step: Charles McCarter, Lawrence McCarter, Margarette McCarter, Maxine Smith, Eunice Voyles Smith, Zelma Crowe Bowen, baby Delbert Bowen.

Mary Margrette "Granny" Crum and great-granddaughter Ruth Wilbanks, 1924.

Charlie and Mollie Crum

Judy Gale Allen, daughter of Frank and Daisy (Forman) Allen.

Billy Dale Crum, Judy (Allen) Crum, Billy Joe and Tiffany Crum, 1984.

July (Allen) Crum, Billy Dale Crum, Tiffany and Billy Joe Crum, 1986.

Tiffany Gale Crum, daughter of Billy Dale and Judy (Allen) Crum, 1998

Judy (Allen) Crum and Billy Dale Crum.

Billy Dale Crum and Billy Joe Crum.

Billy Joe Crum, son of Billy Dale and July (Allen) Crum, 10th grade.

Tiffany (Crum) Gifford and Kylie Gifford.

Henry and Liline Dalton. Henry published two books of poems, Hill Born in 1944 and Process of Becoming in 1977.

Marcus Taylor Dancer, son of William Walter and Narcissa (Brown) Dancer (b. October 27, 1873 in Alcorn County, MS) married Dollie Oaks (b. November 17, 1881), daughter of Leonard and Millie (Johnson) Oaks. They had four children, pictured are William, Marcus, Polly, Dollie and Ruby. Not yet born was their fourth child, Jennie.

W.W. Dancer Family Home in the Hopewell Community, ca. 1910. Pictured are Bricy Mullins (third from left), Bell Dancer (fourth from left), Lucy Jane Dancer (fifth from left) and Josie Dancer (second from left). Unable to identify the others.

Johnny Dancer was often a topic of conversation during his annual birthday celebration which was usually celebrated by more than 100 people. At age 99, he was recorded as "one of Alcorn County's oldest citizens, having lived all his life on the same hill in the Hopewell Community." During an interview, it was stated that "blindness hadn't slowed Johnny much," at that time he was still going to town to transact business and visit old friends. Johnny's parents, W.W. Dancer and Narcissa (Brown) Dancer, were married in old Tishomingo County on February 17, 1853. Johnny never married and is buried in the Hopewell Cemetery.

Parker-Bell-Dancer: Pictured is the family of David Allen Parker. Dave and his first wife, Lecy Alene Bell had 12 children. Front row, L-R: Leon, Opal, Ivanell, Jewell, Dorothy and Alton Earl. Second row, R-L, Arnold, Evelyn, Betty, Levon, Laveda and Paulette. In the center is Mary Narcissus "Polly" Dancer Parker, Dave's second wife. Their children Patricia and David are in the back row, left to right.

Pretty dresses, pretty women, Myrtle Smith Pitts and Willie Smith Dean.

Dr. and Mrs. Davis and Hull Davis and family at celebration for Dr. Davis having practiced medicine for 50 years in 1984.

The Dancer Girls: Polly, Jennie and Ruby, daughters of Marcus Taylor Dancer and Dollie Oaks Dancer, were raised in the Hopewell Community in Alcorn County. Years after raising their children, they would all three move back in together to share their golden years until such time as they required separate care. Many people will remember visiting them during occasions when their Uncle Johnny had his birthday celebration, which was a big event.

Ada Maddox (Mrs. Alec) Dean

Thomas Franklin Dean, only child of Ada Maddox Dean and Alec Dean, ca. 1937.

Dustin Devers, 10 years old, son of Mike and Rhonda (Allen) Devers.

Hillie Deese and wife Bell Rickman Deese

Alfred Martin Dilworth (b. 1853, b. 1903) and S.A. (Quinnie Caldwell) married July 23, 1873.

The William Denver Eshee Family: Judy, Denver, Emily and Judge W.D. Eshee, Starkville, MS.

Front, L-R: James B. Dillingham, Joshua H. Dillingham. Standing: Anna Eliza Dillingham, Alice Ellen Dillingham, Ida Elizabeth Dillingham.

33

Ruby Dilworth and James Douglas Morton were married October 26, 1913. She was the daughter of Cora and Henry Dilworth. He was the son of Jane Ellen (Jennie) Fitzgerald and Wilson M. Morton Sr., all of the Biggersville area in Alcorn County, MS. Their children: Robert, Roy, Marcus, Jennie Mae, Louise, Pauline, Margaret, Frances, Tommie and Frank Morton. Ruby Morton (b. October 27, 1894, d. September 29, 1939) and Douglas Morton (b. December 14, 1886, d. November 21, 1965) are buried in New Hope Presbyterian Church Cemetery at Biggersville, MS.

Standing, L-R: Miller Dilworth, Beatrice Dilworth. Sitting, L-R: Mary Dilworth, Dimple Dilworth, Jennie Dilworth.

Abe and Ben Dilworth

Beatrice and Dimple Dilworth

Abe and Mary Dilworth and grandchildren: Geraldine, Margaret Ann, Peggy Bowers and Ralph Coleman.

Dilworth Reunion in 1936, made at the Walker Dalton Home. First row, L-R: Louise Morton, Mildred Day (Roberts), Margaret Morton, Pauline Morton, Imogene Morris, Frances Morton, Mable Meeks, Sally Day's grandson, Tommie Morton, Barney Morris, R. Nell Morris, Ruth Morris, Estelle Morris, Ruby Morton, Frank Morton held by Douglas Morton. Second row, L-R: Jack Conn, Mary Katherine Dearman, Dora Dilworth, Ben Dilworth, Walker Dalton, Mary Dalton, Jennie Dilworth, Sally Day, Abe Dilworth, Mary "Abe" Dilworth, Mary Lee Dilworth (Bridges), Albert Morris, Sally Day's granddaughter, Velma Dilworth. Back row, L-R: Roger Conn, Katherine Dilworth, Jennie Mae Morton, Dorothy Dilworth, Mamie Dalton Meeks, Grady Meeks, Beatrice Dilworth, Robert Patterson, Mary Dilworth, George Day, Margueritte Dilworth, Anita Morris, Sarah Dilworth, Dimple Dilworth, Tom Day, Frank Conn, Gifford Morris.

Miller Dilworth, MD

Back row: Christy (Brown) Burcham, Scottie Lane Dix. Front row: Misty Dawn Brown Dix (adopted by Scottie) and Mary Ann (Childers, Brown) Dix.

Lon Dixon and Tom Dixon

Ruth (Dixon) Wooten, Elmo Dixon, Tom Dixon, Ruby (Dixon) Osborne, Minnie (Nelms) Dixon and Lola (Dixon) Barnes at the homeplace built by Tom located by Kings Mountain School, ca. 1917.

Sarah Louvinia (DeLoach) Dixon, mother of Thomas Jefferson Dixon.

Ruby (Dixon) Osborne, Rosa (Dixon) Burrow and Jenny (Dixon) Pittman. Daughters of Tom and Minnie (Nelms) Dixon.

Thomas Jefferson Dixon and Minnie (Nelms) Dixon, mid 1940s in Chewalla, TN.

Homeplace of Thomas Jefferson Dixon and Minnie (Nelms) Dixon in Chewalla, TN. They moved to Tishomingo County, MS in 1948.

Wanda Gail (Armstrong) Day, Elmo Dixon, Billy Armstrong, Nelletta (Dixon) Armstrong, Velma (Barnes) Dixon, early 1960s.

Elonza Neeley Dixon taken on his 60th birthday, December 25, 1959.

Front row: Billy Armstrong, Kenneth Wooten (Ruth (Dixon) Wooten's son), Gaines Hill Dixon. Back row: Thelma Ray Pittman (Jenny (Dixon) Pittman's son), Loyd Dixon, Robert Burrow (Rosa (Dixon) Burrow's son), J. W. Dixon, Elmo Dixon holding Thelma's son.

Five generations of Dixons: standing is Charles "Sonny" Watkins holding his daughter. Seated are Sidney Jefferson Dixon, Minnie (Nelms) Dixon and Pearl (Dixon) Wadkins.

Front row: Erma Wooten(Kenneth's wife), Nell (Burrow) Butler. Second row: Ola Mae (Wooten) King, Ruby (Dixon) Osborne, Hallie (Burrow) Harbin, Betty Pittman (Thelma's wife), Velma (Barnes) Dixon (Elmo's wife). Back row: Nelletta (Dixon) Armstrong (Elmo's daughter), Rosa (Dixon) Burrow, Mattie Bell (Henson) Burrow (Robert's wife).

Earl and Juanita Driver

Carolyn Duffer (daughter of Bill Pundt), Brian Duffer (grandson of Bill Pundt), Jessica Duffer (great-granddaughter of Bill Pundt).

Ed Driver Family. Seated is Maggie; second row Earl, Dexter and Susie; third row Herman, Lillian and J.G.; in back is Ed Driver.

Carolyn Duffer and sons Jeff and Brian

Jessica Duffer

Bob Dunn and Nina Jones Dunn, parents of Dessie Ree Dunn Lassiter, J.T. Dunn and Kerry L. Dunn.

Sidney Ishmael Duncan

Back row: Willie Mai Durm and Douglas Durm. Front row: Harriet Durm Clardy, Homer Appleton, Chris Clardy, 1996.

J.T. and Josephine Johnson Dunn, parents of John R. Dunn, Betty Dunn Barres and Linda Dunn Turner.

Willie Mai, Harriet and Douglas Durm, 1963.

Harriet Durm, "Miss Corinth" 1976

Georgia Ellen Eaker (b. 1889, d. 1975) wife of Archie Randolph Hurley.

Louis F. Earthman Family, Rienzi, MS, ca. 1876. Louis (b. 1845, Corinth, Alcorn County, MS) son of Lucinda (Earhart) and John H. Earthman. He was a private in Ham's Regiment during the War Between the States. One battle in Corinth, he was taken as Prisoner of War and held in several Union prisons, one being Fort Delaware. Wife, Mary Ann Margaret (Savage) (b. 1846, Rienzi, Alcorn County, MS) daughter of Eleanor Jane (Shields) and Rev. Hamilton "Ham" Giles Savage. Mary Ann Margaret taught school at the "Savage School" located at Hinkle Creek near present site of Hinkle Creek Baptist Church. Nannie Kate (b. 1872, Rienzi, Alcorn County, MS), daughter of Louis and Mary Earthman seated on far right.

Sisters, L-R: Judy Hudson Eshee, Betty Hudson McAnally, Kay Hudson Beavo

The Elliott Family. In front is Roy (b. 1912, d. 1998). Seated, L-R: Grady (b. 1921), Jewel Goforth (b. 1905, d. 2001), Ruby Miller (b. 1915), Erma Rhodes (b. 1909), Boyd (b. 1907, d. 2000).

Bryan and Lavonia Essary, and daughters Alexis and April, October 1995.

Bill and Cheryl Essary and sons Jason, Jeremy and Joshua, October 1995.

Seated, L-R: Josephine (Essary) Hindman, Ruby (Borden) Essary, Larry Hill Essary and Betty Joan (Essary) Bullard. Standing, L-R: James Larry Essary, Judy (Essary) Hughes, Martin Ray Essary, Cosette (Essary) Hardin and Bobby Eugene Essary, 1963.

This picture was made in front of the Joe Walker Faircloth house on Foote Street in Corinth, MS. Front row, L-R: John R. Alvis, Frances (Taylor) Bennett, Birdie (Faircloth) Alvis, Onada (Alvis) Bennett, Inez (Faircloth) Bennett and Dora (Faircloth) Thompson. Back row, L-R: Joe Walker Faircloth, Roy Bennett, Lloyd E. Bennett holding daughter Martha Lee Bennett, Sue Faircloth, Wllie Bennett, Homer Bennett and Beatrice (Lloyd) Faircloth.

John Robert Alvis and his wife, Martha Alberta Faircloth Alvis. After their marriage in 1887, they continued to live in Alcorn County where John and his brother-in-law, Robert Allen Bennett, operated a store, which they bought from Jack Ginn at Hightown. The Alvis family moved to Ripley, MS in 1910 to take care of John's mother.

Christopher Ludwig Fink born in Hamburg, Germany, grandfather of Josephine Johnson Dunn.

Mildred Brock Faulkner and children: Buddy Faulkner, Wanda Gotcher, Janet Lee, Barbara Thomas and Kathy Garrison, February 1993.

Gladys Ferguson and Marie Anderson

Elvie Fisher and Velma Lancaster

Nancy Jane (Newman) Flanagan, Martha Elvera (Mrs. G.V.) Bingham, Sara E. (Mrs. Hardy) Smith and Emily ?, daughters of Adam and Ailsa Newman.

The second girl from left is Joyce (Thomas) Forman; girl at far right is Verna (Thomas) Harris; other children are unknown. Joyce and Verna are the daughters of Russell and Hallie (Wilson) Thomas, 1946.

Claud Forman and Julie Bell (Thrasher) Forman. Parents of Clyde, Carl, Cleatus, John Robert, Clinton, James, Richard, Billy, Daisy (Forman) Allen, Mable (Forman) Allen and three other daughters. Claud had one daughter, Gladys (Forman) Elam, Morgan, Potts by a previous marriage.

Nancy J. Newman Flanagan and her sister Martha Newman Bingham

Julie Bell (Thrasher) Forman on her 82nd birthday September 1982 (Richard Forman's mother).

Thomas Allen Flanagan and Effie Florence (Tolar) Flanagan (first wife).

Usley Jane (Flanagan) Abel and Luther Abel (Ables)

Thomas Allen Flanagan, Opal (baby), Callie (Floyd) Flanagan (second wife).

Three generations: baby Terry Wayne Forman, Danny Wayne Forman and Billy Wayne Forman.

Richard Aaron Forman, Ronnie Forman and Betty (Griffin) Forman, 1981.

Terry Wayne Forman, son of Danny Wayne and Teresa (Michael) Forman, 2000.

Seated, L-R: Arthur F. Hoyle (principal of Hoyle High School), Celia Fry (teacher), ___Hoyle, Semalle Hoyle (teacher), Jennie Hoyle Hayes (teacher). Standing, L-R: Minnie Hoyle Turner (teacher), Hattie Hoyle Fry, Maggie Hoyle (teacher), Helen Hoyle (RN).

Willie Odle Forsythe and Etoy Langston Odle with sons in both chairs, James Russell and Edwin Eugene Odle.

Burwell Pope Fullilove (b. April 4, 1856, d. May 20, 1940) began preaching at age 14. In 1878 he was licensed to preach and served many churches in north Mississippi until 1922.

Jennie Fuell, age 80.

Holt, McCord and Gammel Family Reunion, 1924.

Charlene (Lancaster) Gatewood, daughter of Charlie Lancaster.

Mervin Gatewood and nephew Jason Gatewood

Cora Mae Gifford (b. April 1, 1872, d. July 21, 1904) and Henry Terry Dilworth (b. October 13, 1873, d. December 25, 1944) were married December 7, 1892. Born to them were: Ruby (Morton), Estelle (Morris), Mae Henry (Elam), Glenn and Eveline (Goddard).

Paralee Gilton and children in 1909. Marshall Gilton, wife Lillie Lambert Gilton, Tennessee Gilton Roberts, Julia Gilton Bingham and Loudell Gilton Knight. Not pictured is daughter Mattie Gilton Lambert.

Sons of Sally Jones Gooch and Nicholas Gooch. They lived in Alcorn County, MS and moved to Texas in the 1870's migration.

The home of Joseph W. and Jennie L. Green located on Old Stage Road west of Rienzi, MS in 1901. L-R: Joe F. (b. 1893, d. 1963), Joseph Watson (b. 1858, d. 1935), Jennie V. (b. 1896, d. 1987), Jennie Luelah (b. 1868, d. 1941), sitting in her lap Jessie Ray (b. 1901, d. 1951), Minnie Kate (b. 1894, d. 1978), Kittie C. (b. 1891, d. 1980). Standing in back is Annie F. (b. 1888, d. 1949) and Effie L. (b. 1889, d. 1938).

Kittie C. Green (Suitor) (b. August 1, 1891, d. June 29, 1980). Picture was made before marriage October 17, 1910.

Family of Joseph Watson and Jennie Luelah Green, ca. 1921. Bottom row, L-R: Henry McCord, Robert Taylor, Clara McCord, Mable Suitor, Beatrice Suitor, Christine Suitor, Albert Suitor, Joseph Suitor. Children back of them: Franklin McCord, Ruth Taylor, Viola Taylor. Adults, L-R: Effie and Andrew McCord, Mark and Annie Taylor (back of his shoulder sitting: Joseph W. and Jennie L. Green, behind them Kittie and Robert Suitor, he is holding Lorraine, Elbert holding Howard and Minnie Kate Suitor. Back row: Jessie Morris, Jennie and Edward Marecle, Joe F. and Carrie (McCord) Green, he is holding Cecil.

George Ann (Mitchell) Griffin and John Price Griffin, taken before 1918.

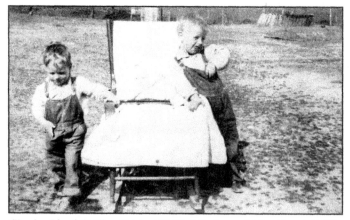

Charles Lloyd Griffin, Shirley (Griffin) Butler and Glen Oneal Griffin. Children of Clarence and Fanny Griffin, 1932.

John Price Griffin and Clarence Floyd Griffin, early 1940s.

Kate (Farris) Griffin and Claud Griffin, ca. 1925.

Clarence Floyd Griffin, 1945.

Leffie Lillie (Pounds) Lefever and twin Effie Willie (Pounds) Griffin, ca. 1953.

Fanny (McCrary) Griffin, May 1973.

David Lawrence Griffin, son of Charles and Effie (Pounds) Griffin, ca. 1961.

Cynthia Jodene (Griffin) Burress, May 1987.

Betty (Griffin) Forman, Shirley (Griffin) Butler, Fanny (McCrary) Griffin and Glen Oneal Griffin. Fanny and three of her four children, July 15, 1984.

Fanny (McCrary) Griffin, Shirley (Griffin) Butler and Elizabeth Diane (Butler) Miller, May 1973.

Danny Floyd Griffin, August 1990.

Valerie (Griffin) Webb, daughter of Ricky Griffin.

Glen Oneal Griffin and Betty Sue (Fagg) Griffin, August 15, 1992.

Katherine Aileen (Griffin) Chuck, Glen Morton "Morty" Griffin and in front is Joanna Sue Griffin. Children of Glen Oneal Griffin and Betty Sue (Fagg) Griffin, May 11, 1983.

Charles Lloyd Griffin, Effie Willie (Pounds) Griffin, David Lawrence Griffin. Front row: Danny Floyd Griffin and Cynthia Jodene (Griffin) Burress, May 1975.

Rev. A.D. Gurley, pastor of First Pentecostal Church. A.D. Gurley, wife Mickey, children: Ruth, Joe, Doris and Wrence.

Jim and Carrie Hinton Hamlin with Roy Hamlin Jr. Jim Hamlin died and Carried married Bill Madden. Her great-grandchildren are David, Gayle and Ruth Hamlin, ca. 1920.

Dora and Maude Hancock

Three Hanley sisters: Doris, Dixie and Dot, 1920s.

Perry A. Johns and Benjamin Henry Hanley just before WWI.

John J. Harden (b. 1879, MS, d, 1966, MS) a Pentecostal minister and Sarah Elizabeth Timmons (b. 1883, AL, d. 1966, MS) married 1897 in Mississippi.

Ervin W. Hardin (b. 1901, d. 1978) and wife Lou Annie Burcham Hardin (b. 1904, d. 1947).

Napoleon Bonaparte Hardwick and wife Nancy Emaline Elledge Hardwick

Hardin Grocery across from Humphrie Home; Henry Lee Hardin and brother Alton Hardin.

Lillie Rachel (McCrary) Harvey, early 1950s.

49

Dorothy Hanley Hasseltine, 1916.

Family of William Payton Hathcock and wife Janie South Hathcock. L-R: Isdo, Edow, Pauline, William, Frank, Janie, Pearl and William Odell, who was the father of Jimmy Hathcock, owner of Jimmy's Jewelry Store in Corinth. The picture was taken about 1917-18 in front of the First Presbyterian Church located on the corner of Foote and Franklin Streets.

Anne Haynie and daughter Evie Haynie, 1942.

Zelma Hearn, daughter of Carl and Lucy Whittemore Hearn; Nancy Rinehart, daughter of Lorenzo Dow and Caroline Branstutters Rinehart (Nancy lived to be almost 100 years old, never married).

Zelma Lucille Hearn and Annie Mae Hearn, daughters of Carl and Lucy Hearn in the Hickory Flat area, Alcorn County.

Lee. L. Hasseltine, MD; Dorothy Hanley Hasseltine and Lee Luther Hasseltine Jr., 1940.

Benjamin and Donie Gwyn Hearn; six of their eight children and Donie's mother.

John Samuel Hearn and wife Flora Ann Yarber. Children Clarence, Sylvia, Dossey, Herbert and Hubert.

Monsie and Callie Hearn with children Vardeman and Ruby.

Back row: Zelma, Carl, Lucy holding Elizabeth, Annie Mae. Middle: Marvin, Oner Dee, Cecil and in front David Carl, ca. 1924.

Miss Maude Herman (b. July 27, 1884, d. November 16, 1958) daughter of Dr. J.K. Herman of Kossuth, seated on lawn in front of Herman home. Miss Herman gave the photo to her friend, Grace Walker Lamberth.

Marion Lodusky Elizabeth Marsh Henderson (b. 1850, d. 1923), wife of Green Berry Henderson, pioneer settlers near Lone Oak Church. She was the daughter of William Elston Marsh and Elizabeth Bullock Marsh and the mother of Sarah Elizabeth "Sallie" Henderson Smith, Robert Henderson, James Samuel "Sam" Henderson, Margaret Jane "Maggie" Henderson Spencer and Minnie Henderson, ca. 1920.

Tom Hinton and Lula Bingham McMullar Hinton

Melvin Elmo "Bill" Hood and Thelma Bingham married October 29, 1932.

Melvin Garfield Hood and Mary Victoria Hood, Whitfield Pharmacy July 1966.

1987, Hoyt Horn (on left) founder of Horn Real Estate and former Alcorn County Circuit Clerk, 1940-48.

Les Horn played professional baseball and was former Mayor of Corinth 1946-58.

David Burton Horn (b. 1855, d. 1937) and Laura Francis Emmons (b. 1860, d. 1947) in front of the home they built on Bunch Street (currently Rosa's).

Ginger Jones Holland, daughter of Sam and Virginia Jones and her family: Wade, Julia 4-1/2 years and Hannah 7 years, May 2001.

Harriett B. Hopkins and her great-grandchildren Charles Moore and Linda Jo Moore.

Harriett B. Hopkins, 22 years old.

Daughters of Sara and Carroll Hudson: Elizabeth "Betty," Kay and Judy Hudson.

Onslow Whitfield Hudson Family

William Hubbard (b. 1869, d. 1957) and Willie Idella Cox Rorie (b. 1874, d. 1944). William's children: Irvin, Gilbert, Dena and Fannie. Their children: Leonard, Irene, Minnie, Virginia and Leslie, ca. 1900.

Katherine Hopper, Virginia McCalla, Nelle Payne, Sara Hudson, sisters.

Mr. and Mrs. Carroll Hudson, Christmas 1987.

Children of John "Jack" Randolph Hurley and Martha Ann Arnold Hurley. Front row, L-R: Cynthia Elizabeth Hurley, Tempie Louvenia Hurley. Second row, L-R: Nicy Jane Hurley, Thomas Jefferson Hurley and twin brother, George Washington Hurley, Lucretia Katherine Hurley. Third row, L-R: Rebecca Ann Hurley, John Ira Hurley, Martha Josephine Hurley, Leander Hurley, Sarah Ellen Hurley.

The Hurley's. Seated is Mary Josephine Surratt Hurley and Arvie Glenn Hurley. Standing, L-R: Havis Hurley, Billy Hurley, Jimmy Hurley, ca. 1962.

Fred and Carrie Hutchins, parents of Loriane Wammack.

Everet Hutchins

Fred Hutchins, Carrie Hutchins and daughter Loraine, 1936.

Carrie Hutchins with children Kenneth and Loraine.

O.C. and Lula Belle Isbell on large logs going to the lumber yard, 1930s.

Willie Eubanks and Herbert Isbell, 1950s.

Back row, L-R: Dr. Bill Jackson and wife Linda. Front row, L-R: Morgan Jackson, Lindsey Jackson, Candace Jackson, Patty Jackson, W. C. Jackson.

John Jobe (b. 1801, d. 1889) served with Andrew Jackson in the Indian wars. Moved to the Alcorn County area from Tennessee in 1833; employed as a surveyor and served the Confederacy under General Reuben Davis. He married four wives and fathered at least 21 children, is believed to be the ancestor of all Jobes in northeast Mississippi.

First row: Rachel and Sarah Johnson. Second row: Bernice and Burton Whirley, Dorothy Johnson, Granny and Grandpa Johnson (Audie and Lon), Molly and Melvin Johnson, Jane Johnson, baby is Joanne Mills. Third row: Juanita Mills, Vera Johnson, Mary Lee and Arnold Killough, Safronia and Levi Johnson, Jesse and Jim Mills, 1936.

Brant Johnson "O'Pa" with Nelda Boatman holding his watch, ca. 1827.

Jennifer Smith Johnson and Allen Johnson, children Katey and Mark.

The Brant Johnson Extended Family. "Springer Place," Wenesoga Road, Corinth, MS, November 21, 1936. Front row, L-R: R.C. Johnson, Lessie (Strickland) Johnson, "Buddy" Johnson O'Pa (Howel Brant) Johnson with R.C. Jr. "Buddy" Johnson, O'Ma, Mae Johnson Miller with Joanne Johnson, Manelle Johnson, Nell (Dickey) Johnson, Wanza Johnson, W. Printis Johnson, Luna (Johnson) Boatman, James "Sonny" Boatman, W.E. "Ester" Boatman. Second row: Price Johnson, Lucille (McKinsey) Johnson, Wilford "Bud" Johnson, Max Johnson, Nelda Boatman, William W. Johnson, Cliff Boatman, Victor "Dude" Johnson, "Kat" Kathleen Johnson, Katie Pearl Johnson.

1932, Hatchie River Bridge Lookout. J.A. "Jim" Jones (b. 1873, d. 1950 and second wife, Annie Hodum Jones (b. 1878, d. 1945).

1932, Lookout Bridge, Hatchie River. J.A. "Jim" Jones' grandchildren. Front row: Billy Brooks, Imogene Jones, Thaniel Jones, Elva Jones. Middle row: Vernell Brooks, J.W. Jones, Geneva Jones, Kerry Dunn, Odis Jones, R.G. Jones. Back row: J.T. Dunn, Fredra Brooks, Dessie Ree Dunn, Truit Brooks.

Jack Jones Homeplace, Kossuth, MS.

Kevin and Dana LeAnn (Allen) Jones, April 2001.

Jesse Walker Jones (b. October 27, 1898, AR, d. 1963, Bald Knob, AR) married Nettie Velma Crum February 5, 1923. Nettie, the daughter of Van Lansing Crum and Myra Martha Coke of Alcorn County, MS died August 1995 in Bald Knob, AR.

Bessie Jones at Maude Hermon home.

O.C. and Luevada Jones, August 1986.

Ida and Henry "Baby" Jones, 1989.

Helen Virginia Kemp Jones, seventh child and fourth daughter of Annie Moore and Charlie Odell Kemp, born April 25, 1924 in Alcorn County. Virginia was the first Alcorn County woman elected to a full term of office of Justice Court Judge which she served from 1972 until 1980. She served as president of the Mississippi Justice Court Officers Association in 1979 and 1980, appeared in Who's Who in Mississippi and was inducted into the 1978-79 edition of Personalities of America.

O.N. (Noland) Jones (son of Robert E. Lee Jones) in front of his store which was located next to Smithbridge Road in the Jones/Gift Community.

Dannye B. Jones, 1978.

Robert U. Jones, teacher, 1953.

James Newton Jones (b. 1812, d. 1894) and Mary Blandina Gordon Jones (b. 1824, d. 1897). They are who the Jones/Gift Community are named for. James died while hunting in the bottom on land now owned by his great-great-grandson Prentiss Turner. Mary died suddenly and no one ever knew what happened to her. Their daughter Susan and Terrell never married. They lived at the old homeplace and took care of their parents.

Uncle Terrell Jones (b. 1853, d. 1939) known throughout the Jones/Gift Community. A bachelor who lived with his sister Susan at the old homeplace pictured here. The home was built by his father, James Newton Jones along with Terrell and his brothers. He was robbed and killed. They placed him in a bedroom he never slept in and tucked him in. This has been a mystery to this good day. Who killed him?

Aunt Susan Jones (b. 1843, d. 1935) lived with her brother Terrell and was known throughout the Jones/Gift Community. In later years she went blind. She went to get firewood and picked up a snake. The last few years she lived with her brother Lee down the road from Terrell.

Joyce (Jones) James

Hettie Mae (Collins) Jones (mother of Herschel, Billy and J.C. Jones) with her sister Irene (Collins) Rolby.

L-R: Hubert Jones, Will Jones, Jenny Jones, Mildred Jones and Brooksey Jones. Hubert was the daddy of Herschel, Billy and J.C. Jones.

L-R: Billy N. Jones, Ada (Chandler) Jones, in front J.C. Jones, Hubert Jones and Herschel C. Jones. This was taken on Salem Road at their old homeplace. The boy's mother died very young, this was their stepmother. She was very good to them. They would have never got to go to school if it hadn't been for her, 1930s.

Back row: Georgia (Childers) Morgan, Herschel C. Jones holding David W. Jones, Ellie Mae (Morgan) Jones, LuevernieKnight. Middle row: Lola (Knight) Morgan, Joyce (Jones) James, Betty (Morgan) Gear, Lonnie Jones, Eddie Sellers, J.R. Morgan. Front Row: Jetti (Sellers) Kliesch and Barbara Morgan. This picture was taken by the railroad on Oakland School Road (home of Herschel and Mae Jones), 1950s.

Standing in front is Dannye Bernard Jones. Back row: Jamie K. Patton, Frankie Jones, Robert Jones, Tracy Presley and Neil A. Jones, 1986.

Front row, L-R: Robert U., Frankie and Neil Jones. Back row, L-R: Martinal, Maria D., Jocelyn A. and Robert Norman Jones, 1994.

Front row, L-R: Frankie Jones and Robin E. Jones. Back row, L-R: Norman, Neila, Jocelyn and Robert Jones, 1998.

Jon K. Jones, 1974.

H.B.B. Jones house built about 1870 in Alcorn County, MS has been home to four generations of Jones. It was destroyed by fire in 1949. This picture dates ca. 1910.

Henry Booker Bascomb Jones and Mary Elizabeth Babb Jones family. Standing, L-R: Margaret Neronah Jones (Howell), Erda Jones (Snyder), Walter Winifred Jones. Seated, L-R: H.B.B. Jones, Laura Alice (Bynum), Sam B., mother Mary Elizabeth, Octavia Bruce (Hurley), ca. 1889.

Typical dwelling house built ca. 1914, owned by Sam Booker Jones. In 1917-18 it was occupied by his sisters Lena Jones Murray, son Elmo, Olivia Jones and Octavia Jones. During this time it was operated as a hospital.

Henry Booker Bascomb Jones Family ca. 1920-21. Old Marvin Methodist Church. Back row, L-R: Octavia Jones Hurley, W.P. Hurley, Zena Jones, W.M. Jones, Erie Jones, Walter W. Jones, Lena Jones Murray, Sam B. Jones. Seated: Margaret Jones Howell, Lena Mae, Dr. J.G. Howell, Mary Elizabeth, George W. Bynum, Howard Bynum, Laura Alice (holding baby), H.B.B. Jones with second wife Ava Louella Marrett Jones. Children seated on ground: John Bynum, Elmo Murray, G.W. Bynum Jr.

Nancy Ellar Miller Kellum and grandson J.W. Kellum at Kellum home, Hatchie near Kossuth, 1935.

Kellus Family Reunion at Winford Matlax home near Union Church, Kossuth, MS.

Walter Kellum, grandson Michael Gurley, son-in-law Joe Gurley at store at Saulsbury, TN, 1980.

L-R: Rev. William V. Kemp in 1945 was the youngest ministerial student in Corinth Methodist District. Rev. Virginia Ann Jones Finzel on graduation day May 1999, Memphis Theological Seminary. Both Methodist ministers. Virginia Kemp Jones member First United Methodist Church since 1933. She is a sister to William and mother of Virginia Ann.

Laurie Marecle Kerut living in Vicksburg, MS. She is 19 years old and attending school at Mississippi State.

Children of Leslie and Virdie Key: Virginia Key, Katherine Key and Sara Key.

Mrs. Leslie Key, daughter Sara Hudson and granddaughter Betty Hudson.

Virginia Key, Katherine Key, Sara Key and Nell Key

Leslie Key Family, 1934.

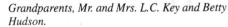

Grandparents, Mr. and Mrs. L.C. Key and Betty Hudson.

William Ebenezer and Alice Saphira (Carlock) Killough and their identical twin sons, James McClarity Killough sitting on lap of father and Thomas David Killough sitting on lap of mother.

James Oliver Knighton, Nannie (Flanagan) Knighton, Willie "Jack" and Madison Knighton.

Family of Thomas David and Lena Thompson Killough. Seated, L-R: Clell Killough, Arnold Killough, Myrtle Killough Calvery, Lena Thompson Killough, Thomas David Killough, Eula Killough Mattox. Standing, L-R: Maudie Killough Spencer, Annie Bell Killough Michael, Clifton Killough, Gertrude Killough Rodgers, Edna Killough Alexander, Lois Killough, Milton Killough.

Watermelon King. Edmond Beauregard King was known as Watermelon King in Corinth. The picture is taken at downtown Corinth, ca. 1930. He once had a watermelon that weighed 149 pounds. Unless he got a good price for his melons, he carried them back home. He was born in 1859 and died in 1952, had 14 children and outlived three wives. His father was in the Battle of Shiloh and is buried at Salem Christian Church in Alcorn County. Watermelon King was grandfather to Donald O. King Sr. and father to Everett "Hooker" King.

Marylane Louise Wade Koch, her hair was not cut for 13 years, granddaughter of Dick and Beulah Wade, ca. 1964.

Family reunion at Daniel F. Lamberth in the Pleasant Hill Community near Kossuth about 1921. Mr. Lamberth is seated on the right in the center of picture. Several of his children, grandchildren, brothers and sisters are in the picture.

E.S. Lancaster, carpenter ca. 1904. Houses were built by Mr. Lancaster.

Aaron Ben Lancaster, Margurite Ann Essary Lancaster

Hollis and Nell Lancaster

J.R. and Ida (Leatherwood) Lancaster, son of Charlie Lancaster.

R.T. Lasley with Clydesdale horse pulling wagon.

R.T. Lasley with Clydesdale horse.

Minnie Bell Brawner Latch (b. 1882, d. 1930), wife of John David Latch, mother of Florence Latch Allen, Frankie Latch Cook and Roy Clinton Latch, early 1900s.

Leatherwood Family gathering. Seated: Fannie and Buster Leatherwood, Sarah "Sally" Leatherwood and John Leatherwood. Standing: Clara Mae (Rodgers) Shaw (daughter of Will and Docia (Leatherwood) Rodgers), Lillie and Jess Leatherwood, Will and Jane (Leatherwood) Miller, Docia (Leatherwood) and Will Rodgers and Viola (Rodgers) Talley.

Miss Effie L. Lokey (b. 1888, d. 1985) lived in Kossuth, MS where she attended both grammar and high school. She then attended Bethel College in Tennessee. She taught her first school at Deerlick, 1915-16, Alcorn County, MS. This was a one-teacher school with grades 1 through 8 and averaged 45 pupils. The last 25 years were taught at the Kossuth Grammar School teaching 1st grade.

Heather Nicole Lollis, 1982.

Lisa Nicole "Nikki" Luker, age 1 year, daughter of Tim Luker and Diane (Butler) Luker Miller.

Lisa Nicole "Nikki" Luker, age 16, daughter of Tim Luker and Diane (Butler) Miller, September 2000.

Lillian Maddox (Mrs. James E. "Tubby") Mays (b. February 14, 1914), 1932-33.

Nelda Miller MacIntyre

Isaac Jasper "Ike" Lynch (B. 1862, d. 1931) and wife Hattie Suzhannah Pearlie White Lynch (b. 1860, d. 1939), early 1900s.

Ben Maddox and his sister Amanda Tucker on her visit from Bluewater, NM.

George L. Maddox, Mary Shelby (Flanagan) Maddox, late 1950s.

Mrs. Dovie and Milton Maddox at their house in Roswell, NM.

Minnie Vera, Ben F. Maddox, Herman Otto and Becky (Doty) Maddox

Luxora Wheeler and Wilda Jean Maddox, ca. 1950.

J.W. Maddox Family. Sitting, L-R: Ginny, father J.W. Maddox with grandson Nolie on lap. Granny Abel and Mary. Standing, L-R: John, Ben, Richard, Mandy and Frank.

John Wilson Maddox and Martha (Nash) Maddox, Spring 1923 near Rider Creek.

Ernest and Bernice Maddox

Earnest Maddox, second son of George L. Maddox.

James Allen Maddox, Willa Dean Newman, grandmother Mary Shelby Flanagan Maddox, Annette Maddox, Ezralee Maddox, ca. 1933 in Macedonia Community.

Nolie Maddox, Uncle George's oldest son before WWI.

John Wilson Maddox, father of George L. Maddox.

Lillian Maddox about 1929.

L-R: Mary Shelby (Flanagan) Amanda (Maddox) Tucker, Ezralee and James Allen Maddox.

Back row, L-R: Minnie (sister), Duell, Bremer, P.J., Herman Maddox. Middle row: Becky (Doty) Maddox and Ben Maddox. Front row: Thelma and Alice Ben.

G.L. Maddox and family. Names from oldest down: George, Mary, Ezra, Adah, John, Lee, Lillian and Paul the baby.

James Harrison "Jim" Mattox and Lorena Moore Mattox family picture. L-R: Raymond Mattox, Jim Mattox, Lorena Mattox, Harold Mattox and Winford Mattox, June 11, 1944.

Being readied for baptism: Luxora Wheeler, Becky Doty (Mrs. Ben) Maddox and Mary Shelby Flanangan (Mrs. G.L.) Maddox

Wilda Jean Maddox now living in Kenosha, WI.

Jerry Allen Maddox, now married and living in Kenosha, WI.

Mary Nell "Snooks" Maddox, now Mrs. Tom Eidsor, Kenosha, WI.

James E. Mays Jr., George L. Maddox, Willa Dean Newman, Mary Shelby (Flanagan) Maddox on west porch of the home of G.L. Maddox, 1942.

Ezra Homer Maddox, Alec Dean, Willa Dean Newman, James E. "Tubby" Mays, Bobby Wayne Mays, Lucy Lillian Mays, James E. Mays Jr. in front of the Corinth (MS) Fire Station in 1940.

Cherry Gail Maddox, only child of Paul T. Maddox and Pansy Rhodes Maddox, Corinth, MS 1946.

Harold Ray "Bud" Maddox, now married and living in Waukegan, IL.

Wilda Jean Maddox, now widowed and living in Kenosha, WI.

Leroy Maddox in his youth. Photo taped to note paper from Willa Dean Newman Trumbore's home when it was being sent back to its owner, Duell Maddox Reece, his first cousin.

Ada Alma Maddox, ca. 1927, Corinth, MS.

Frank Maddox and Maude (Maness) Vanderford, brother and sister. Frank was raised by his grandfather John Wilson Maddox.

Family of John Wilson Maddox and wife Nancy Addeline. Seated: John Wilson Maddox holding daughter Jennie Rose on his knee, mother-in-law Mary Ann Abels. The children positioned (clockwise l-r) are Amanda, Benjamin, Richard, George, Della, John and Mary.

July 1952, Macedonia Community at the home of George L. Maddox. Sitting, L-R: Mary Shelby(Flanagan) Maddox, George L. Maddox, Lillian (Maddox) Mays holding Keith. Standing: Billy Maness, J.E. "Tubby" Mays, Janie Rose Balough, James Mays Jr. and Bobby Mays.

Last known photo of Mary Shelby (Flanagan) Maddox and George L. Maddox at the home of daughter, Lillian Mays, Macedonia Community, 1959.

George L. Maddox and Duell (Maddox) Reece, ca. 1955.

Milford Maness, son of Floyd and Dollie Hardin Maness, ca. 1950, Alcorn County, MS.

Floyd and Dollie (Harden) Maness and family.

Maness Family. Front row: Robert "Bob" Marcus (b. 1854, d. 1949) and Mary Elizabeth Brown Maness (b. 1859, d. 1933). Back row: John Maness (b. 1893, d. 1976) and Lillie Mae Maness Childers, ca. 1910.

Christmas in a Juliette Community home. Ettie L. Owen (b. 1899, d. 1977) and John G. Maness (b. 1893, d. 1976), ca. 1955.

Maness sisters, L-R: Neal Maness married Mark Vanderford and Emma Maness (b. 1887, d. 1958) married Albert Vanderford (b. 1887, d. 1969), ca. 1949.

Mamie Manning, Mr. Smith and Velma Lancaster, July 1969.

Ruby Marecle Mask, Elic Marecle (father), Word Yancy Marecle (mother) and Roy Marecle (son) lived in Hinkle Creek Community. Mr. and Mrs. Marecle are buried in Hinkle Cemetery in Rienzi, MS.

Ray and Grace Odle Marecle's first home living in Hinkle Creek, now living in Corinth, MS.

Wesley Elic Marecle (d. November 21, 1968) married Word Yancy (d. 1967) December 21, 1919. Both are buried in Hinkle Cemetery.

Ray and Grace Odle Marecle Family. L-R: Darrell Lynn and Donna Bumpas Marecle with son Wesley Ray and daughter Carley Grace, Grace and Ray Marecle, Dr. Donald Ray Marecle, Christy, Lindsey and Haley, 1997.

Harold Ray Marecle and Grace Odle Marecle, 1971, now living in Corinth, MS.

Dr. Donald Ray Marecle, Ray Marecle (father), Lindsey Marie, Grace Marecle (mother), Haley Marecle, Darrel Lynn (father) and Wesley Ray (son).

Dr. Donald Ray Marecle with daughters Lindsey and Haley, Grace (mother), Ray (father) and brother Darrell Lynn Marecle, summer of 2001.

Dr. Don Marecle, daughters Haley and Lindsey, and niece Linda Dalan, 2001.

Richard and Susanna (Boyd) Mauldin. Susanna is the daughter of Andrew and Nancy (Scarborough) Boyd.

Alvin and Louise Marler with a prize catch of crappie fish.

The Hooked Rug Club, 1952, L-R: Mrs. Genevieve Maxedon, Mrs. Adeline Penny, Mrs. Sarah Biggers, Mrs. Ruby Barkley, Mrs. Julia Biggers, Mrs. Adrienne Biggers, Mrs. Mattie Green Striplin.

Willa Dean Newman, Nancy Pearl Mays, James E. Mays Jr., Bobby Wayne Mays in 1943. Photo made at Corinth, MS., probably McCord's Studio on Waldron Street.

Bob Mays and Keith Mays (in front), 1953.

Bob Mays wearing hand-me-down suit and tie from Uncle Paul T. Maddox, 1955. First attempt at beard.

Lucy Lillian Maddox Mays, 1963, just a short time before her death in January 1964 at Spottswood Avenue, home of her first cousin Duell Maddox Reece, Memphis, TN.

Paul Keith Mays, 1st grade.

James Emmett Mays Jr., Rienzi High School, Rienzi, MS, ca. 1952.

Dr. and Mrs. Lon W. McAnally (Elizabeth Hudson McAnally), Charleston, SC.

Amy Belinda Mays, Alan Wayne Hosch, Cindi Gail Mays, 1980.

Keith, Willa Dean and Bob Mays at Keith's house in 1980; Bob's motor home in rear.

John Byrum McCalister and Bertie Mae (Jackson) McCalister.

Stanley George and Jimmy H. McCalister at the Curlee house on Jimmy's wedding day, June 29, 1984.

Jimmy Harold McCalister and Kathy (Jones) McCalister in front of an old trailer Jimmy bought. They rode 12 miles on their bikes that day. This was taken in the yard of Jimmy's parents, Jim Ed and Clara McCalister (Farm Road).

Front row: Virgil McCollum, Brenda (Harben) McCollum, Rachel (Rushing) McCollum, Kathy (McCollum) Patrick. Back row: Larry W. McCollum, Sandra (McCollum) Carpenter.

Rachel McCollum, James H. Rushing and Maud Rushing.

Rachel Tawanda (Rushing) McCollum and Virgil Alfred McCollum.

Andrew J. McCord (b. 1889, d. 1961) and Effie (Green) McCord (b. 1889, d. 1938) daughter of Joseph W. and Jennie (Walker) Green married December 25, 1911. Children, Clara (b. 1912, d. 2000) and Franklin (b. 1915, d. 1967).

Friends, Kitty Mitchell McCord and Virdie Dilworth Key.

Effie Lorena Green McCord (b. October 5, 1889, d. October 7, 1938) daughter of Joseph W. and Jennie L. (Walker) Green.

Thomas Jefferson McCrary, great-grandfather of Betty Forman.

Galvin Millard McCrary, Fanny (McCrary) Griffin, Mary Louvinia (Dixon) McCrary and John Thomas McCrary, 1913.

Front row: Jewell (Castile, Byrd) McCrary, Barry McCrary, George Allen McCrary Sr. Back row: Stevan Lloyd McCrary, Brenda Jean (McCrary) Stachan, Eddie Byrd and George Allen "Buddy" McCrary Jr. Taken November 1983 before Allen died in January.

John Thomas McCrary and Mary Ellen (Nellie Hughes) McCrary. Taken in 1948, a short time after she came to America from Ireland to become John's wife in 1947.

Mary Louvinia (Dixon) McCrary, daughter of Tom and Minnie (Nelms) Dixon.

W.S. McDonald and W.W. Sandlin in some of the first pine seedling set out in Alcorn County. W.S. McDonald won an award from Sears Roebuck for this.

Beulah and Peggy McDonald in pine trees set out by W.S. McDonald and family, May 1961.

W.S. and Beulah McDonald at old homeplace in Farmington Community, 1959.

Rev. Elias C. (b. 1822, TN) and Nancy (b. 1821, TN) McElyea. A Methodist minister, he was chaplain, (F-S) Hamm's Mississippi Regt. Cav., CSA and 23rd Mississippi Regt. Inf., CSA.

Jimmy and Lillian McFalls married December 2, 1933.

Seated, L-R: Lonnie, Jessie, Violet and Effie Hearn McLemore. Standing, L-R: Grace, Flossie and Robert McLemore.

Whit McLemore and Willie (Flanagan) McLemore.

Scott and Katie McKinney, February 1892.

Hugh McMullar and Lula Bingham McMullar.

George Washington McNair (b. 1853, d. 1921) and a young lady believed to be Pauline Ledbetter, ca. 1919. George was the father of John Sylvester McNair.

McNair Family ca. 1915. L-R: Ed Clinton, John Sylvester, Robert, George Washington and Margaret Lula.

John Sylvester McNair and wife Pearl Ethel Keen McNair, ca. 1955.

Annie Dee Rider Miller children: Front, L-R: Charlotte Miller Winstead, Annie Rider Miller, Nelda Miller MacIntyre, Marie Miller Anderson. Back, L-R: John Miller, Don Miller, Jim Miller.

Dr. William McRae, Dr. Leroy Bracksone, Dr. Maury McRae, 1932.

Bertha Elizabeth Taylor McNeeley, wife of William Thomas and daughter of James Major and Mattie Jane Pinkard Taylor.

Christopher Miller, age 8 months, October 1991, son of Jim and Diane Miller.

Earl Miller, Annie Rider Miller and son Jim Miller, 1957.

Five generations: Annie Miller, Marie Miller Anderson, Diane Anderson Payne, Danna Payne Ivie and Ariel Ivie.

Christopher Miller age 9, son of Jim and Diane (Butler) Miller, September 2000.

Charles Mincy (son of James and Mattie Mincy who are grandparents to James and Matt Mincy also) father of Charles James Mincy, age 4 and Samuel Anthony Mincy, age 4 months. Their mother is Elizabeth Mincy and the family lives in Godfrey, IL.

The James Reid Mills Family, 1931. Front row: Jim Mills, Marie, Ruby and Laura Mills. Second row: Vernon, Jimmy Lee, Merle, Lillie, Nan and Johnny Mills.

Four generations: Great-grandfather James Roy Mincy, age 87 here. He lives in Farmington Community and is now 92 years old; grandfather James Wesley Mincy, age 62 at time of photo, lives in Clear Creek Community on CR 301; Perry Neal Mincy, age 30 when photo was taken and Ashley Michell Mincy age 2 months, daughter of Perry and Mary K. Mincy.

The Mitchell Family, ca. 1942, Rienzi, MS.

J.S. and Sarah Mitchell, Martha, Mollie and Hubert.

Family photograph in early 1900s of Henry Stevenson (son of Franklin and Octavia Katherine (Burnett) Monroe) and Mary Katherine "Kate" (daughter of Frederick and Mary (Stevenson) Hamlin) Monroe and their four children, L-R: Annice, Laura Katherine, Curtis Ray and Rupert.

The Monroe Brothers, sons of Franklin (son of William Robert Monroe and Harriet (McPhatter) Monroe) and Octavia Katherine (Burnett) Monroe. Seated L-R: Benjamin F. "Bennie," Walter Edward and Charles Franklin "Charley." Standing, L-R: Henry Stevenson and George Lee.

The Curtis Monroe Family: Curtis Ray (son of Henry S. and Kate (Hamlin) Monroe) and Florence Erie (daughter of Johnie L. and Doshia Edna (Michaels) Green) Monroe. Front row, L-R: Behind Curtis and Florence are Hermie Florence (Monroe) Turner, Ray Ann (Monroe) Woodruff and Franklin Dale "Frank" Monroe.

Mary Russell Montgomery, 1932.

Beatrice Lancaster Moore, Wesley Moore in the 1930s.

Wesley Moore on a visit to Burke, VA with his grandson Jay Tolleson.

The Irma Bennett Moore Family: Ernest, Herman, Mack, Malcom, Wesley, Felix, Ruth, Ray, Lorena and Irma.

Lela Moore (b. August 9, 1907, d. 1939) daughter of Charley and Tishie Erma Moore.

Felix and Lela Moore, 1987.

Felix Moore, age 23 (b. March 25, 1913, d. August 30, 1996).

Beatrice Lancaster Moore, Wesley Moore, Virginia Lancaster Moore, Ernest Moore.

Moore homeplace built by Manuel Moore in 1883, he cut the logs. There was a chimney at each end of the house. His son, Charley was 6 years old when the house was built. He later married and raised a family of 10 children in this home.

Greg Moore, 1963

Greg and Denise Moore

Mitch, Christy and Sarah Grace Moore, November 1996.

Top row, L-R: Eldon Howell Morgan, Lula (Knight) Morgan and John R. Morgan. Bottom, L-R: Ellie Mae (Morgan) Jones and Beatrice (Morgan) Sellers, 1941.

Arnell Morris at Corinth Post Office, 1945.

The Robert Franklin Morrison Family in front of the Morrison Homeplace, ca. 1896. Back row, L-R: Robert Jr., Dora, Sara Annie, Laura Esther, Mamie. Front row: Neal, Robert Franklin Sr., Errett, Laura Ellen, Marcus. Robert Franklin Morrison was the son of Neal and Sarah Rushing Morrison. He was their eighth child. Robert Franklin Morrison and Laura Ellen Brooks Morrison and seven of their children are buried in the Antioch Cemetery. It is near the Old Morrison's Mill Community, about six miles southeast of Corinth and adjacent to their old homeplace site.

On the left is Sara Annie Morrison who married J.D. Biggers Sr. On the right is her sister Dora Morrison who married Walter Hinton, ca. 1889.

Family of Wilson and Mary (Allen) Morton. Back row, L-R: Wilson McKenney Morton, Mary (Allen) Morton, Berniece (Morton) Parvin, Gladys (Morton) Able, Kate (Morton) Elliott, J.W. Morton, Clovis Morton. Front row, L-R: Howard Morton, Carroll Morton Sr., Geraldean (Morton) West, Willie Mae (Morton) Ketcham, Vance Morton, Ammie Lou (Morton) Kuykendall.

Morton Reunion in 1986. Front row: Joe Frank Morton Jr., Pauline Kuykendall, Amanda Witt, Byron Ginn, Casey Wegmann, Bryant Ginn, Tom Wegmann. Middle row: Brent Pittman, Susan Morton, Marcus Morton, Florene Morton, Paulette Pittman (face barely showing), Pauline Morton, Frances Ramer, Tina Morton, Robert Morton, Blake Ginn, Ginger Pittman, Billie Wegmann, Jennie Harmon, Frank Haley, Vickie Witt. Third row: Bettie Ginn, Steve Ginn, Frank Morton, Stanley Pittman, a friend, Roy Morton, Dora Nell Morton, Margaret Haley, Louise Lancaster, Howard Lancaster.

Jack and Millie Mellon Mullins, 1930.

Andy and Marie Mullins

Manuel V. Mullens Sr., Rhoda Gustava James Mullens. Standing is Gladys Ruth Mullens Grimes and on Rhoda's lap is Margaret Louetta Mullens Morton.

Manuel V. Mullens Sr. and child on mule is M.V. Mullens Jr., Biggersville, 1943.

Horse drawn buggy, driver is Rufus Nash visiting his parents, Robert "Bob" and Nannie Elizabeth Rorie Nash, ca. 1915.

Robert "Bob" Nash and sons take a ride in their Model T, one of the first in Alcorn County. Driver is Earie and dad, Bob Nash. Back seat, L-R: Elgin "Dick," Leslie "Dess" Archie and Allie, ca. 1920.

House of Robert "Bob" and Nannie Rorie Nash (Rienzi-Jacinto Road, ca. 1918). L-R: Leathie holding Roscoe, Bob, Mabel, Earie, Avie, Jane Rinehart Nash, Nannie, Dick. Back row: Allie, Susie, Dess and Archie Nash.

Great-granddaughter Meredith Grace Wade Koch is taking good care o "Granny" Beulah Vanderford Nash, ca. 1996.

Gardens give fresh food, m-m-good. Giffie Nash and daughter Jewell "Bittie" Felks picking fresh vegetables, summer 1963.

James Jefferson Nelson (b. April 24, 1862, d. June 29, 1928) married first Alice Catherine Jordan, January 6, 1884; married second Hester Hill, July 24, 1912 in Tishomingo County, MS. J.J. and Alice had the following children: Jessie Lee, Essie M. Sarah G., Oscar O'Neil, James Omer, Charles O., Elie M. Marshall Price "Mark," Eula Odell, David Eugene, Stella Alma, John Thomas "Tom," and Cayce Ione. Most of these children raised their families in Alcorn and Tishomingo County where many still reside and own/operate businesses today. Front row: Oscar, Omer, Eugene (baby), J.J., Eula, Alice, Marshall. Back row: Essie, Sarah and Jessie.

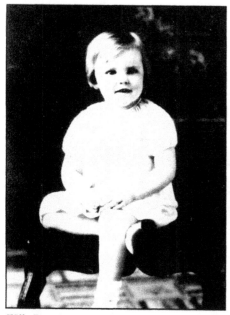

Willa Dean Newman (b. June 11, 1931), ca. 1932.

Twins Annie (Norman) McPeters and Mary (Norman) Lorick, October 28, 1894

Twins Effie (Norman) Lorick Jones and Essier (Norman) Boyd Galloway, Feb. 20,1897

Jimmy Norman (Dec. 25 1861-Oct. 9, 1927) and Cornellia (Shorter) Norman (?-Oct. 25, 1935).

Twins Minnie (Norman) Hurd and James Norman, May 6, 1899

Lonnie Norman. 28, 1888

Henry Norman, July 19, 1890

Neallie (Norman) Orange, Aug. 30, 1901

Paul Norman Oct. 18, 1902

Twins Victoria (Norman) Jones and Robert Norman Aug 28, 1892

Christmas gathering, L-R: O.P. Norvell, Roy Norvell, Lillie Norvell, Eunice Norvell, Shellia Steen Surratt, Troy Norvell, Velma Norvell. Children, L-R: Bobby Norvell, Dorothy Surratt, Sidney Surratt, ca. 1935-36.

Husband and wife, Troy and Velma Norvell, 1966, Wenasoga, MS.

James O'Riley Odle (son of William A. and Nancy Odle) and Sarah Jane (Clark) Odle.

Family of James Francis and Alice Nora (Mauldin) Odle. Standing in rear, L-R: Mary Helen (Parvin) Odle wife of James W. Odle, James W. Odle (husband of Helen Parvin and son of James and Alice Odle), Mona J. Odle (daughter of and in arms of her father J.W. Odle), Melvin M. Odle (husband of M. Ruby Killough and son of James and Alice Odle), Mary Ruby (Killough) Odle (wife of Melvin and daughter of James and Eliza Killough), Otis Rhinehart (friend and neighbor of family), Arrie Rachel Odle (daughter of James F. and Alice N. Odle), Lester F. Odle (son of James F. and Alice N. Odle), James R. Killough (husband of Arnie E. Odle and father of Janeice, son of James M and Eliza (Langston) Killough). Middle row seated, L-R: James Francis Odle (husband to Alice Nora (Mauldin) Odle and son of James O'Riley and Sarah Jane (Clark) Odle), Alice Nora (Mauldin) Odle (wife of James Francis Odle and daughter of William Benjamin and Rachell (Harrell) Mauldin), Arnie Etta (Odle) Killough (wife of James R. Killough, mother of Janeice Killough and daughter of James and Alice Odle). Front row seated and kneeling L-R: Baby Schakelford (neighbor's son and family friend), Charlie Hester Odle (son of James and Alice Odle), Maudie Mae Odle (daughter of James and Alice Odle), Hillie Hugh "Jack" Odle (son of James and Alice Odle, holding his niece, E. Janeice Killough and daughter of Arnie and James R. Killough), E. Janeice Killough (in lap of her uncle "Jack" Odle and daughter of James R. and Arnie E (Odle) Killough), Joseph Edward Killough (son of James and Mary Eliza Killough and brother of Ruby and James R. Killough).

Russell Odle, Kathrine Odle Foss, Edwin Odle, Grace Odle Marecle, Billie Sue Odle Stanton, Doris Odle Choat. Children of Mr. and Mrs. Sam Bob Odle.

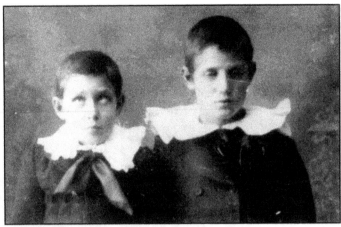

Sam Bob (Robert Forrest) Odle (age 96) at Care Inn Nursing Home, Corinth and daughter Grace (Odle) Marecle, 1998.

George and Armistead Odle. Blind at birth in Talladega, AL. Blindness was caused by their mother being bitten by an infected mosquito before they were born.

Esker Moronie Osborn and wife Alma Zettie Butler Osborn, ca. 1925.

Osborn Family in 1952. Back row: Eddra Irene, J.C., Mattie Jo. Front: Esker Moronie Osborn and wife Alma Zettie Butler Osborn.

Sadie Odle, blind at birth in Talladega, AL. Blindness was caused by their mother being bitten by an infected mosquito before Sadie was born.

Ruby (Dixon) Osborne and Onnie Osborne.

Palmer Family. Seated: Henry Lee (b. 1912, d. 1999), Jasper Odell (father, b. 1889, d. 1964), Bessie Rebecca Cox (mother, b. 1884, d. 1969), Jerry David. Standing: Phyllis Marie Baker (b. 1926, d. 1993), Jasper Bonnie (b. 1919, d. 1996), Howard Mitchel (b. 1913, d. 1988), Gladys Lucille Calvary, Wesley Rupert (b. 1929, d. 2001), Jasper Odell Jr. "Junie" (b. 1924, d. 1992), Mary Lou "Susie" Taylor (b. 1934, d. 1968).

L-R: Martha (Flanagan) Palmer holding John Henry and William Calvin "Bill" Palmer holding Callie Mary Jane before moving to central Texas, ca. 1897-98

David Allen "Dave" Parker, son of John Thomas and Sarah Elizabeth (Morris/Morrison) Parker, was born October 24, 1898, probably Guys, TN. Dave married first Lecy Alene Bell (above right with David), daughter of John Edmond and Emma Latisha (Thomason) Bell on September 7, 1919 in Tennessee. They had the following children: Leon, Opal, Ivanell, Jewell, Dorothy, Alton Earl, Arnold Lee, Evelyn, Betty, Levon, Laveda and Paulette. Perhaps work and a desire to be close to his siblings brought Dave and Lecy to Alcorn County where he tended ground on the old Rube Choate place and sawmilled, and where three of their children were born. Many of their children still live in Alcorn County. He married second Mary Narcissus "Polly" Dancer and they had two children. Dave, a carpenter, lived in the Hopewell Community on the old Hopewell (Iuka/Corinth) Road as well as in Tennessee, Arkansas and California. He died February 15, 1966 at the age of 66.

The Clifford R. Parrish Family, 1963. Clifford, Lanita "Hootie," Nelda and standing, LuAnne.

Mr. and Mrs. Walter Parsons, 1942

Clarence O. Phifer and Gertie (Dillon) Phifer, October 1962.

Greg, Tammy and Tage Philamlee, June 1995

L-R: Nellie Eve (Clark) Philpot and her grandmother Lula Elizabeth (Knight) Morgan, 1940s.

R.J. Pinkard and wife, Sara Ann Newman, parents of Mattie Jane Pinkard Taylor. They lived in the Farmington Community and were married August 23, 1857 in this county which was formerly Tishomingo County, MS.

Mattie Jane Pinkard (b. 1860, d. 1936) wife of James Major Taylor (b. 1861, d. 1919) daughter of R.J. Pinkard and Sarah Ann Newman Pinkard shown here with their nine children. Front row, L-R: Benny Ellen, Sarah Ann, Laura Lee on mother's lap, Fillmore Baxter. Back row, L-R: Florence, Myrtle Annie, Moncie Dell, Bertha Elizabeth and Willis Morgan. This picture was made in front of their home in the Farmington Community around 1900.

Family of James Madison Pittman and Eliza Jane Seago Pittman. Back row: Samuel "Sam," Luceal, Annie, Tom, Henderson. Front row: Charlie Edgar, Emma, Ruthie "Ruth" and Eliza Jane.

Family of William E. "Will" Potts and Sarah Jane Haynes Potts. Back row, L-R: Charlie, Heber, Jess, James "Jim," William C. "Corb." Front row, L-R: Maude, Lula, Sara Jane Haynes, Lucille. William E. Potts was born July 4, 1862 in Corinth, MS. His parents were Elisha and Magaret Bowie Potts. At the time of William's birth, Abraham Lincoln was the 16th president, the Civil War was raging and the bloody battle at Shiloh had taken place only three months earlier. When William was about six months old, his father, Elisha, left to fight the war. Elisha returned from war and the family made their home near the Farmington Baptist Church. On November 2, 1885, William married Sarah Jane Haynes. They made their home in the Farmington area and had nine children. William was a farmer and beekeeper. He died March 3, 1927. Sarah Jane Haynes Potts was born in Waterloo, AL on February 11, 1863, died in 1954 at the age of 91.

Steve and Stella Pundt, son and daughter-in-law of Grace Pundt; Jessica Duffer, great-granddaughter of Bill and Grace Pundt.

Fred Alexander Rast

Ann Elizabeth Rutherford Rast

Johnnie Cuthon Rast, Bonitha Bowen Rast, 1998.

The Rast Sisters: Dimple Rast Caldwell, Shirley Rast Voyles and Nell Rast Heauner, 1992.

Sisters: in front Theresa Calhoun Dolaway, back: Shirie Rast Felks and Connie Rast Vatalaro, August 1966.

Donald, Bill and Kenneth Rencher, 1949.

Family of Ed and Effie Ballard Rencher. Back row: Eunice, Ed, Effie, Oral, Juanita and Dimple. Front row: Ora, Wilma, Genelle, Bill, Kenneth and Donald, 1948.

Jim and Kim Andrew Rhodes' wedding rehearsal on Filmore St., Corinth, MS Little Chapel. Max Rhodes and sons: Max (b. 1936, d. 1999), John (b. 1964), Jim (born 1968) and Paul (b. 1959).

Joy Dale Wilbanks Rhodes' grandchildren, L-R: Mark Rhodes, Luke Rhodes, B.J. Owings, Andrew Rhodes, Hollye Rhodes (holding Suzanne Rhodes), Nathan Rhodes, November 27, 1999.

Faithful to get the church wood heater going each church night, always walked two or more miles. Willie H. Rinehart (b. 1874, d. 1941) and Annie Whittemore Rhinehart (b. 1879, d. 1956) ca. 1990.

Lottie Bass Rinehart (94 years young) teacher at Hickory Flat School in 1924, wife of Columbus Rinehart, ca. 1998.

Sara Ann "Sallie" (Rorie) Rice (b. 1886, d. 1981) with her brother James Frederick Withers Rorie (b. 1874, d. 1957). They are the children of James Frederick Withers and Sarah (Cheek) Rorie.

Children playing dolls, ca. 1919. L-R: Verna Nash Richardson (b. 1913, d. 1995), Laura Mabel Nash Tucker Glidewell (b. 1907, d. 1973), Robert Roscoe Nash (b. 1918, d. 1993), Avis Leoner Nash Burcham, Albie Smith Nash (b. 1917, d. 1998).

Characters in play The Black Cat *at old Hickory Flat School. Seated: Hazel Richardson, Bonnie Palmer, Dess Nash. Standing: Douglas Richardson, Christine Walden, Eveline Palmer, Cordelia Calvary, Billy Crowe, Sue Smith, Cleve Smith, ca. 1960*

John Wesley Richardson and his wife Frances Louisa Spier/Spear when they were young about 1871.

John Wesley Richardson family lived and raised their children on Proper Street in Corinth.

Bob and Alice Dees Rider at their home near Kossuth, 1943.

W.F. Rider family at their home near Kossuth, 1907. Arch, Minnie, Lora, Martha Ann, W.F. "Frank and Kennel.

Singing group: Bob Rider, Jasper Green, Brew Anderson, Kittie Green Suitor, Florence Anderson, Effie Green McCord, Annie Green Taylor.

Sons of Arnold and Beatrice Rider: Donald Ray, James Robert and Billy Wayne.

Velma Rider, daughter of Bob and Alice Rider (b. October 19, 1913, d. August 23, 1933).

The daughters of Arnold and Beatrice Rider, front: Brenda Joyce, Sandra Lynn, Gleada Faye, Linda Maye. Back row: Betty Jane, Doris Jean and Ruby Frances.

Arnold and Beatrice Marecle Rider

A 1925 picture of the Roaten Family. Front row, L-R: Eugene, Estell, Hubert Talley, Emma Ellis, James Monroe, Anna Priscilla, Eliza Jane, Mary Elizabeth, babies are Hillie D. and Willie B. Back row, L-R: James Marlin, Jewell Vastie, John H. and James Bonnie.

William L. "Billy" Roten (Roaten), ca. 1900.

Back row: Emma Roaten and Mary Elizabeth Roaten. Front row seated is Eugene Roaten, the mother of all, Eliza Jane Crum Roaten and James Monroe Roaten, ca. 1930.

Wanza Marie Robbins, daughter of Bobby Robbins.

Hatchie Bottom brothers and sister in 1929. Back row: James Bonnie Roaten and Jewell Vastie. Front row: James Marlin, Hillie D., twin brother Willie B. and John H.

Bobby Lloyd Robbins, Dawn (Rasco) Greshem and Lynda Gayle (Rasco) Robbins. Dawn is Lynda's daughter. Taken December 23, 1988 on Bobby and Lynda's wedding day.

Bobby Lloyd Robbins and Lynda Gayle (Rasco) Robbins

Kelsie A. Rogers holding Ronnie Rogers, Emma K. Bynog Rogers holding Patricia Ann Rogers. Standing L-R: Jeanette and Shirley Jean Rogers.

Henry Clinton Rogers, Cherry Castile Rogers, 1902s

Eugene and Della Rogers Family. Children, Clifford, Benjamin Tillman and Helen.

Margaret Greene Rogers (center) poses with Tommy Lasorda, former manager of the Los Angeles Dodgers and keynote speaker at the 2001 Blue Cross and Blue Shield Ageless Hero ceremony and former first lady of Mississippi, Pat Fordice. Mrs. Rogers, a Prentiss County native, graduated from Corinth High School, Virginia Intermont College and received a bachelor's degree from Mississippi University for Women and a master's degree from the University of Mississippi. She is not only a retired third grade school teacher but is also the retired executive director of the Northeast Mississippi Museum. Her book, Civil War Corinth, is in its fifth printing and she speaks to numerous groups and frequently does historic and genealogical research. Some of her many honors are: 1988 Junior Auxiliary Citizen of the Year, 1989 Corinth/Alcorn County Chamber of Commerce Ambassador of the Year Award for Volunteerism, 1998 Mississippi Governor's Volunteer of the Year, 1998 Alliance Spirit of Service Award and in 2000 the Museum Library was dedicated to her honor. Mrs. Rogers was married to the late Fred E. Rogers and has one son, Bill.

Stanford Stanley Rorie with L-R: wife Clara Sue, daughter Eva Arminta (b. January 1908) and mother Sariah Frances Cheek Rorie, widow of J.F.W. Rorie, winter 1908.

George Cheek (known by many as a "real" fiddler) son of Silas and Edieth Cheek, brother of Sariah Frances Cheek Rorie.

Sariah Frances Cheek Rorie (b. 1846, d. 1924), daughter of Silas and Edieth Cheek, widow of J.F.W. Rorie (b. 1838, d. 1885). Children, L-R: Eugene Bailey, Sanford Stanley and Sarah A.

Spring 1912 - Children of Sanford and Clara Sue Rorie and grandchildren of James F.W. and Sarah (Cheek) Rorie. L-R: Ollis Roy (1909-1993), Virgie Aval (1912-1985) and Eva Arminta (1908-1993).

Family of Eugene Rorie (b. 1882, d. 1940), E.E. "Bud" Rorie (b. 1910, d. 1982), Ruby Ione Rorie Brown (b. 1912, d. 1996). Standing: Eppie Vanderford Rowsey (b. 1901, d. 1988), Lois Rorie (b. 1908, d. 1988). Not pictured is Oner Rorie Hearn, ca. 1930s.

Five generations: William Hubbard Rorie (b. 1869, d. 1957) and Willie Idella Cox Rorie (b. 1874, d. 1944). L-R: Virginia Eveline Rorie Vanderford (b. 1910, d. 1998), Ruby Marie Hendrix Burkes, Carolyn Sue Hendrix Warren Caughman, Tina Sue Warren Stubbs, Whitney Jo Stubbs, Hallie Elizabeth Stubbs, ca. 1995.

James Frederick Withers Rorie and his wife Sarah Elizabeth "Bettie" (Denson) Rorie late in life.

Sarah (Cheek) Rorie (b. 1846, d. 1924) wife of James Frederick Wither Rorie, daughter of Silas and Edith (Phillips) Cheek.

Ruby Ione Rorie (b. 1912, d. 1996), daughter of Eugene and Lena Rorie and granddaughter of J.F.W. Rorie and Sarah (Cheek) Rorie.

Lois Rorie (b. 1908, d. 1988), daughter of Eugene and Lena Rorie, granddaughter of J.F.W. and Sarah (Cheek) Rorie.

(Right) Mary Elizabeth "Polly" Rorie (b. April 7, 1805, d. February 14, 1892) came with her husband Reuben (b. August 30, 1799, d. August 6, 1862) and eight of their nine children from Stewart County, TN in January 1837. James Frederick Withers was born in Mississippi. They settled near Jacinto (old Tishomingo County). Polly was a midwife and rode horseback to tend the sick. She educated her children at the Academy.

Seated, L-R: Sanford Rorie (b. 1881, d. 1960) and James Frederick Withers Rorie (b. 1874, d. 1957). Standing, their wives Clara Sue (Smith) Rorie (b. 1887, d. 1971) and Sarah Elizabeth "Bettie" (Denson) Rorie (b. 1879, d. 1957).

James Frederick Withers Rorie (b. 1874, d. 1957) with his daughter Ruby Bell Rorie (b. 1894, d. 1966). Fred was the son of James Frederick Wither and Sarah (Cheek) Rorie. The picture was made at the W.H. Rowsey Studio in Corinth, MS.

Collins Ross and wife Ray Moore Ross, Kossuth, MS.

James Frederick Withers Rorie (b. July 6, 1838, d. October 8, 1885), son of Reuben and Polly Rorie. J.F.W. married Sariah Frances Cheek and had 10 children. J.F.W. served one term as Alcorn County tax assessor, one term as Alcorn County treasurer of school funds and one term as country treasurer of Alcorn County.

First row, L-R: Robert Ross, unknown, James Ross. Second row: unknown, Rev. Mims, unknown, Ranwnell Ross, Flora Ross, Indian Battle, unknown. Third row: West Daniel, unknown, Shurkita Roby, Leon Bates, Marcell Baldwin, Mable Jones, unknown, Ethel Rerd. Top row: Robert Jones, Rena McMillan, Alfred McMillan, Rosemary Bowden, Minnie Stiger, unknown.

Ray Moore Ross and Ruth Moore Stevens.

William Elijah (b. 1870, d. 1946) and Laura Rowsey (b. 1880, d. 1958). Nash Family. Children: Lorena Richardson, Major Nash, Arlin Nash, Velma Harris, Howard Nash, Verna Richardson and Sybil Nash. All lived near Hickory Flat School, ca. 1946.

John Bell Rowsey (b. 1875, d. 1954) and Leslie Burcham (b. 1895, d. 1991).

This is Mrs. Opal Miller Rutledge on her 95th birthday, March 28, 2001. Her three granddaughters are from left Deborah Jackson, teacher of business at Kossuth, MS; Melinda Hamlin, teacher of nursing at North East Junior College and Denise Tweddle, teacher at Alcorn Central.

Mr. and Mrs. Blain and Anner Russell, 1935

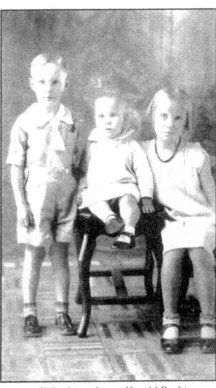

Eugene T. Rushing, James Harold Rushing and Rachel (Rushing) McCollum.

Maud (Miller) Rushing and Thomas Richard Rushing.

Mr. and Mrs. G. F. Sargant operated a small nursery in the Farmington area. They are the parents of three daughters: Betty Hamm, Jo Ann Seargant and Mary O. Gurley.

Dr. Giles Christopher Savage, son of Eleanor Jane (Shields) and Rev. Hamilton "Ham" Giles Savage. Dr. Chris Savage was a noted ophthalmologist in Nashville, TN. He was a professor of ophthalmology at Vanderbilt University Medical Department.

Savage brothers and sisters, four of the nine children born to Eleanor Jane (Shields) and Rev. Hamilton "Ham" Giles Savage. Front row: Mary Ann Margaret Earthman, George Martin. Back row: Giles Christopher "Chris" and unknown sister.

Hardy Sellers Family, Macedonia Community. Seated: Hardy Hollis Sellers (b. 1867, d. 1946), wife Dora Haynie (b. 1869, d. 1954), Eula Burcham (b. 1893, d. 1974). Standing: Thomas Franklin (b. 1896, d. 1919), Mellie E. Tolar (b. 1891, d. 1964), Susie Nash (b. 1899, d. 1978) and Cordelia Whittemore (b. 1889, d. 1970), ca. 1915.

Mildred Walker (Sawyer) (b. 1908, d. 1999), daughter of Joe L. and Mary (Suitor) Walker.

Front row, L-R: Raymond "Doc" Simons, Floyce Fowler. Standing: Christen Keeton, Unice Fowler, Thurmon Simmons.

Jef and Melissa Moore Sheirwagen and daughter Lauren.

L-R: James Abner, Bob, Alec Smith, sons of Joseph B. Smith, Co. A, 32nd Mississippi Infantry, CSA.

Back row, L-R: Charlie Smith, Allen Smith, Walter Smith, Mary Smith Splann, Nora Smith, Tom Smith. Front row, L-R: Jack Smith, Mary Lou Smith, Louella Greer Smith and Robert Smith.

L-R: Lizzie Smith, brothers Jeff and Calvin Smith before 1922.

Annie Sargent Smith and son, Grady Smith were the wife and son of Harm Berry "Bee" Smith. Annie and Grady died in the early 1920s. Annie was the daughter of Jim Sargent and Martha Crum Sargent.

Bryant Gaines and Mary Cordelia Richardson Smith at their home in the Jones/Gift Community. Their daughter Mallie Smith married Edward Arthur Turner.

Members of the C.D. Smith family are pictured at their home in the Farmington Community, ca. 1950. Front row, L-R: Vandel Smith, Vernon Smith. Back row, L-R: Vera (Smith) Reed, Verlene (Smith) Strickland and Mr. and Mrs. C.D. Smith.

Smith-Burcham Family, ca. 1915. Seated: Annie "Sis" Owens Burcham, Ora Bell Burcham Smith, John Henry Burcham. Standing: Jim "Buster" Burcham, Hermia Burcham Cowan, Lou Annie (Bay) Burcham Hardin, Arch Burcham.

Louise and H.B. Smith picking their crop in 1963. They made their living from cotton and always picked it by hand.

The Bee Smith Family ca. 1937. They were a farm family who lived in the Kossuth area. Picture shows Harm Berry "Bee" Smith, Maggie Annie Louise Fitzgerald Smith, Opal Olean Smith, Hazel Lavern Smith and Helen Marie Smith.

Martha Melinda Crum Smith (b. 1805, 1875)

Joseph Smith (b. 1810, d. 1885) and wife Martha Melinda Crum Smith (b. 1805, d. 1875) were early settlers in the Brush Creek area in western Alcorn County. They were the parents of Martha Jane Smith Burrow, Lenora Smith, Harm Marion "Bud" Smith, Julia Ann Smith Faulkner, Fannie Smith Coleman and Joseph Henry Smith.

C.D. and Bertha Smith

Tracy and Karen Hughes Smith and daughter Megan.

Myra Kathryn and Vernon Smith

Brad and Lorie McKee Smith and twin daughters Hayley and Heather.

Katey Johnson, Megan Smith, Mark Johnson, Heather Smith, Hayley Smith, grandchildren of Kathryn and Vernon Smith.

Children of C.D. and Bertha Smith. Front row, L-R: Verlene Strickland, Virl Smith Verlon Smith, Viola Simmons. Back row, L-R: Varnell Smith, Virgil Smith, Van Smith, Vandel Smith, Vera Reed, Vernice Coffman, Vernon Smith, Vadie Pittman, Vester Smith.

Grandchildren of C.D. and Bertha Smith.

Joseph Sohm (b. 1912 (?), d. 1993) son of Sallie and Henry Sohm.

Margurite Sohm (b. 1915, d. 1972) and Joseph Sohm (b. 1912 (?), d. 1993).

Willie D. South and Ruth Bingham South, 1945.

Willie M. South, 1944.

Joe C. and Margaret (Atkins) South, son Willie D. South, mid 1920s.

Ruth Bingham South, Beatrice Bingham, Bernice Bingham Kiddy, 1945.

Willie D. South, D. Mullins, Ida Mae Mullins, Maggie Lee Mullins at the old Atkins home at Glen, Alcorn County, MS.

Three generations, 1929. Back row, L-R: Myra Sue Stewart, Nancy Geonetle Harrison Surratt. Front row, L-R: Mary Frances "Fannie" Surratt Stewart, Mary Nell Stewart.

Wedding picture, February 28, 1913 of Brown Stewart (b. 1882, d. 1967) and Mary Frances "Fannie" Surratt (b. 1888, d. 1976).

John Spears and wife Ethel Harrison Spears, daughter of Lon Harrison.

Harry Steen, 1926.

John William Stewart (b. 1845, d. 1918) and wife Susan S. Woods Stewart (b. 1849, d. 1926). John W. Stewart enlisted in the CSA in 1861 at the age of 16 and fought through the entire war. He died in the flu epidemic of 1918 and is buried in Holly Cemetery.

Seated center: Susan S. Woods Stewart (b. 1849, d. 1926) with her children. Back row, L-R: Donald, Ossyth, Kennon. Front row, L-R: Winston, Susan holding granddaughter Myra Sue Stewart, Brown (Myra's father).

L-R: Velma Stoop, Kyle Stoop, Claude Stoop, Lillian Stoop, Willie Lou Stoop, Evelyn Stoop, Velma Stoop, Ethelyn Stoop.

Willie Lou Stoop, Claude Stoop, Ethelyn Stoop, Evelyn Stoop and Kyle Stoop. Granddaddy Stoop worked for the State Highway Department while Lincoln was president.

Willie Lou (b. 1893, d. 1977) and Claude Walter Stoop (b. 1893, 1983).

Claude Walter and Willie Lou Stoop, ca. 1967.

Edith, William, J.C., Harold, Donald, Kenneth, Willard and Lillie Strachan.

Wanda (Driver) Strachan, Harold Strachan, Todd Strachan and Tracy Strachan, 1963.

L-R: William Newton Suitor, second wife Ella (Davis) Suitor. Children: W.N. and Alice (Lusk) Suitor's – Rufe, Lewis, Sallie, George, Mary, Nellie, Robert and Elbert, 1910.

Alice (Lusk) Suitor (b. 1845, d. 1891) born in Maury County, TN, daughter of James and Ellen Lusk.

William Newton and Alice (Lusk) Suitor

Herman Roy Suitor (b. December 14, 1904, d. March 8, 1920) second child of Lewis and Jennie Sue Suitor.

Sallie Margaret Suitor (b. 1877, d. 1917) and Henry Sohm of St. Louis, MO were married December 24, 1905. They had two children, Joseph and Margurite.

Three first cousins in the 1930s. Lucille Suitor (b. 1914, d. 1993) daughter of Lewis and Jennie Sue Suitor; Alice (b. 1915) daughter of Rufe and Mamie Suitor; Edith Suitor (b. 1907, b. 1995), daughter of George and Annie Suitor.

Elbert Newton Suitor (b. 1891, d. 1960), Minnie Kate (Green) suitor (b. 1894, d. 1978). Back, L-R: Albert Franklin (b. 1914, d. 1986), Joseph Newton (b. 1916, d. 2001). Center front is William Howard (b. 1919).

Elbert and Minnie Kate Suitor on the occasion of her 50th birthday. Sons Albert and Howard were given leave to celebrate this time. Elbert's brother Robert, her brother Joe F. Green and their families surprised her with a dinner September 28, 1944.

Oda Miller Suitor on her 97th birthday and husband George Suitor (age 93). Mrs. Suitor was known for her wood carvings and handiwork. She was the daughter of E.S. Lancaster, wood carver and carpenter. Mrs. Suitor (d. July 3, 1973) and Mr. Suitor (d. September 1974) resided on Route 2, Rienzi, MS.

Picture taken in October 1979 in Joseph N. and Mabel Suitor's home. He is the son of Elbert N. and Minnie Kate Suitor. Top to bottom: Joe Jr. and Linda Suitor, Joseph III in her lap; Joseph N. and Mabel Suitor, she has Joe Jr.'s daughter Jennie in her lap; youngest child of theirs Robert W. is in center back, James Elbert and Barbara with sons Sam and David; Kenneth and Mabeth Cortner and Will.

Elbert Newton Suitor (b. 1891, d. 1960) and Minnie Kate (Green) Suitor (b. 1894, d. 1978).

Archie and Minnie (McCrary) Strebeck Family. Front row: Clinton Lee Strebeck. Second row: twins Eddie Strebeck and Evelyn (Strebeck) Arinder, Douglas Strebeck and Alice (Strebeck) Hudson, Donald Strebeck. Back row: Dorothy (Strebeck) Wade, Minnie (McCrary) Strebeck holding Thomas Strebeck and Archie Strebeck. Richard Strebeck was born in the early 1950s, picture taken late 1940s.

Josephine Surratt, 4 years old, 1916.

Front row: William H. Surratt, Guy Ledbetter, Mary Ann Sprinkles Surratt. Back row: Mary Lee Ledbetter, Sam Ledbetter, Mary Caroline Surratt Ledbetter (b. 1876, d. 1962).

Standing, L-R: Julia Harrison Wygul, Watt Jones Surratt (Lorenzo's wife), Octavia Harrison, Hattie Surratt (Sid's wife), Lonietoos "Lon" Harrison, Etta Harrison, Lorenzo Surratt and Sidney "Sid" Surratt. Seated adults, L-R: John Morgan "Robe" Surratt, wife Nancy Geonetle Harrison Surratt. Seated children, L-R: Sidney Surratt and Gloria Jean Surratt.

Children of John Morgan and Nancy Geonetle Harrison Surratt. Standing, L-R: Mary Frances Surratt, Frank Surratt, Lonnie Surratt. Seated, L-R: Lorenzo Surratt, Sidney Surratt, ca. 1906.

Cousins, L-R: Patsy Surratt, Nelda Hamlin, Jo Ellen Surratt, Betty Hamlin, Jimmy Hurley and Louis Surratt, 1938.

Portrait of the James Thomas "Tom" Talley family in 1936. Standing, L-R: Rudell, Chester, Roy, Charley, Raymond, Ronnell and Lester. Seated, L-R: Virdie, Ruby, Loyce, Ozell, Kizzie, Tom, Modena, Lillie and Vadie.

Family portrait in 1936 of Tom and Kizzie Talley's children, spouses and grandchildren.

Talley – Thompson Mule Barn, northeast corner of Tate and Franklin Streets, 1934-59. L-R: Guy Thompson, J.R. Talley, Linnie Talley and John Bowers.

Tatum Family. Seated: William Riley "Bill" Tatum, father; Ecie Christina Potts Tatum, mother. Children: Charlie Tatum, Mary Etta Tatum (Kellum), Sidney Tatum, Cora Tatum (Warren), Willie Tatum, Thelma Mae Tatum (Glissen), Zach Tatum, Birdie Tatum (Dellinger), ca. 1920.

Mark Taylor (b. 1891, d. 1961) and Annie F. (Green) Taylor (b. 1888, d. 1949) with daughter Ruth Taylor (Davidson) (b. 1912). Mark and Annie married October 12, 1910, she was the daughter of Joe W. and Jennie L. Green.

James Major Taylor (b. 1861, d. 1919) son of James W. and Amanda Cumby Taylor as he heads out on his rural mail delivery. Pictured with him are his daughters, Florence and Dell.

Mrs. Gladys Taylor and daughter Jane E. Taylor. Mrs. Taylor died in 2001 and is buried in Hinkle Cemetery.

Theo Coleman Taylor, Jimmy and Frank Taylor, ca. 1942.

Russell Thomas and Hallie (Wilson) Thomas, 1982-83. Parents of Joyce Forman. Russell made the musical instruments shown in the picture.

Four generations, L-R: Joyce (Thomas) Forman, baby Casey Wayne Bearden, Janet (Forman) Bearden and Hallie (Wilson) Thomas.

Matthias H. Toler (b. 1825, d. 1901) Jacinto, MS.

The Tice children: Carl Tice, O'Vera Tice and Van Tice.

Eric Talley and Jay Tolleson hunting birds on Effie Lancaster's farm.

Jay Tolleson and Eric Talley having fun at Papa Moore's home.

Sybil Moore Tolleson, Jay Tolleson and Dwight Tolleson on a visit to Mississippi in search of a college for Jay.

William Martin Turner (b. 1820, d. 1877), grandfather of Col. Roscoe Turner and J.W. Turner is pictured with his Confederate uniform on. He became a prisoner of war and his health suffered terribly. He never recovered and is buried at Lebanon Cemetery. He raised his family on land now owned by his great-great-grandson, Prentiss Turner.

James William "Jim" Turner (b. 1873, d. 1916) and Georgia Alma Young Turner (b. 1873, d. 1956). J.W. and Georgia lived in the Jones/Gift Community most of their lives. They had seven children: Agnes married C.E. (Lige) Kennedy, Arthur married Mallie Smith, Payton married Frances Potts and Lottie Austin, Holley married Essie King; Beulah, Leonard and Vernon died young and are buried in Paoli, OK.

Mary Elizabeth Young Turner (b. 1828, d. 1916) wife of William Martin Turner. She was Col. Roscoe Turner's grandmother and buried at Lebanon Cemetery in the Jones/Gift Community along with numerous other Turner kin.

James David Turner (b. 1848, d. 1937) father of J.W., Frank, Gordon, Josie Lamberth, Delight Rogers and Lula Nelms, 1907 in Oklahoma Territory.

Turner Family, Oklahoma Territory August 17, 1907. Back, L-R: Agnes Turner Kennedy (daughter of J.W.), J.W. "Jim" Turner, Georgia Young Turner (wife of J.W.), James Vernon Turner (son of J.W.), James David Turner (father of J.W.) and Sarah Agnes Jones Turner (mother of J.W.). Front: Edward Arthur Turner (son of J.W.) and Mary Beulah Turner (daughter of J.W.). J.W. was a first cousin to Col. Roscoe Turner. James David was a brother to Robert Lee Turner, father of Roscoe.

James David "Dave" (son of David William and Mary Elisabeth (Young) Turner and wife Sarah Agnes (Jones) Turner and sisters, Susan Jones and Jennie (Jones) Bell. Taken by a traveling photographer in the early 1900s.

James David "Dave" Turner on a hunting trip with cousins, Clyde and Vester Coke.

Uncle Dave Turner on his mule "Old Bill" in the Gift Community in front of his home.

Family get-together in 1955 at David Frank (son of James David "Dave" and Sarah Agnes (Jones) Turner) and Sallie (daughter of John and Mary (Leatherwood) Nelms) Turner's home located on Smithbridge Road in the Jones/Gift community. First row, seated, L-R: Velma Turner Duckworth and daughter Jeri Lynn, Irene Turner, Sandra Turner Talley, Gloria Turner Roberts, Susan Turner Talley, Joe Turner, Johnny Turner, Jamie Turner and Junior Turner. Second row, seated: David Frank Turner, Sallie Nelms Turner, Amy Turner Taylor (baby in Sallie's lap) and David Turner. Third row, standing: Price "Pud" Turner, F.L. Turner, Macon Rickman, Neal James Turner, Hillie Turner, Bessie Turner Rickman, Clayton Turner, Annie (Hagy) Turner and Hermie Monroe Turner.

Portrait of the James Thomas "Tom" Talley family. Tom was the son of Richard and Caroline (Dennis) Talley. He married Kizzie Adelene Cartwright, daughter of James Monroe and Ellen (Medford) Cartwright. Back row, standing, L-R: Modena, Lillie, Vadie and Lester. Front row: Ronnel, Raymond in Tom's lap, Tom, Charley, Roy in Kizzie's lap and Kizzie.

Edward Arthur Turner (b. 1903, d. 1992) and Mallie Smith Turner (b. 1909, d. 1975).

The Tyson Clan of Alcorn County, 1920. Pictured in the dark suit is Joseph Albert Tyson (b. August 20, 1860, d. September 15, 1927). Joseph's wife Eliza is seated beside him.

Back row, L-R: Ella Mae Utley, Charles Utley, Mary Bynum, David Babb, Eliza Babb, Myrtle Gann Parker and Joe Dickson. Front row, L-R: Tommy Hynmen, Pearl Utley, Mary Benize Cratey.

Louise (Powers) Vanderford, Leonard Vanderford, Mary (Driver) Vanderford (second wife of Christopher Pleasant Vanderford). Dave Vanderford's mother and brother.

William Jackson "Jack" Vanstory in his Blacksmith Shop at Rienzi, MS, 1923.

L-R: Ann Vanstory, Margaret Harwood Vanstory, Tommy Vanstory, Kittie Mae and Happy Vanstory, December 1966, Kemps Chapel Church.

Margaret, Mary and Tommy Vanstory at 1206 N. Parkway, Corinth, MS, 1992.

Jeffrey Wyatt Vatalaro and Connie Rast Vatalaro, 1994.

John Martin Voyles and Florence (Griffin) Voyles, late 1940s.

Edward Voyles, Naomi (Voyles) Wall, Dora (Griffin) Voyles, Allen Voyles, Hershell Voyles, 1956.

Back row: Carolyn (Wall) Duhon, Dewey Wall, Naomi (Voyles) Wall, Mickey Lambert, Faye (Wall, Lambert) Franks. Front row: Bobby Robbins and Terry Wall. Dewey Wall Family and Bobby Robbins, 1956.

Naomi (Voyles) Wall, Allen Voyles, Edward Voyles, Dora (Griffin) Voyles, Hershell Voyles. Allen and Dora's 50th wedding anniversary, June 23, 1962.

Elvira Frances (Dilworth) Walker (b. 1842, North Carolina, d. 1915, Mississippi) married Alexander A. Walker September 28, 1856.

Alexander Allison Walker (b. 1828, North Carolina, d. 1895, Mississippi), husband of Elvira Frances Dilworth.

Elvira Frances Walker (b. 1842, North Carolina, d. 1915). Second from left: Joseph Anderson Walker, Minnie (b. 1873, d. 1913), John, Lylia (ca. 1858) and Edgar Oneal. Back row: Jennie (b. 1868, d. 1941), Mary Edna (Eddie b. 1862, d. 1944), Sarah E. (Sallie b. 1860, d. 1899) and a neighbor.

James Newton Walker (b. 1911, d. 1966) and Mildred Walker (Sawyer) (b. 1908, d. 1999). Children of Joseph L. and Mary Suitor Walker.

James Newton Walker on his farm in 1950. This farm was named "Ann Arbor."

Walker siblings gather to celebrate Barry Walker's birthday, late 1950s. their parents were David Settle Walker (b. 1858, d. 1920) and Minnie Barry Walker (b. 1862, d. 1933). The Walkers are buried in Wheeler Cemetery. L-R: Lollie Walker Kitchens (b. 1900, d. 1967), Kendall Walker (b. 1887, d. 1969), Grace Walker Lamberth (b. 1894, d. 1966) and Barry Walker (b. 1886, d. 1962).

Four generations. Front row: Mary Suitor Walker, great-grandson Ben Walker Dilworth, granddaughter Gwen Walker Dilworth West. In back is son Milton Wheeler Walker.

Gillian and Jack Wallace

Ruth (Wallace) Suggs, Charlene (Wallace) Hurley, Maxine (Wallace) Barnes, Doris (Wallace) Barnes, Kenneth Rae Wallace, March 7, 1992.

John Wammack at work at Tyrone September 1985, C.S. Department.

Adrienne Combs Webb (b. 1896, d. 1987) was the daughter of J.B. Combs, principal of the Colored School. After high school, Adrienne attended Normal College for teachers. She served as a substitute teacher, as well as pianist at the St. Mark Baptist Church. Adrienne was married to William Dakota Webb and they had six children.

Lester Whirley Sr. and Eula Mae (Crouch) Whirley were married April 18, 1931 in Montgomery County, MS. Leck, as he was fondly known, was born in Alcorn County to Jessie Whirley and Fannie (Crum) Whirley. Mae, as she was fondly known, was born in Atwood, AL. They have four children: Lester Jr., Bertha, Jessie and Lloyd C.

Lloyd Chester Whirley, son of Lester and Eul[a] Mae (Crouch) Whirley was born January 17[,] 1945 at the Pinkey Adkin's place in Glen, Alcor[n] County, MS. Lloyd, also known as Chester o[r] Cooter, married Lecy Paulette Parker born Ma[y] 18, 1945 in Prescott, AR to David Allen and Lec[y] Alene (Bell) Parker. They have five children[.] Front row: Anthony, Teresa, Rickey, Lloy[d] Chester holding Randy, Paulette and Cindy.

Ethel White, Olen Woods and Pauline Edwards, brother and sisters, summer 1984.

Sitting: Will and Mary Beth Nash Whittemore[.] Standing: Vickey and Dora Whittemore.

William Dakota Webb (b. 1892, d. 1975) was born in Rienzi. At the age of 19 he started employment at the US Post Office as a messenger custodian. He held this job for over 50 years, retiring in 1962. He was active in church and Boy Scouts. As an entrepreneur, Dakota raised chickens. His Tryme Chicken Farm raised Plymouth Rock chickens, which he sold locally and to neighboring towns. The Webb homestead on Meigg Street was donated to the City of Corinth in 1990.

J.J. Whittemore Family. Seated: Eunice Vera Burcham (b. 1914, d. 1979), Cordelia Sellers Whittemore (b. 1889, d. 1970), John Jonas (b. 1887, d. 1970), Perry Dalton (b. 1913, d. 1987), Herman Hardy, Jodie "James" Terrell (b. 1919, d 1988), Ira Cecil and John Curtis Whittemore, ca. 1970.

First row: John C. Wilbanks, Zena Wilbanks, Kit Bobo Wilbanks. Second row: Ish Crum, Martha Clark, Cora Russell, 1908.

The Emert Wilbanks Family, 1949. Bessie Barnes Wilbanks, Paul Wilbanks, Emert Wilbanks, Levoyd Wilbanks, Bobby Wilbanks.

Donie Wilbanks with her children in 1940. She was the widow of Harling Wilbanks who died in 1940, leaving her with eight children. In 1946, her sister-in-law died shortly after giving birth to twin daughters and Donie adopted the babies. She raised the 10 children alone. Shown here with Donie are Maedeen, Irene, Evelena, Floyd, Dorothy, Pauline, Helen and Kenneth Wilbanks.

Bluford Wilbanks and Myrtle Coleman Wilbanks

John West and Comfort Wilbanks, ca. 1915. They were early settlers in western Alcorn County and came from Union County, SC, ca. 1850.

Bluford Wilbanks and Jimmy Taylor

Emert Wilbanks in the country store he operated in the mid 1950s in Goosepond Bottom, western Alcorn County.

The Emert Wilbanks Family, 1993. Levoyd Wilbanks, Shirley Wilbanks Hollis, Emert Wilbanks, Paul Wilbanks, Bessie Barnes Wilbanks, Pat Wilbanks Malone, Bobby Wilbanks.

Mark L. Wilbanks (b. 1913, d. 1983) and wife Fredra Brooks Wilbanks (b. 1917).

Sarah Beth Wilbanks, daughter of Rickey and Sarah (Allen) Wilbanks, 1998.

Rickey Brenton Wilbanks, son of Rickey and Sarah (Allen) Wilbanks, 1993.

Vadeen Wilbanks

Wood Family, August 5, 1904. Standing, L-R: Eldred K. Wood, Mattie Wood Taylor, Nora Louisa Wood, Callie Pearl Wood Strachan. Sitting, L-R: William Macajah Wood (father), Claudia May Wood Martin, Margaret Jane Jones Wood (mother), Bannie Wood Moore in mother's lap, Orval Meeks Wood and Grandma Beene.

Sunday afternoon, 1942. L-R: Olen Woods, Dessie Woods, Maude Woods, Andrew Woods, Mr. A. Jackson, neighbor.

Grandpa (Andrew) Woods resting from his labor in the vegetable garden, summer 1941.

Mr. and Mrs. Andrew Woods of Glen, MS sitting on their front porch.

Dr. L. W. Worsham

Corinth and Vicinity, Alcorn County, MS.

Second Corinth Courthouse. The cornerstone was laid in 1880 and it burned in 1917.

The old county jail located on Taylor Street by the railroad tracks. Located in the top of the jail was the "hanging gallows."

Waldron Hotel, ca. 1910

Union Depot, Corinth, MS

The Opera House located on the corner of Foote and Franklin Street, ca. early 1920s.

Greyhound Bus Station, 1940 in Corinth, MS.

The Corinth fire of December 29, 1924. This scene is of the Post Office which was gutted by flames. The picture was taken looking southeast.

An entire city block was consumed by the fire of 1924. This photo was taken looking northeast toward the block where 50 businesses were destroyed including the "Opera House." The fire consumed the entire block from Foote Street to Waldron and from Fillmore Street to Franklin Street.

Scene looking towards the southwest. The court House is on the left out of scene where the three cars are parked.

This shot was taken looking southeast from Foote Street, the Court House can be seen in the back left of the picture.

A closer view of the destruction caused by the fire looking south.

This scene was taken looking north.

Looking south two business names can still be seen on portions of some of the remaining brick walls.

Rubel Building, downtown Corinth

Arlin Davis's Gulf Station located on the corner of Foote and Taylor Street. In the picture is his brother Lee Davis, ca. mid 1950s.

(Right) Corinth Post Office new 1920s and Personnel Building now used as SouthBank," Fillmore Street. Pictured: Mark Potts on motorcycle, Jobe Leeth in front of post office, Elbert Lamberth, Hillman Mathis, E.J. Duncan (at top), Garfield King, H.L. Hardin, Sam B. Jones, Elmer Martin, M.A. Candler, R.E. L. Mitchell, J.M. Brady, Elgin Wright, P.M. Fred Elgin, Ledford Dickerson, Jim Brice, Jim Taylor, Alex Modlin, Bud Felker, Charlie Bennett, unknown by light post.

Retirement party for C.W. Galbraith from Southern Bell Telephone and Telegraph Co. with senior manager T.E. Harris.

Pickwick Theater, 1940 in Corinth, MS.

Elvie Byron Austin (man standing with straw hat). He was part owner of the Ray & Austin Shoes.

Ray and Margaret Hamlin home on Proper Street. Whitfield bought the house and it became Corinth Hospital. In 1995 it became Whitfield Nursing Home.

Boatman Meat Market, ca. 1927. William Ester Boatman and his father, Will Tom Boatman. Located on corner of Fillmore and Wick Street, across from Mitchell Department Store.

Mr. Vic Box of Victor Box Company in Corinth, MS. Mr. Box was demonstrating his new tractor for the local farmers in front of the courthouse, 1952.

Home of Dr. L.W. Worsham, 117 Main Street.

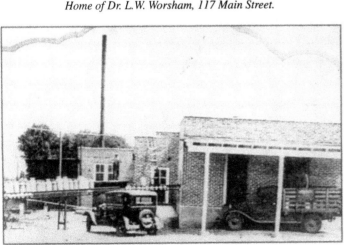

Cheese Plant about 1934. John Oscar Brown's truck is setting under the shed.

The Fish Pond House was built in 1856 by I.P. Young for his daughter Mattie Neely. This photograph dates from 1862 and is the earliest available of the house at 708 Kilpatrick Street. It shows clearly the ornate railing surrounding a tin-lined basin on the roof. This architectural design was called a Fish Pond Top and is only seen on a few remaining antebellum homes. The windows underneath provided cooling and the water container may have assisted with indoor "facilities." Also, shown in the photo are modifications made by the general's headquarters there. Canvas flaps protected sentries from the afternoon sun and another kept rain out at the office window on the south side of the house. The tent in the yard probably housed an Aide. Another interesting note, the US blanket thrown across the corral fence adjacent to headquarters probably dates this picture to the summer of 1862 when the Union forces took command at Corinth.

115

Waldron Street, downtown Corinth, 1906.

Court Square, downtown Corinth, ca. 1926.

W.S. McDonald receiving $5 for the toughest rooster in Alcorn County.

Corinth Centennial, Monday, May 22, 1954. W. S. McDonald leading team. Beulah and Peggy McDonald driving team. South side of Corinth Courthouse. Advertising by Swift's Liberty Cash.

Championship bowlers from Corinth. Marvin Kreel, Martin Essary, Alton Sargent, Larry Essary and Jim Philamlee, September 1980.

Whittlers on Courthouse Square. Pictured are: Lee Essary (father of Clovis), Junior Boyd, Elmo Hurst, unknown, Aud Mask (father of Gertrude Dunn), unknown, early 1980s.

Picnic group of Black and White Store in 1940s.

Ray Stenett, Bert Mills, Jim Buck Ross and John D. Merceir.

County Officials, 1950s. L-R: Bubba Coleman, 4th District Supervisor; Jeff Briggs, 1st District Supervisor; unknown, Clarence Edge, 3rd District Supervisor; J.G. Driver, 2nd District Supervisor; Herman Madden, Chancery Court Clerk; Mark Dillingham, 5th District Supervisor; N.S. Sweat, Lawyer. Ladies L-R: Madge Wilkinson and Gladys Vanderford.

Zeke Martin and Kitty Scott with other entertainers at WCMA.

Daniel F. Lamberth on left, Alcorn County Agriculture Commissioner and unidentified man look over corn in 1920s.

Glen Group. First row: Ada Leitch Strachan, Francis Potts, Callie Dancer, Allie Potts, Jim Brown, Willard Potts, Noel Potts. Second row: Charlie Strachan, Luke Dancer, Bose Wood, James Strachan, Author Roy, John Anderson, Bill Dancer, John Choate, Haywood White. Third row: Jim Strachan, E.D. Wood, Billy Atkins, Luke Choate, Joe Joslin, William Strachan, Johnny Dancer, Tom Lewis. Fourth row: Walter Brown, Saul Choate, Sandy Roy, Dave Strachan, Taylor Dancer, Mark Choate, John Roy, Jimmy Leitch, Frank Joslin, John Potts.

"Big Ike" located in Tuscumbia Bottom south of Corinth near Highway 145. Said to be one of the largest pecan trees in the state of Mississippi. It was destroyed by the State Highway Department when widening the highway. Sam B. Jones is standing by the tree to indicate its size, January 7, 1989.

Abe Dilworth place at Hinkle on Mitchell Hill Road.

Biggersville, Alcorn County, MS.

A most interesting picture of oxen and a group of men, women and children. It looks like a sawmill. Perhaps in the early 1900s. This came from Biggersville, MS.

The R.C. Cates house at Kossuth was built shortly after the Civil War and burned about 1917.

The old Kossuth Post Office, former Matt Dixon Store.

Louis Kossuth (b. 1802, d. 1894) a Hungarian freedom fighter for whom the town of Kossuth was named in 1853.

This hotel in Kossuth, MS was owned by Joh Savage.

This sign is at the west entrance on Highway that goes through the town of Kossuth. Erecte in 1996 by the Kossuth Community Club. L-R Cleo Wilbanks, Ruby Collins, Virginia Moore Charles and Elizabeth Frederick.

This sign was erected on Highway 2 in Kossuth in 1996 by the Kossuth Historical Society.

Leedy, Alcorn County, MS.

Leedy Depot

Rienzi, Alcorn County, MS.

Postal employees Rienzi Post Office around 1950. Barney Burnett, Postmaster; W.C. Graves, F.E. Wicks, P.A. Hudson, Cleveland Green, mail carriers; Stacy Rutledge, postal clerk and Arlin Johnson, sub clerk.

C.B. Curlee store, demolished during 1913 cyclone in Rienzi. Looking north the Livery Stable and Dr. Perry's two-story home was untouched.

Wenasoga, Alcorn County, MS.

Post Office/General Store, Wenasoga, MS. L-R: Levi "Dee" Smith (owner), Sarah Smith, Maude (friend of family) Evner Smith, Green Lee Smith (owner), Anne Smith (wife of Green), ca. 1910.

1950 V.M. Box Motor Co. Back row: Donnie Berlin, Frank Benjamin, Wallace Benjamin, Amos Bearden, Ray Gibbs, Bill Scott, Jay Bearden, A.J. Benjamin, Arlin Davis. Front row: unknown, Willard Palmer, Milton Benjamin, Jimmy McFalls, Jay Henderson, Ellis Rencher. Jimmy McFalls worked at the Ford Motor Co. for 37 years, retiring in 1965.

1964 "Grand Opening" on Highway 72 West, Corinth, MS. Car salesmen, Steve C. Coleman and Mark L. Wilbanks.

V.M. Box Motors, 1937. Back row: Owen Angle, unknown, Willie Gilliland, Reese Kennedy, V.M. Box, Evelyn Fowler, unknown, Clovis Henderson. First row: Jimmy McFalls, Lonnie Richards, Arlin Davis, unknown Canon, J. D. Crawford.

M. Byrnes Hardware, Est. 1885

Johnnie C. Rast (right), Century Electric Mfg., 1965.

Mrs. Una Sanders, Daisy Queen & BBQ at Leck Fraleys.

Horton Brothers' new office building located on Highway 45 North.

Dolan Bugg and Harold Isbell, Dean Truck Line, May 1969.

Gaultney Motor Company, ca. 1935-36. Back row: Willie Gilliland, unknown, David Gaultney, unknown, unknown, V.M. Box. Front row: unknown, unknown, unknown, J.D. Crawford, unknown, Jimmy McFalls.

Hughes Motor Company, 1949. L-R: unknown, Cletus Gatlin, Bratton Burgess, Ben T. Rogers and Tom Smith.

Herbert Isbell in front of O.C. Isbell's Meat Market on Bunch Street, 1950s.

Robert and O.C. Isbell in O.C. Isbell's Meat Market, hams in background.

On May 12, 1993 the doors of Magnolia Funeral Home, located at 1223 Tate Street in Corinth, were opened to serve the needs of the people of Corinth/Alcorn County and the surrounding area with dignity and respect. Magnolia Funeral Home is locally owned and operated by Jim Johnson, Jimmy Calvary, James Cornelius, Leroy Brown and Charlie Browning.

P.W. North Sr. (left), Grocery Store & Jewelry

C.F. Palmer General Merchandise, Rienzi, MS.

Waits is the oldest jewelry store in Corinth, MS. It was founded in 1865 and is now owned by 94 year old Mrs. Eugenie Lynch Waits and operated by her niece Betty Lynch Ashcroft.

Office employees of Weaver Pants Factory, 1948. Standing, second from left, is Hilda Sherrod Brawner; standing far right is Gilbert Sherrod; sitting front on right is Mary Sue Faircloth and sitting behind her is Betty Jo Simmons (Armstrong).

Henry Vanderford, third from right, organized the Vanderford Funeral Home in the 1920 to 1950s. It was located at the New Blat for 30 years. He passed away Christmas Day, 1932. His co-workers were Goldie Wells, J.P. Watson, Henry Vanderford, wife Adra, Lila Watson and Mary Wells.

Weavers Pants Corporation, Union Local 707 Officers, 1957. First row, L-R: Emma Garrett, W.A. Stevens, Effie Kuykendall, Jonnie Sassar, James King, Lela Moore, Billy Brawner, Larry Brinkley, Doyle Moore, Rodney Haynie, Nathan Richardson, Sid Stevenson, G.B. Voyles. Second row, L-R: Ardeen Howell, Alford Dillon, Leroy Mask, Doris Miller, Tom Shults, Milton Bain, Auttie Holley, Earl Price, Stanley Bennett, Goddard Callahan, James Nunley, Mr. Doggett.

Johnnie C. Rast with Worsham's Brother's Construction, breaking up concrete to build a new Sears Roebuck building, corner of Foote and Taylor Street, Corinth, MS.

Rev. James Thomas Killough, ordained Baptist minister, son of Thomas David and Sarah Jane (Perry) Killough, brother of Margaret, William Ebenezer, John Pryor, Mary Jane and half-brother to David Harrison Killough.

August 14, 1918, Brush Creek Baptist Church, Alcorn County, MS. Ann Burrow Jones' funeral. Standing in door, back row, husband Oscar Jones (b. 1890, d. 1965) holding son Willie James Jones (b. 1909, d. 1992). Joe Allen Roten is in the buggy. Bud Bennett is sitting on second row, fifth from the right.

Rev. Richard Clements, pastor East Corinth Baptist Church.

Kemp's Chapel Baptist Church founded 1923, 853 Road 356. Dedication of minister's home, 1972. First row, L-R: Harold Graves, Leslie Clay (Dess) Nash (b. 1901, d 1986), Howard Nash (b. 1910, d. 1980), Lewis Cleatus Rowsey (b. 1924, d. 1988), Grady Nash, James Chase, Jimmy Robinson, Clifford Rinehart, Jesse V. Perry (b. 1905, d. 1994), Mrs. Gentry, Mr. Gentry, Jessie F. Rinehart (b. 1900, d. 1991), Renee Nash, Jill Nash, Anthony Perry. Second row, L-R: June Chase Brown, Judy Palmer, Evelyn "Sissy" Kennedy McLemore, Tammie Nash Prior, Cindy Robinson, Debbie Nash Price, Diane Graves Weathers, Beulah Vanderford Nash (b. 1903, d. 1999), Lizzie Felks (b. 1913, d. 1997), Avis Nash Burcham Crum, Cora Gunthorp, Ludie B. Childers (b. 1908, d. 1988), Thelma Rinehart, Eva Richardson, Greta Robinson, Douglas Richardson (b. 1898, d. 1981), Iva Burcham Perry (b. 1914, d. 1998), Albie Smith Nash (b. 1917, d. 1998), Barney Nash, Jankey Nash. Third row, L-R: Earlene Rowsey, Gwen Nash, Brosure Y. Nash (b. 1914, d. 1988), Tammie Robinson, Evelyn Bobo Rinehart, Lena Rippie, Sarah Whitley Brackeen, Linda Suitor Rowsey, Danny Rowsey, Genette Brackeen Chase, Odie Nash, Donnie Chase, visitor and husband.

Vacation Bible School, First Baptist Church, Corinth, MS, early 1940s, southeast corner of Fillmore and Childs Streets.

Dedication of the First Baptist Church, Corinth, 1954. Pastor D.L. Hill, seated center aisle, back left, minister at that time. Former pastors are front row center aisle.

Hinkle Creek Baptist Church was organized November 2, 1853. Savage School House was the first meeting place and Hamilton Giles Savage was its first pastor. Dr. George Martin Savage, so of Rev. Hamilton Giles Savage is shown standing in front, ca. 1900s.

Holly Baptist Church Vacation Bible School, Class of 1946.

Macedonia dress up "Old Times Day," Freewill Baptist Church, ca. 1975.

Tishomingo Chapel Baptist Church

Sardis Primitive Baptist Church east of Rienzi, MS, 1958.

1914 Thanksgiving dinner on the ground, Bethel Church, Highway 45. Beginning on the left: Mrs. Jim Epps and son Ruby Epps, Hilbert and Walter Hearn, William and James Epps, Jim Epps, Lillian Epps, Clarence and Mamie Edge, Annie Maud Epps, Ruth Bynum, Ella Edge, Kate Bynum. A teacher Irene Blackwell, Katie Ward Bynum, Didge Blackwell, Fannie Blackwell, Bessie Kilpatrick, Walter Blackwell, Edward Hearn, Arthur Blackwell, Boy, Elsie Kilpatrick, Frank Blackwell, child, Rufe Suitor, Clayton Suitor, Mrs. Lon Dilworth, Mamie Suitor, Louella Hamilton, Annie Suitor, Lon Dilworth, Joseph Bynum, child, Mrs. Jessie Bynum, Bud Bynum, Edith Suitor, Joshua Blackwell, Gertrude Blackwell.

A Sunday School Class on the front steps of Waldron St. Christian Church in the early 1900s. Those identified include: O.M. Wood Sr., Lorena George, Lillian George, Sam Richardson, Byrd Ijams Stone, M.T. Sharp.

St. Paul's Episcopal Church, established 1903 on Taylor Street, Corinth, MS, old location. Moved to new building in new location 2001.

Calvary Pentecostal Church, Bunch Street, 1960s. Rev. H.O. Duncan, pastor.

St. Paul's Episcopal Church, corner of Highway 2 and Shiloh Road, new location in 2001.

First Pentecostal Church, choir in he mid 1930s, Tate Street, Corinth, MS.

First Pentecostal Church, Tate Street, 1948. The church burned in 1951. The new church was relocated at the corner of Cruise and Proper Streets.

First Pentecostal Church at Cruise and Proper Streets, Corinth, MS from 1953 to 1999. Moved to new location on Highway 72 East, November 1999.

First Pentecostal Church, choir director Gilbert Hillard, mid to late 1950s, located at Cruise and Proper Streets.

Mark Cornelius Sunday School Class, First Pentecostal Church at Cruise and Proper Streets.

First Pentecostal Church Men's Sunday School Class "The Bereans." Rev. A.D. Gurley pastor, third from right on first row, located at Cruise and Proper Streets.

First Pentecostal Church, 2037 Highway 72 East, Corinth, MS. Pastor, Nelson Hight at new location, November 1999.

Hatchie Chapel Church, established 1952, Floyd Crum, pastor.

Pastor of Hatchie Chapel Church, Floyd Crum with his wife, Dean Nelson Crum, April 2000.

1911 photo of the Macedonia church members. Standing at the far right is Zachariah Garrett Prince.

Shown are members and neighbors of an African Methodist Episcopal Church, which until Urban Renewal of the 1960s sat near the meeting point of the west side of block 500-600 on old King Street. The pastoring couple at the late 1930s date was Rev. Mims and wife, second and third from the left on the second row from the bottom.

"Singing School" at Old Bethel Methodist Church, Rienzi, MS in the grove south of the church on Highway 45. Instructor, Florence Anderson, ca. 1910. Children in front on ground: Opal Miller (Rutledge), Ruby Epps, William Epps, Edward Massengale. Second row: Rufe Suitor, Clayton Suitor, Roy Suitor, Minnie (Walker) Suitor, Lizzie Bardhman, Jim Epps, Barney Epps, Mrs. Jim Epps, Mrs. Josie Lancaster, Minnie Kate Green, Annie (Storey) Suitor, Edith Suitor, George Suitor. Third row: __Green, Jennie V. Green, Odell Green, Ruby Dalton, Edna Carpenter, Ida Lancaster, Virdie Massengale, Kate Hamilton, Joe F. Green, Hillie Green, Elmo Elam, unknown, Keith Anderson, Annie Green, Monato Carpenter, Annie Maude Epps, Lillian Epps, Mamie Edge, Claude Hearn, Vivian Massengale, Edward Hearn, Bessie Storey, __ Storey, unknown. Back row: Claude Carpenter, Maude Carpenter, Hugh McCord, Louella Hamilton, William Carpenter, Cora Carpenter, Charlie Dilworth, Jasper Green, Leander Massengale.

The First Methodist Church was organized in the early 19th century. In 1858 the first church was built in the downtown center. The old church served as a hospital during the Civil War. Its men's Bible Class has won National honors. It has been the seat of a large number of Annual Conferences of the First Methodist Church. The congregation of the First Methodist Church is now worshipping in one of the most up-to-date churches in the south. Rev. Roy A. Grisham is the present pastor.

Kossuth Methodist Church Homecoming, ca. 1941.

Gaines Chapel United Methodist Church, 1854-2001. This building was built in 1912 as a modest one-room frame building on a lot adjacent to the Bell School.

Rienzi United Methodist Church, 1988.

New Hope Church, 1890.

New Hope Presbyterian Church, Biggersville MS. This picture was made in 1983 of the present building.

The congregation of Corinth's First Presbyterian Church purchased property on the northeast corner of Foote and Franklin Streets in 1887. The edifice was built there in 1894. Extensive renovations and the installation of a pipe organ occurred in 1926. This building was abandoned when the congregation moved to its present location on Shiloh Road in 1953, later is was torn down.

1900 Get-together of New Hope Church. Ely Mitchell and wife, Vick Hill, Will Settle, Barbara Settle, Oscar Dilworth, Virdie Dilworth, Marcus Morrison, Minnie Dilworth Morrison, Sam Settle and Maud Settle. Seated R.E. Honnoll, others not identified.

New Hope Presbyterian Church, Biggersville, MS, May 1988. 150th year celebration, many attended for services and dinner. A great day!

Pleasant Ridge Cumberland Presbyterian Church built ca. 1890 on an one-acre lot given by E.J. Green. P.A. Honnoll, W.N. Suitor and J.F. McCord, Trustees. Located near Wesley Chapel Methodist Church in the Hinkle Community.

Pleasant Ridge Presbyterian Church USA, built in 1934 in the Hinkle community located on the main road.

Pleasant Ridge Presbyterian Church, Hinkle, MS. In November 1950 the congregation held Thanksgiving and Centennial Services in the church. It was a beautiful warm day, dinner was enjoyed on the ground, snow fell that night. "A day of homecoming for many." The church was dissolved in 1982.

Clarence E. Lamberth of the Pleasant Hill community near Kossuth, served on Alcorn ASCS Committee in 1960s. He is shown making a presentation at Annual Convention in Biloxi.

4-H Resource Development June 1976 Conference Fontana Village Resort, NC. Pictured: Mrs. Sam (Virginia) Jones, Sam B. Jones, Lon Perry (leader), Linda Wolfe, Ginger Jones, __ Wilbanks, unknown.

Lions Club, L-R: Henry Arnold, Jessie Clausel and Robert Wolfe.

Hanley Erwin Hasseltine, MD Eagle Scout, God and Country Award, 1961.

Alcorn Bar Association meeting honoring B.F. Worsham Sr., W.C. Sweat Sr. and Ely Mitchell on 50 years of practice of law in Corinth, October 27, 1955 at Cannoneer Restaurant. (1A) Frank Worsham, (1) Dot Worsham, (2) Betty Shirley, (3) Bob Shirley, (4) W.C. Sweat Jr., (5) Dot Sweat, (6) N.S. Sweat Jr., (7) Joe Burge Mitchell, (8) unknown, (9) Cary Stovall, (10) Lillian Stovall, (11) Vivian Sweat, (12) Spurgon Sweat, (13) Ely Mitchell, (14) Judge Raymond Jarvis, (15) Mattie Lee Sweat, (16), W.C. Sweat, (17) Helen Boone Worsham, (18) B.F. Worsham, (19) Judge Kyle, (20) Mary Kirk Adams, (21) W.C. Adams, (22) Margaret Smith, (23), Hack Smith, (24) Clifford Worsham, (25) Mildred Worsham, (26) Rubel Phillips, (27) Doris Price, (28) Margaret Phillips, (29) Jimmy Price, (30) H.M. Ray, (31) Christine Hopper, (32) Merle Ray, (33) Hugh Hopper, (34) Essie Dean, (35) William Sharp, (36) Johnny Louise Young, (37) unknown, (38) Vannie Godwin, (39) unknown, (40) Martin Shelton, (41) Frances Shelton, (42) unknown, (43) unknown, (44) unknown, (45) Chester Sumners, (46) Mrs. Chester Sumners, (47) unknown.

Alcorn County Farm Bureau picnic at Settles Grove in Biggersville, 1930s. Known members, first row: Lottie Brooks, Howard Brooks, Cleo Bridges and Hillie Bridges. Third row: Tom Brooks and Mrs. Tom Brooks.

Daughters of the American Revolution La Salle Chapter, Corinth, MS. Frances Ramer, Regent. First row: Nancy Kizer and Kathryn Sewell. Second row: France Ramer, Bobbie Anthony, Minnie Ulmer, Virginia Chambers, Sara Hudson and Nita Dees, 2001.

The 4-H Clubs parade downtown, Corinth, MS. Bro. Harris Counce Jr. is driving the tractor, Geneva Shipman is to the left of Bro. Counce, Max Rhodes is to the right of Bro. Counce and the queen is Marjorie Dees (others unknown), ca. 1950.

The Majors Little League baseball team of 1968 at the YMCA when it was located at Fourth and Washington Streets in Corinth.

Lee Luther Hasseltine Jr. (b. 1940, d. 1996) Eagle Scout. Receiving the God and Country Award April 1956 in the First Methodist Church on Taylor Street with his parents and brother Hanley.

Brownie and Girl Scout leaders, West Corinth School, 1960. Front row, L-R: Louie Cantrell, Dorothy Dees, Velma Norvell. Back row: ParaLee Stewart and Mrs. Mancel Rowland.

Girl Scout Troop No. 35. R-L: Theresa Ann (Rast) Calhoun and cousin Cheryl Denise Bowen.

United Daughters of America, 2001 meeting.

Alpha Class, May 24, 1921. Corinth Lodge of Perfection, Ancient and Accepted Scottish Rite of Freemasonry, Corinth, MS. (1) F.K. McRae, Corinth. (2) W.R. Nelson, Vice President. (3) G.R. Mitchell, Booneville. (4) J.W. Sanders, Booneville. (5) J.M. Witt, Tupelo. (6) S.M. Hamm, Booneville. (7) H.M. McAmis, Corinth. (8) C.E. Campbell, Booneville.(9) W.D. Patrick, Booneville. (10) F.H. Muse, Booneville. (11) W.C. Graves, Rienzi. (12) J.R. Galyean, Corinth. (13) O.L. Meeks, President. (14) S.R. Hinds, Tupelo. (15) S.D. Bramlett Sr., Corinth. (16) Dr. A.C. Jones, Booneville. (17) J.R. Cates, Kossuth. (18) W.C. Adams, Orator. (19) P.T. Jones Jr., Corinth. (20) H.E. Stephenson, Corinth. (21) J.Y. Bell, Corinth. (22) C.L. Bryan, Corinth. (23) J.F. Perkins, Corinth. (24) Dr. S. L. Stephenson, Corinth. (25) C.V. Taylor, Corinth. (26) W.O. Shoemaker, Corinth. (27) W.F. Riley, Tupelo, Secretary. (28) C.A. Nichols, Corinth. (29) J.M. Hanley, Corinth. (30) H. E. Roebke, Rienzi. (31) J.R. McCarter, Rienzi. (32) C.G. Fairchild, Tupelo. (33) F. P. Weaver, Corinth. (34) H.C. Wardlow, Corinth. (35) J.H. Shalliday, Corinth. (36) N.L. Armistead, Corinth. (37) A. L. Johnsey, Corinth. (38) J.C. Bishop, Corinth. (39) W.C. Peeler Jr., Booneville, (40) J.C. Jones, Corinth. (41) L.E. Spencer, Tupelo. (42) Joe Brandt, Corinth.

Corinth Chapter No. 333 of the United Daughters of the Confederacy, organized September 13, 1899. Katherine Sewell, president.

Corinth Lodge Freemasonry

Corinth YMCA All Star Basketball team traveled to Vicksburg in 1959. Front row, L-R: Hull Davis, Jimmy Wheeler, Mickey Linder, Andre Dodd, Jimmy Shackelford. Back row, L-R: Tommy "Red" Harmon, Tommy Robertson, Walter Green, Edwin Coleman, John Burton Williams, Steve Davis.

Corinth Fire Department, ca. 1920s. Kneeling in front, L-R: Brodie Jackson, Mike Byrnes, Jesse Bynum. Back row, L-R: Dr. W. L. Stroup, Paul Timlake, Bud Pace, John Timlake, Mark Strickland, Ed Byrnes, Red James, Herbert Denton, Garnett Lanning, Albert Pace and John Pace.

Corinth Fire Department, 1953, Christmas toys rebuilt by Byrd, Forsythe, Caster, Wammack, Switzer and Stevenson.

Corinth Fire Department, 1954. Bill Switzer, Robert Caster, Charlie Forsythe, Bill Wammack and two unknown.

Corinth Fire Department, 1954, with first fire truck, a 1927 LaFranc (Ole Betsey).

Fireman Banquet, December 1954.

Corinth City Firefighters compete in North American Combat Challenge for the first time April 2000. There were two teams, both qualifying to compete in the World Challenge held in Las Vegas, NV. Standing, L-R: Sky Wood, Chris Bullock, Chris Duncan, Shawn Nelms, Jamie Judkins and Ronnie Taylor. Kneeling: Jeff Hilliard, David Stanley, Greg Hopkins, Clint Green.

Corinth City Firefighters competed again in 2001, also qualifying for the World Competition held in Memphis, TN. This year they finished fifth. Back row, L-R: Chris Duncan, Ronnie Taylor, Shawn Nelms. Front row, L-R: Clay Talley, Jeff Hilliard.

Corinth Police Department officers, ca. late 1930s. Chief of police is on the left. Sitting on the motorcycle is Hillie Coleman.

This group picture of the Corinth Police Force was made August 1948. Back row, L-R: Carmon Johnson, Joseph Archie Tyson, W.D. "Boots" Carroll, James Marlin Roaten, Harold Hinton and Candler Steen. Front row, L-R: Ed Allen, Ed Morgan, Albert Simpson, Coleman Rogers and Conn Wardlow.

On the left is James Marlin Roaten and to his right is Harold Hinton, 1948.

Corinth Police Department, 1960. Front row: M.W. Baggett, Chief Harold Hinton, Carmon Johnson, Robert Burns. Second row: Tandy Null, Benny Gann, Don Watkins, James Young, Lee Ellenburg, John Howard Payne. Back row: Lawrence Phifer, Delbert Ray Burns, C.T. Bullard, Max Carroll, Ray King, J.W. Dixon.

Corinth Police Department, 1963.

Corinth Police Department, 1964.

Corinth Police Department, 1968.

Corinth Police Department, 1988, L-R: Chuck Hinds and Mike Shipman.

Union Station

Illinois Central Railroad Depot, 1903.

Rienzi, MS Depot on Mobile and Ohio Railroad (then called) running north and south from Corinth. White and colored waiting rooms. Six passenger trains a day.

Corinth & Counce Railroad personnel, Counce, TN. Original locomotive 901. Top row, L-R: J.R. Parrish, Frt. Agent; E.E. "Gene" Amerson, L.R. Ragan, Iddo "Bear" Allen, unknown, Leonard Kirk, W.E. Roberts, Junior Worley, J.C. Manning, Tom Henry Prather. Bottom row: E.H. King, Sherry House, Vicki Jean, Adolph Dalton, W.H. Keltner, C.W. Byrd, general manager, CCR Co.; F.B. Schelhorn, resident manager, TRP&P Co.; Sam B. Jones, Earl M. Overton, section foreman and Lem McKinney, 1971.

Embarrassing moment on the Corinth and Counce Railroad when someone pulled the wrong pin. Sam Jones and Randy Johnson looking it over.

The main office across from the train depot where cotton and other produce sales were transacted, ca. mid 1920s.

The Corinth & Counce Railroad Company road switcher No. 1004, mid 1980s. Sam B. Jones, engineer and Ransom Junior Roland, Cdr.

Scene of the activity at the train depot, ca. mid 1920s.

Gulf, Mobile & Ohio Railroad Freight Depot, Corinth, MS was located on Cruise Street (corner of Cruise and Jackson Streets) which has since been torn down, 1949.

GM&O Railroad Freight Office force, Corinth, MS, May 7, 1952. A.H. Taylor, Grady N. Pankey, Joseph C. White, Virginia Dell Staggs, Harry Archer, Hoyl Phillips, Ornie Holland, Thad Gipson, Dwight Strickland, Lawrence Gann, Walter E. Kemp, Howard H. Hahn.

Standing in front of the GM&O Railroad Freight Office building are Agent J.C. White and Supt. W.H. Forlines of Jackson, TN, August 1956.

Picture made inside GM&O Railroad Freight Office during Corinth Centennial Celebration, May 1954; Betty Walker and Virginia Staggs.

GM&O Railroad Office, commercial agent Bob Kelley of Jackson, TN greeted by Miss Virginia Staggs, steno-clerk and traveling auditor J.M. Putt, 1956.

SCHOOLS

1908-12, the first Alcorn County Agricultural High School.

Alcorn Central High School, 1965. Top to bottom, L-R: Billy Parker, Diane Fowler, Ronald Gray, Barbara Whittemore, Faye Lambert (reporter), Margaret Harwood (treasurer), Sue Harris (secretary), Horace Gray (reporter), Diane Fowler, Henry Dunn, Suzanne Haynie, Gary Rowsey, Don Taylor, Faye Brooks, Johnny White, Charlene Smith (vice president), Mrs. Frances Young (sponsor), Ray Potts (sponsor), W.C. Williams (principal), Mrs. Barbara Bullock (sponsor), Don Crouch (president), Frank Phillips, Ruby Lancaster, Barry Rickman, Larry Barnes, Cathy Davis, Lanny Marlar, Nicky Wiginton, Stella Baxter, Erbie Massengill, Jimmie Richardson, Bobbie Streetman, Jerry Grisham, Jo Ann Brown, Joyce Russell, Danny Walls, Janice Lancaster, Donald Johnson, Johnny Baswell, Violet Hickman, Philip Rowsey, Norma Whittemore, Harris Stickland, Wayne Grisham, Johnny Price, Danny McGee, Carolyn White, Wendell Nagle, Darlene Hunziker, Tommy Whittemore, Jimmy Kiddy, Brenda Davis, Jimmy Lancaster, Teresa Glover, Ricky Cornelius, Jimmy Swindle, Scottie Smith, Jannie Nelms, Larry Newcomb, Sarah Bingham, Jack Lewis, Frankie Braddock, Linda Pace, Kenneth Roaten, Margaret Down, Billy James, Larry Duncan, Larry Robinson, Bobby Smith, Mary Knight, Cecil Phillips, Helen Bain, Ray Lambert.

This is believed to be the second A.A.H.S., the first building burned in 1912.

Alcorn County Agricultural High School 1909-1960. In 1960 A.A.H.S. was changed to K.H.S., Kossuth High School. In 1961 this wood frame structure was torn down and replaced with a brick structure.

Kossuth High School (A.A.H.S.). The first agricultural building was constructed in the 1920s. Later an addition was added with rock applied on the outside.

133

Kossuth School, A.A.H.S. This wood frame building, gymnasium was built in 1930-31.

Kossuth High School. The teacher's home.

Alcorn Agricultural High School dormitory students, 1912-13. To right of center post and second from post is Lottie Jones Brooks.

A.A.H.S. Group, 1912-13. Grace Walker, 2nd from R., top row; Acton Mills, 7th from L., 3rd row; Clarence Lambert, 2nd from L., back row; Ed Strickland, seated far R. in chair.

A.A.H.S., 1920. Students (not in order): Hugh Allen Boren, Gladys Dickson, Anne Maude Epps, Herbert Hamlin, Jewel Ginn, Grace Hall, Zenobia Harris, Ruth Hudson, Cullen Irwin, Ezra Johnson, Julian Kendrick, Dale Kimmons, Illa V. Kitchens, Mabel Lambert, Mary Lindley, Beatrice Martin, Cecil Meeks, Ruby Moore, Irene Phillips, Irene Strickland.

A.A.H.S., 1926-27 Seniors. First row, L-R: Avis Pirkle, Millard Dilworth, Lucille Leggett, Willie Kilcrease, Clara Mills, Everett Cobb, Miss Hemeter (class sponsor), Red Lamberth, Vivian Hollingworth, Tandy Counce, Bernice Oakley, Lon Dilworth. Second row: Turner Childs, Sue Lamberth, Bernice Henry, Cleo Parish, Lessie D. Killough, Bessie Smith, Bertha McDowell, Katie M. Skinner, Ruby Mills, Bertha Allen.

Kossuth (Alcorn Agricultural High School) Class of 1925 on the steps of an old building. Mildred Walker Sawyer, student (third from left in back row.

The Alcorn Agricultural High School, 1933-34. Ione Mills, Evelyn Howard, Dimple Dilworth, Margaret Dilworth, Bernice Rogers, Gladys Smith, Carrie Lee, Fredra Brooks and Ruby Mills, teacher and coach.

Kossuth School. This wood frame building, "Home Economics," was constructed in the 1902s.

Kossuth (A.A.H.S.) Home Economics Club, 1934-35. Ola Fortenberry, teacher, first row on left.

Miss McMillan
English
and
Music

Mr. Dalton
English

FACULTY
OF
A.A.HS

Mr. Smith
Coach & Sci.

A.A.H.S. 1934 Graduating Class. First row, sitting: Thelma Gwyn, Lamount Richardson, Lillie M. Melvin, Hubert Carroll, Elizabeth Dillon, Arnet Crum, Fredra Brooks, Truit Brooks, Vera M. Duncan. Second row, standing: Ruth Walker Dalton, Edwin Lambert Madeline Long, Juanita McCowan, Ralph Honnell, Mary Emma Coleman, Alva Dalton, Dimple Dilworth, Ronel Coleman, Stella M. Rogers, Leon Howard, Carice Norman, Addean Ray (sponsor and English teacher). Third row: Hillie Mills, Ola Arnett, B.A. Jones, Fleetie Burrow, Cecil Shields, Edith McClintock, Wilbur Jones, Grace Parish, Henry Keith J. Franklin, Carrie Lee, Beecher Calvary, Venice Crow, Lavaughin Feruson, Inez Wilbanks, Luther Crum, Hazel Aldridge (not pictured).

Miss Cox
Commercial

Mr. Davis
Mathematics

Miss Mills
History

Mr. Hurt
Agriculture

Mrs. Walker
Home Economics

Mrs. Long
Matron

A.A.H.S. 1936 Seniors. First row: L.M. Huff, Very Talley, Lillian Essary, Lena Alexandra, Helen Bennett, Evelyn Bell, Mary Gant. Second row: Harley Smith, Ruth Louise Green, Rubel Shelton, Elizabeth Latta, Sarah Martin, Elizabeth Murphee, Dorothy Goodman, Effie Dunn. Third row: Myrtle Lee, Susie Driver, Gladys Smith, Mabel Morris, Jimmie Lee Mills, Stella Rainey, Christine Jones, Cora Wilbanks, Watt Martin. Fourth row: E.E. Long (school superintendent), Earl Driver, J.F. Sherrard, Carl King, Mark Wilbanks, Aaron Layton, Ruby Mills (teacher), Mack Wilbanks, Dee Crow, Charlie Wegman, Nadine Lamberth, Jesse Calausel, Leslie Seago, (not pictured, Arlin Simpson).

Faculty of A.A.H.S., 1936.

A.A.H.S. 1939 Graduating Class. First row: L-R: Miss Mary Frances Roebke (class sponsor), Ruth Lancaster, Scally Mathis, Mattie V. Jobe, Vera Suitor, Evelyn Stoope, Marcell Carter, Miriam Lamberth, Principal E.E. Long, Dorothy Dewberry, Nell Nelms, Estelle Carter, Ethelyn Stoope, Viola Bonds, Mary Anna Evans. Second row: Howell DeLoach, Juanita Aldridge, Mary Anna Jones, Tell Mathis, Pansy Gatlin, Sylvester Nash, Eloise Rencher, Celestrial Dixon, Hazel Carter, Odell Barnett, James Goodman, Esba Bobo Crum, J.T. Wilbanks, Jettie Hall, Harvey Crow, Fred Cole (sponsor). Third row: Jeff Balfour, Norman Davis, J.T. Smith, Herman Miller, Grady Elliot, T.C. Jones, Marvin Rainey, Vance Wilbanks, Jimmy McKenzie, Hal Underwood, Thomas Hill Coleman, Billy Ray Briggs, Charlene Trantham, Hal Phillips, Halla B. Barker.

A.A.H.S. 1939 Alumni Reunion, 1990. L-R: Walter Ed Monroe (husband of deceased alumni Pansy D. Catlin), Marvin Rainey, Jewel Coleman Rainey (Class of 1938), Ruth Mathis (wife of Scally Mathis), Miss Mary Frances Roebke (class sponsor), Scally Mathis, Miriam Lamberth Rinehart, Howell DeLoach, Vera Suitor Johnson, Charlene Trantham Felker, Mary Anna Jones Hoffman, Billy Ray Briggs, Mattie V. Jobe Switcher, Juanita Aldridge Reynolds, Norman Davis, unknown, T.C. Jones.

Pictured in 1995 at the Class of 1941 Reunion, A.A.H.S., Kossuth, MS. Front row, Rosie Mae Smith, Elba Coleman, Ruth Bullard, Dorothy Johnson, Hilda Brawner. Back row: Nita Dees, Francis Leeth, Rachael McCollum, Patricia Johnson, Daisy Caldwell, Gladis Rencher.

School board of Kossuth, 1941. L-R: Amos Monroe, T.J. Newman, David "Buster" Horn (d. December 1941), H.C. Poindexter, William Young Rogers (chairman), E.E. Long (superintendent 1932-41).

Alcorn Agriculture High School, Class of 1939.

1951-52, the Alcorn County Agricultural High School. L-R: Abie Coleman, Max Rhodes, Curtis Rogers, Shorty Coleman, Irby Talley, Moon Parks, John Grimes, Jake Mills, Lawrence Meeks, Leiman Wilbanks. Front: Joe Bonds and Buster Davis, coach.

A.A.H.S. Class of 1942: Ray Allen, Clinton Boals, Elvie Bright, Lassie Briggs, Eugene Brooks, Myrtle Brown, Laverna Burns, Marie Clingham, Nonie Sue Coleman, Willie Bea Coleman, Beatrice Coleman, Georgia Crum, Sarah Dilworth, William Russell Hamm, Mary Brice Hancock, Virginia Hancock, Murke Harrison, Aunita Muriel Johnson, Hugh B. Jones, Ruth Marie Kimmons, Clovis Walker Kitchens, Avice Nabors Mann, Mildred Martin, Erst Mathis, Marie Mauney, Thomas McClintock, Robert Melvin, Michael Kimbrough, Artie Mills, Jewel Morris, Tulon J. Nelson, Furman Mitchell Odle, Ruby Phillips, Myra Frances Russell, Edward Andrew Shelton, Mary Frances Shelton, Rachael Shields, Gladys Marie Suitor, Gladys Eubanks Suitor, Velma Turner, Addie v. White, Hershel Wilbanks.

Bell School. The first two-teacher school, grades 1st through 8th was built in the early 1900s. In 1922 a new wood frame structure was built for $1000 and had three teachers. Later Bell was consolidated with Biggersvile, Kossuth and Corinth.

Alcorn Agricultural High School, Tombigbee Conference, 1953. Jake Mills #27 (b. 1937, d. 2000) and Max Rhodes #33 (b. 1937, d. 1999).

Bethel School, ca. 1880s. Top row: Willie Taylor, Charlie Bynum, Jim Edge, John Palmer, Edd Dilworth, Bill Palmer, Will Bynum, Henry Dilworth, John Edge Next row: two names are missing in this row, Taylor Jobe, Charles Monroe, Annie Bynum, Alice Epps, Fannie Taylor, Houston Mitchell, Ben Dilworth: Next row, Buddie West, Beulah Taylor, Katie (?) Monroe, Annie Powell, Fannie Bynum, Lena Taylor, Katie Taylor, Susie West, Mollie Monroe, Mary Jobe, Zilpha Jobe: Next row: Henry Monroe, Henry Taylor, Aubrey Epps, Lutha Taylor, George Monroe, Abe Dilworth, Reed Bynum, Walter Monroe, George Bynum.

School group beside old Bethel School House, 1906. Back row: Kate Hamilton, Lizzie Hamilton, Mary Fannie Scott, Sulu Dilworth, Louella Hamilton, Elbert Suitor, Robert Suitor, Charlie Dilworth. Middle row: Lettie Crowder, Mamie Edge, unknown, Dalton Mitchell, Laura Savage (teacher), unknown, unknown, unknown, Lester Rodgers. Front row: Maudie Rodgers, Bessie Kilpatrick, Sally Rodgers, Lillian Epps, Ruby Epps, Nellie Kilpatrick, Margaret Mitchell, Annie Maud Epps.

Old Bethel School group. No names or date, find your relatives.

Bethel School group beside old Bethel Church. Back row: unknown, Alfred Wren, unknown, Claud Hearn, Lillian Epps, Charlie Dilworth, Mamie Edge, Leander Massengill. Third row: Edd Massengill, Annie Maud Epps, Arthur Blackwell, Frank Blackwell, Baxter Rodgers, Ruth Bynum, Vivian Massengill, unknown, unknown, Edward Hearn. Second row: Katie Ward Bynum, Ruby Epps, Vardie Hearn, Maudie Rodgers, Hubert Hearn, Clayton Suitor, Jim Kilpatrick, Charlie Rogers, Richard Rogers, unknown. First row: Walter Hearn, unknown, Clarence Edge, Hilbert Hearn, unknown, Hermon Suitor, unknown, Calvin Kilpatrick, William Epps, Lester Rogers and Florence Anderson, teacher, 1912.

A group of students from Bethel School. Willie Mae Suitor is probably third from left on second row and Mable McHaffey is next to her.

Biggersville Grammar and High School with grades kindergarten through the 12th, 2001.

B.H.S. Biggersville's teachers' home.

Biggersville High School, Corinth, MS, Senior Class 1942. Harold Carpenter (president), H.M. Ray (vice-president), Sereda Dobbs (secretary/treasurer), Marie Bridges, Katherine Suitor, Vernon Bryson, Juanita Sowell, Pauline Morton, Merle Thompson. R.A. Timbes (Superintendent), W.B. Brand (class sponsor).

Burcham School established before 1904. Moved later to Macedonia School, one-teacher school.

Corinth Colored High School Football Team, 1937. (1) Sylvester Burton, (2) Arthur Long, (3) Samuel Gunn, (4) Willie Cragton, (5) James Lacey, (6) unknown, (7) James Wallace, (8) Leonard Warren, (9) James Webb, (10) Eddie Coleman, (11) Robert Taylor, (12) Henry D. Fowler (13) Thomas Warren, (14) Preston Vanderford, (15) James Peterson (coach), (16) Willie Ed Beauregard, (17) Gene Tyler, (18) Sylvester Freeman, (19) Charlie Betts, (20) Johnny Wilson, (21) Vonny Warren, (22) Robert Settle.

Boneyard School group in early 1920s. Hazel (Aldridge) Jones at far le, in white.

Brush Creek School. This school was established before 1908 as a one-teache school. The picture was made several years later with Willie Crum as teache Charlie Deloach is a visitor. Names not in order: Fleetie Burrow, Paulin Fallin, Anita Wilbanks, Odell Bright, Jewel Kennedy, Wardie Burrow, Ange and James Crabb, Katie James and Valeria Sanders, Elsie and Early Crum Irene and Lee Wilbanks, Wilbur and Opal Markle, Hestor, Edith and Syb Thrasher, Nathaniel Hicks, Wayne Follin, Elbie Miles. Some unable to identify Brush Creek was consolidated with Union Center in 1958.

Carpenter School. In 1902 the teachers were Misses Maude Wood an Mollie McClamrock. In 1926 this school was consolidated with the Gif School. First row: Jim Mask, Jodie Garrett, J.B. Mills, Clarence Switcher Ackle Garrett, Herman Harrison, Curtiss Brawner. Second row: Billy Brawner, Mildridge Harrison, Maydell Felker, Jennie V. Brawner, Lol Mae Felker, Lottie B. Suitor, Avis Morgan, Elvie Switcher, Ione Mills, Oberi Williams, Lena Morgan, Ruby Brawner. Third row: Laura Felker (teacher) Edith McClintock, Elvie Beavers, Annie Brawner, Mamie Smith, Bernice Williams, Ola Mask, Earnest Brawner, Bruce Williams, Gertie Harrison Ophelia Parks. Fourth row: Ray Morgan, Bob Beavers, Virdie Strickland James Beavers, Katie Mae Suitor, Lucy Beavers, Earlie Strickland, Leotie Morgan, J.R. Switcher, Mittie McClintock.

Old Corinth High School, ca. 1918.

Old Corinth High School, Corinth, MS located on 5th Street.

Corinth Public School Class, 6th grade, 1911.

Corinth High School Graduation, 1924. Roy R. Biggers Sr. is sixth from left on the middle row.

Corinth High School football team of 1926, C.E. Russell, coach. Back row, second from left is Les Horn.

Charlie Betts, Patrick Miller Selected for Scholarships. CHS seniors Charlie Betts (above left) and Patrick Miller (above right) have been chosen by Tuskeegee Institute for "working" scholarships. The scholarships offer the boys the opportunity to earn their engineering degrees while being paid to gain work experience at the Oak Ridge, TN and Paducah, KY Union Carbide facilities.

The starting backfield for the Corinth Warriors against the Clarksdale Wildcats is pictured with head coach and athletic director Jack Frost (kneeling left). The backfield includes quarterback Charlie Bette (22), tailback Dan McLemore (42), fullback Gerald McRae(44) and wingback Gary King. All are seniors except King, he is a junior. Action at Warrior Stadium closed out the 1969 campaign for Corinth.

Mrs. Roy Goforth, principal and teacher, 1st Grade, West Corinth Elementary School.

Starting team, 1941, Corinth High School. Front row, L-R: Jimmy Burns, Leonard McCullough, H.R. Tyson, Richard Hinton, J. Travis Butler, Bill Kemp and Gerald Strickland. Back row, L-R: Dorsey Strickland, Charles Wright, Aaron S. Timmons and Auther Doyle.

Mrs. Roy Goforth, 1st Grade Class, 1966-67.

West Corinth Elementary School, 1968-69. Mrs. Roy Goforth, principal and teacher, 1st Grade.

Mrs. Louise Bennett's Kindergarten class in band uniforms, 1963-64: Shanda Wilbanks, Brenda Essary, Beverly Hardin, Becky Glisson, Navara Wallace, Regena Holloway, Cindy Rogers, Lanita Parrish, Brenda Locke, Keith Phillips, Kenny Vanderford, Mike Deaton, David Carroll, John Austin, Larry Hudson, Joyce Whisenhunt, Nan Franks, Don Nelms, Debbie Briggs, David King, Greg Taylor, Steve Mills, Donna Faulkner Anita Deaton, Sammy Tull, Denise Dodd, Eddie Strickland, Roger White, Chip Purvis, Ricky James, Randy Lancaster, Mitzie Baggett, Phil Barker, Debbie Lewis, Chris Mills, Jan Taylor, Donna Dillingham, Greg Moore.

Cruise Street Elementary School, 1st Grade. Principal Mabel Barnes; teacher Mrs. Hill. First row, L-R: Sallie Davis, Patricia Gray, Betty King, Shelia Simpson, Phyllis Rhoads, Estelle Morgan, Barbara Ann Burns, Camilla Isom. Second row, L-R: Charlotte Harwell, Judy Marlow, Rita McClain, Jan Talent, Charles Tubbs, Tommy Stricklin, Benny Brewster, unknown, Jerry Johnson, teacher. Third row, L-R: Johnny Whitt, Wayne Curtis, unknown, Charles Ray Irvin, Dendy Henson, Johnny Roaten, Larry Prescott, Mike McClamroch and Larry McCoy. 1953-54.

Ms. Bennett's Daycare and kindergarten.

Deerlick School. In 1915 a one-room, wood frame building was constructed for grades 1st through 8th. In 1919 the building was destroyed by fire. School was held in the Bethlehem Baptist Church until 1941 when this two-room block building was built. In 1958 Deerlick was consolidated with Union Center School.

One-teacher school, Deerlick, 1916-17, monthly report. Teacher, Effie Lokey. Pupils as on report: Oyston Boyd, Price Bobo, Walter Bobo, Herbert Bobo, Johny Crum, Luther Crum, Huston Eubanks, Jim Eubanks, Epting Eubanks, Leon Forsythe, Burt Forsythe, Howard Gary, Clay Jones, Mart Mullins, Art Mullins, Vester Mullins, Luna Mullins, Robert Nabors, George Null, Jesse D. Ramer, Massie Ramer, Roy Raines, Willie Raines, Roy Wilbanks, Mack Wilbanks, Ausie Wilbanks, Marlin Wilbanks, Hubert Wilbanks, Alfred Wilbanks, Dovie Boyd, Birdie Boyd, Lena Bobo, Jessie Eubanks, Gertie Forsythe, Birdie Forsythe, Theo Forsythe, Hallie Jones, Maxie Jones, Irrie Mullins, Maudie Mullins, Gracie Mullins, May Mullins, Bessie Mullins, Essie McKelvey, Adelina Null, Lessie Ramer, Daisy Wilbanks, Eula Wilbanks, Zeaner Wilbanks, Birdie Wilbanks, Rubye Wilbanks.

Deerlick School, 1928-29 with Vada Crum teacher. First row: Pearl Bobo, Elbert Crum, Marshall Porterfield, Earl Bobo, Maggie Ferrell, Bernice Mullins, Ruth Wilbanks. Second row: Grady Mullins, Elsie Bobo, Lorene Ferrell, Lovie Nelson, J.B. Bobo, Earlie Crum, King Bobo, Eyla Ferrell, Birdie and Ivola Crum, Nellie Bobo, Alvis Portfield, Bessie Ferrell. Third row: Mark Wilbanks, Luther and Johnnie Crum, Loyd Nabors, Claude Wilbanks, Viola Crum, Ruby Nabors, Essie Crum, Chester Ferrell.

Dilworth School, ca. 1924-25. First row, L-R: Frank Conn. Second row: (last on right) Dorothy Dilworth. Third row: Dimple Dilworth. Fourth row: unknown. Fifth row: Roger Conn, (left seventh) Mary Dilworth, (left eighth) Jennie Dilworth.

Eula School near Lone Oak Church, ca. 1915. Pupils identified, first row: Roscoe Follin, Walter Mills, Roy Follin, Anderson Mills. Second row: Callie Mills, Velma Follin. Third row: Kelse Follin, Mattie Elam, Minnie Austin, Vonnie Coleman, Velma Tatum, Ruthie Spencer, Odis "Dyke" Henderson. Fourth row: Lester Settlemires, John Henry Crum, Stanley Glisson, Ernest Crum, Ed Hartley, Ollie Chapman, Bonnie Mitchell. Fifth row: Richard Follin, AB Rogers, Berton Henderson, Esther Parish, Harm Berry "Bee" Smith.

Farmington Elementary School, 5th Grade, Peggy McDonald Isbell teacher, 1966.

Farmington Elementary School

Farmington Elementary School, Kindergarten Class of 1971 and 1972.

Miss Onie Potts, teacher, Farmington School.

Farmington School located on the Farmington Road. Pictured here as it looked in 1900.

Farmington School, Class of 1926.

Farmington High School 1945 Basketball Team. Top from left: Coach Bratton Burgess, Talmadge "Tal" Phillips, Perry Bingham (#9), Donald O. King, Sr. (#6), Willie "Bill" King, Jr. (#7) and Harry Jordan. Bottom from left: Joe Seago (#5), William Littlejohn (#10), Edward "Whistle" Voyles (#4), Avon Phillips (#3) and Hershel Pittman (#8). Coach Burgess, the father of Ricky Burgess was known for always chewing tobacco and telling jokes about being raised on the hills of Hatchie.

Class of 1950 30-year Reunion. Farmington High School at Chapman's Restaurant, 1980

Farmington High School, Class of 1950. Top row, L-R: Arvie C. Hamm, James Jones, J.L. Ray (superintendent), Mr. Kitchens, Jeanette Fields, Leon Hopkins, Buddy Jackson. Second row from top, L-R: Loyd Haynes, Leon Fields, Ruth Strickland, Mrs. Margie Ray (sponsor), Johnny Glisson, Paul Brooks, (L) Charles Smith, Ruth Weeks, (R) Eva Hill, Vernell Duncan. Third, L-R: Opal Blankenship, Mary Lou Jernigan, Mavene George, Bernece Brooks, Hazel Faye King, Ruth Burress, Mary Elizabeth Messner. Fourth, L-R: Charles Hathcock, Billy Harold Calvery, Christine Hathcock, Lonnie Oaks, Marjorie Taylor, Dock Oaks, Donald Ray Voyles.

Farmington High School, Class of 1954, J.L. Ray, Principal.

Farmington Class of 1954 40th Class Reunion.

Farmington High School Basketball Team, 1954-55. Front row, L-R: Roy Phillips Jr., Martin Ray Essary, Billy Taylor, Durrell Mills, Bob Elam and David Jernigan, manager. Back row, L-R: Queen Evelene Gann, J.W. Hodum, Ray Brown, Marcus Leatherwood, Charles Vanderford, Vernon Smith and Coach Earl Sitton.

Farmington Seniors of 1956. Front row: Betty Griffin, David Jernigan, Mabel Austin, Marlon Phillips, Norma Hammett, Vernon Smith, Peggy Stevens, James Griffin. Second row: Charles Vanderford, Betty Sargent, Sue Counce, Annie B. Reid, Major Smith, Clara Griffin, Katherine Strickland, Mattie B. Vandiver. Back row: Sue Spencer, Lavonne Potts, Delores Barnes, Martin King, Alice Jobe, Elbert King, Sue Strickland and Billy W. Brooks.

Farmington High School, Class of 1960, J.L. Ray, Principal.

Farmington Gymnasium

Farmington School. The teacher's home.

This picture was taken at the old Field's Schoolhouse at the meeting of a Farmer's Union. Top row, L-R: Bob Barnes, Henry Hyneman, Eugene Babb, Uncle John Bingham, Dossie Brice, John Booker Bingham, Ike Fields, Boge Wallace. Second row, L-R: John Fields, Oscar Barnes, Milas Voyles, Charlie Bingham, Oscar Wallace, Henry Smith, George Marlar.

W.I. Gibson College, established 1885 at Rienzi, MS. It was a co-educational boarding school. Sloan Vanderford was teacher who later was state superintendent of education. Several Rienzi citizens are in picture. C.B. Curlee, Norwood Ellis, Harry Roebke, Orville, Cleveland and Clifford Green, Earl, Robert and Douglas Perry, Jeff Furtick, Emma Furtick, Hattie Roebke, Annie Lou Ellis and many others.

Fields School, 1924.

Field's School. Front Milton Grissom, Robert Seago, Bernice Haley, Kathleen Kiddy, Evelyn Haley, Jim Fields, Virgel Woods, Clyde Hutchens (teacher). Willie D. South, unknown, Louie Hutchens, Mable Marlar, unknown, unknown, Virgel Burgess, Mr. Hardin (principal).

Gift School located west of Corinth in the Gift Community in the 1930s. First row, L-R: Elbert Butler, Beulah Jones, Loretta Duncan, Hazel Garrett, Christine Jones, Myra Wilson, Louise Floyd, Rosie Mae Smith and Clayton Turner. Second row: Vernon Jones, Brooks Martin, J.T. Smith and Ottis Jones. Third row: Arnold Dunn, Robert Burcham, Mr. Floyd (teacher), Walt Briggs (bus driver), Hillie Turner, Ernest Goodman, Ackle Garrett, Mr. Walker (teacher), Wilson Garrett and Morris Wilson.

Gift School. This school was built in the 1920s in honor of J. E. Gift who contributed to the construction of the building at a cost of $20,000. Grades 1 through 12 were taught. Later the high school was transferred to Kossuth and the grammar school followed later.

Gift School. The teacher's home.

Glen School. Grades 1 through 12 were taught. Later consolidated with Alcorn Central. Today grades 1st through 8th are taught.

Glen School. The teacher's home of yester-year.

Glen School, 1936. Dorothy Garrett, Curtis Hardin, Frances Holder, Homer Ray Woodruff, Prentis Hardin, J.P. Leggett, Dwight Strickland, Woodroe Wilson, Lillie Howell.

Glen School gymnasium.

Glendale School #1. In 1874 a teacher was Mrs. Julie Strickland. In 1903 the name changed to Glen. In 1914 a wood frame structure was built for $2500 for four teachers. In 1933 an annex was added and a high school was established. Several years later the high school was consolidated with Alcorn Central.

Glen Reunion Basketball Team. L-R: Cecil Hardwick, J.E. Harris, Rubel Wigginton, Coach Earl Sitton, Billy Wayne Coke and Harold Strachan.

Goose Pond School, Elvie Irene Bright Crum, Teacher. Paul Curtis Bright, Sam Kirby, Odis Mathis, H.P. Crum, Imogene Eubanks, Aaron Junior Miles, Jimmy Fiveash, Larry Norman Crum, Johnny Wayne Forsythe, Roger Lane Crum, Danny Eubanks, Ricky DeWayne Crum, Patsy Ruth Crum, Helen Flake, Dimple Wilbanks and Marie Kirby, ca. 1955-56.

Glen School 1945 Basketball Team. Arland Little, Cecil Hardwick, Billy Wayne Coke, Earl Sitton (coach), Mark Johnson, Harold Strachan.

Goose Pond School Group, 1935. Charlie Deloach in back right-hand corner.

Glendale School. Margaret South is the woman in the white dress.

Senior Class of 1956, Glendale School.

Hickory Flat School. In 1910 a one-room wood structure was built for $3300 where grades 1st through 8th were taught. In 1927-28 in the above building, there were four teachers with J.S. Thornby as principal. This school was consolidated with Rienzi.

Hickory Flat School Group, ca. 1917.

Hickory Flat School about 1925, east of Rienzi. Teachers: Mr. Bellany on left, Miss Addie Harper and Miss Nellie Kemp on right, second row from front and Tom Searcy, middle of back row.

Hickory Flat School, February 14, 1929.

Hickory Flat School Days 1949-50, Mary Richardson.

Hickory Flat School Days 1949-50, Freda Richardson.

Hickory Flat School Days 1939-40, Eveline Rorie.

Hickory Flat School Days 1939-40, Alsie Mae Smith.

Hickory Flat School Days 1948-49, Christine White.

Hickory Flat School Days 1939-40, teacher Lola Mae Brooks.

A part of the students at the old Hickory Flat School. The 8th grade school ceased to be many years ago. First row, L-R: unknown, Erie Faye Moore, Edith Mae Moore, unknown, unknown, teacher Garvin Richardson, Jessie W. Waldren. Back, Estelle Duncan, rest are unknown.

Hickory Flat School, 1951 Graduation. Boys, L-R: Thomas White, Billy Rineheart, Hershel McLemore, Freeman Moody, John Nichols. Girls, L-R: Charlene Sloan, Edith Moore, Jane Hearn, Reba Brown, Peggie Jo Rorie, Helen Brown.

Hickory Flat School Teachers, 1951. L-R: Garvin Richardson, Miss Louisa Smith, Mrs. C.D. Thompson, Mrs. Ray Duncan.

Hinkle School, Rienzi, MS, 1926.

Hinkle School Group, ca. 1891-92. Front row, L-R: Jim Moody, Pick Jones, Walter McCord, Gene Latch, Worth or Joe Jones (twins), Will McCord, Worth or Joe Jones, Jasper Gray, Edwin Honnoll, Charlie Holt. Second row: Priscilla Bray, Alma Tucker, Alice Latch, Becky Jane Moody, unknown, Laura Savage, Kate Johnson, Miss Mattie Reynolds (teacher), Jeese Johnson, Mary Gray, Kate Holt, Maud McCord. Third row: Dick Holt, Joe Moody, Barbara Hill, Alice Bray, Maggie Livingston, Mary Lee Holt, Ester Holt, Pearlie Livingston, Onilla ? Gary, Laura Holt, Annie Holt. Fourth row: Hilbert Savage, Frank Hill, Jim Latch, Edgar Savage, Jim Hill, Mack Bray, John Perkins, Will Hill, Bingham Savage, Ross Hill, Walter Dilworth.

Hinkle (or Wayside) School Group, ca. 1915, Miss Addie Harper (teacher on right end). Not all are identified: fourth from right front, Edwin Dilworth; third from right on front, Benjamin Dilworth; seventh from left, second row, Kathryn Dilworth and to her right Rivers Conn; Raymond Dilworth in front of right door. Others among the group are Vance Holt, Mildred Walker, Melvin Conn, Velma Dilworth.

Basketball team for Hinkle. Mary Emma Coleman (second girl) and Dimple Dilworth (fourth girl).

Hinkle School, 2nd grade, 1937. First row: Earline Robinson, Beth Essary, Frances Morton. Second row: Robert Rinehart, John E. Miller, Ray Marecle, Clarence Benjamin. Third row: Carl Robbins, Jack Odle, Clarence Green.

Hinkle School 1946 Graduates. Front row: Grace Odle, Imogene Green, Dorothy Huggins. Back row: Bob Farris, Kenneth Farris, Kenneth Lancaster, Mrs. Gladys (Henry) Taylor, teacher and principal.

Hinkle Creek School students. Included in the picture is Edwin, Kathrine and Grace Odle (Marecle).

Hinkle School. In 1921 a wood frame structure was built for $1000 and had three teachers. Grades 1 through 8 were taught. This building was built later. Hinkle School was consolidated with Kossuth.

Holly School, 1904. Back row, eighth from left, Lonnie Surratt. Next row to back, fifth from left, Mary Frances "Fannie" Surratt.

Holly Singing School, 1908. Seated second from left, Mary Frances "Fannie" Surratt Stewart. Back row, eighth from left, Donald Stewart.

Hopewell School.

Hopewell School. Some of the students: John Roye, E.D. Driver, Mark Choat, Dave Strachan, Kennie Wright Nash, Alice Driver Bush, Elizabeth Strachan, Callie Cobb, Earlie Cobb, Oscar Vanderford, Brice Mullins and teacher John Romine.

Hoyle High School, ca. 1920s.

Jones Schoolhouse, 1891. The man in front is James David "Uncle Dave" Turner. Pictured here in among this are Frank Turner, Gordon Turner, Delight Turner Rogers, Lula Turner Nelms, Josie Turner Lamberth, James William "Jim" Turner (father of Arthur Turner), members of the Briggs family, McAlister family, Coke family, Jones family, Burgess family, McClintock family, Nelms family, Smith family and Garrett family.

Jacinto School Group Picture, February 1929.

Johns School (possibly), ca. 1899. Picture belonged to John Bynum Smith (b. 1889, d. 1951), brother of Clara Sue Smith Rorie.

Hoyle School juniors and seniors hiking to C.C. Camp, 1938. Sitting: R.H. Richardson, J.C. Boyd. Second row: William Grayson, Ardelia Reid, Pearlener Fowler, James Webb, Ozella Richardson Betts, Ethel Reid. Third row: Lee Henry Ransey, Gladys Burkett, Clarence Baldwin, James Lacey, Lola Collins.

Jones School located in the Jones/Gift Community near Smithbridge Road west of Corinth, ca. 1912. Seated, first row: Lloyd Dixon, unknown, unknown, Walter Jones, Grady Dixon, Benjamin Tillman Rogers, unknown, Troy Jones, Edward Wilson (baby), Noland Jones, Herman Reardon, Leo Turner. Second row: "Bity Sis" Coke, unknown, Leo Long, Louise Jones, Martha Wilson, Cleo Long, Lillie Turner, Beulah Jones, unknown, unknown, Ruland Jones, Anna Lou Goodman. Third row: Lila Mae Clifton (teacher), unknown, Martha Wislon, Helen Rogers, Mary Goodman, Clifford Rogers, John McCalister, Maggie McCalister, Unice Jones, Inez Coke. Fourth row: unknown, Anna Bell McCalister, Ruth Evenlyn Jones, unknown, Bland Jones, unknown, Mr. Raden (principal), Hardy Lee, Tendell Burgess (holding the dog), Will Martin, Joe Garrett.

Juliette School, 1909. Seated: Roy Maness, Ninnie Owen, Dewie Owen, Goldie Owen, Gladys Owen, Vardman Rorie, Fred Owen. Second row: Erskin Rowsey, Charlie Able, Frank Sellers, Susie Sellers, Ethel Rowsey, Ettie Owen, Hazil Linnebeck, Ottie Linnebeck, Clelon Rorie, Cliff Rorie. Third row: Nolie Owen, Lillie Mae Maness, Cleo Vanderford, Willie Rorie, Actie Vanderford, Maggie Vanderford. Last row: Arch Owen, John Able, Cordie Sellers, Dena Vanderford, Mellie Sellers, Elsie McLemore, Eula Sellers, Annie Bell Owen, Teacher was Dougless McCoy (can't see him).

Juliette School, ca. 1923. Known students: Front row, first on right, Ira Lee Rorie. Third row, second from left, Virgie Aval Rorie and fourth from left Roy Ollis Rorie, first from right, Reuben Frederick. Back row, first on left, Eva Arminta Rorie. All children of Sanford Stanley and Clara Sue Smith Rorie.

Kendrick School, students, teachers, "bus" drivers and others. Dr. Kendrick and wife (first row, second and third on left standing). Man with gray beard on far right is James Bingham.

Kendrick School #2. The first school was constructed in 1914 for $1200 with grades 1st through 8th being taught. Later the school was consolidated with Alcorn Central School.

Kossuth School, 1928. First row: Clester Switcher, Alton Phillips, unknown, Reed Miney, unknown, John Bonds, Alton Sherard, Morris Smith, V.S. Ashmore, Orville Ginn. Second row: unknown, unknown, Talmage Carter, Vernon Rogers, Frank Allen, Malcolm Moore, G.B. Ginn. Third row: Maylene Majors, Ruth Moore, Gladys Grimes, Rachel Shields, Ray Moore, Benny S. Walker, Maxine Smith, Elizabeth Simmons, Beatrice Lamberth, Mary Gant. Fourth row: Mary Elezibeth Bonds, Bernice Dalton, unknown, Nulma Crum, unknown, Elvie Thrasher, unknown, Ethel Rogers, Hazel Dildy, Mrs. Avis Purkle.

Kossuth Grammar School. In 1936 this brick structure was built by the Works Project Administration, teaching grades 1st through 8th.

Kossuth Grammar School. Mr. Magers, principal, 1941.

Kossuth Elementary School, 7th Grade Class, 1959-60. First row: Tony Honeycutt, Patsy Allen, Danny Moore. Second row: Harold Switcher, Charles Porterfield, J.D. Hopper, Ann Crum, Tommy Mathis. Third row: Mrs. Lilian Fort Meeks, Doris Harris, Katherine Glidwell, D. Crow III, Paul Tomlinson. Fourth row: Sue Brock, Joan Gann, Jane Follin, Jerry Henderson, Judy Shadburn, Barbara Kuykendall. Fifth row: Janira Essary, Sybil Patrick, Maxine Allen, Barbara Hilburn, Judy Mills, Carlton Butler; Sixth row: Shirley Thompson, Loraine Ridge, Johnny Austin, Kenneth Grimes, Peggy Jones, Jimmie Honeycutt. Seventh row: J.W. Lumpkin, Johnnie Bonds, Linda Crum, Diana Bridges, Betty Gant, Mira Henry. Eighth row: Jimmy Caldwell, James Ashcraft, Rickey Talley, Woodrow Mitchell, Danny Mattox, Jimmy Talley, Gary Hodum.

Kossuth High School, 1965 Senior Class. First row: Gloria Turner, Linda Crum, Carolyn Suitor, Judy Shadburn, Sandra Essary, Paulette Bridges, Jeannette Gurley, Ann Clark, Nona Sue Talley, Peggy Jones, Patricia Lassiter, Peggy Phelps, Mary Riggs, Ann Crum, Barbara Lipford, Linda Turner, Doris Harris, Carolyn Dilworth, Shirley Thompson, Martha Cummings, Era Mae Prather, Donna Davis. Second row: Jerry Brawner, Danny Mattox, Jimmy Talley, Gary Hodum, Jimmy Maricle, Danny Moore, Linda Wilbanks, Nilean Richardson, Jane Follin, Mary Mayfield, Lynette Rogers, Mira Henry, Earlene Box, Maxine Allen, Patsy Allen, Jimmie Honeycutt, Dorothy Wilbanks, Barbara Hilburn, Diane Gwyn, Brenda Wegman, LaDana Rencher, Paul Tomlinson, Carlton Butler, Jimmy Yarber, Charlie Free, D.Crow III, Billy Browder. Third row: James Dunn, Morris Weaver, Elbert Settlemires, Roger Gant, Freddie Phillips, Jerry Borden, Jerry Mathis, Wayne McGee, Harold Switcher, Jerry Henderson, Perry Rencher, Kenneth Grimes, Carrol Wilburn, Fred McCord, Tony Honeycutt, Roger Hilburn, L.D. Wooley, Harold Mills, Soggy Kennedy, Danny Mathis, Jimmy Hodum, Dewey Mercer, Billy Hines, Danny Martin.

Kossuth Grammar School, 1955.

Lone Pine School #2. School #1 was built in 1901. This building was built for $300 as a one-teacher school. Lone Pine consolidated with Union Center School in 1958.

Lookout School. In 1910 this two-teacher wood structure was built for $300. Grades 1st through 8th were taught. In 1958 the school consolidated with Union Center School.

Mathis Grammar School, 1958-59 Girls Basketball Team. First row: Paulette Crum, ? Prince, Nan Bass, Mary Jane Nails, Linda Guynes, Carolyn Crum. Second row: unknown, Peggy Hodum, Shirley ?, Geraldine Dillingham, Gail Hodum, Maureen Nelms.

Macedonia School, 1924-25. Seated row 1, l-r: J.P. Leggett, Terrell Whittemore, Paul T. Maddox, Lee Kennedy, Milburn Vanderford, Calvin Hardin, Vernol Vanderford, Herman Whittemore, Millard Childers. Seated on bench (second row from bottom, l-r: Lee Roy Maddox, Frank Reece, Usona Leggett, Ruby Duncan, Gladys Reece, Jewel Burcham, Sybil Burcham, Beulah Hardin, Arizona Vanderford, Marie Rider, Annie May Kennedy, John Harden, Ella Mae Abel, Vera Whittemore, Zerma Abel, Leo Abel, Ava Childers, __. Standing (third row from bottom, l-r: Willard Childers, Dalton Whittemore, Ruby Reece, Lillian Maddox, Odell Doty, Alma Richardson, Eva Childers, Olive "Otch" Harden, __, Maggie Abel, primary teacher Johnny Harville. Standing 4th row from botton, l-r: teacher John Little, Dora "Kitty" Harden, Liza Reece, Ruby Myrtle Chase, Minnie Harden, Ora Burcham, Letra Josephine Leggett, Lou Annie Singley, Elizabeth Abel, Catharine Rider, Herman Abel, Marvin Leggett, John Marion Chase, Glen Rider.

The teacher's home, McGlathery School.

McGlathery School was organized on or before 1915 as a two-teacher school. In 1922 the building was a wood structure when grades 1st through 8th were taught.

Mount Pleasant Public School, children at Kossuth November 19, 1933.

New Hope School Group, Biggersville, Ms, 1919. William Carpenter, second from right end on second row from back (perhaps you may find your kin).

Oakland School #2. Oakland School #1 was built in 1913. In 1927-28 it was a four-teacher school with Elmer Rhodes as principal. Grades 1st through 8th were taught. Later the school consolidated with Alcorn Central.

Rienzi School, 1920s.

The old Rienzi School building, ca. 1938-39. There has been two or three buildings since this one. Some of them burned.

Rienzi (MS) High School, 1925, second year after formation. Back row: Miller Dilworth, Marie Dalton, Lima Green, William Epps, Annye Carpenter, Birdie Parvin, Rivers Conn, Mattye Mae Surratt, Beatrice Dilworth, Bonnie Sharp, Marvin Smith. Second row: Elmer Cooper, Clifford Rinehart, Rubye Epps, Roy Carpenter, Madgelin Smith, Raymond Green, Ernest Moss, Maybel Lang, Melvin Conn, Opal Miller. Third row: Mr. S.S. Glenn, Guy Johnson, Baxter Smith, Annye Thorn, Hazel Parvin, Alyce Dalton, Winnye Mae Smith, Verona Rinehart, Lewis Earl Perry, Mr. Dabbs. Front: Richard Thorn, Truman Smith, John H. Rinehart.

Alcorn County 1938 Champions! Rienzi High School Basketball Team. L-R: Marcus Henry Morton (b. 1918, d. 1993), Arlen Walker Johnson, D.C. (David Carl) Hearn (b. 1921, d. 1951), J. Lamar Gallaher (b. 1918, d. 1959), Lyle "Pal" Hill, Ray Surratt and Rufus Bynum (submarine sank in WWII, lost at sea, first Rienzi resident killed). Coach Glenn Boyd Williams. D.C. made goal to win championship.

Rienzi High School 1939 Graduates. Seated: Eugenia Miller, Jennie Mae Morton, Arlen Johnson, Junior Crowe Hendrix, Ruby Duncan Whittemore, J.T. Phillips. Standing: Narka Lang, Lynna Dickinson Davis, Loyce Killough, May Maness Rowsey, Vivian Moran, George Smith (principal), Virgie Lancaster, Mozelle Trantham. Not pictured is Rufus Bynum killed in WWII submarine accident.

Rienzi High School Girls Basketball Team, 1941. Seated: Mauvelene Gallaher, Warine Mink, Jean Cox, Elizabeth Johnson, Kathleen Gray. Standing: Bernice Nash, Coach Martha Howell, Louise Winfield, Marjorie Perry, Coach__, Lottie V. Nash.

Rienzi High School 1942 Graduating Class. Seated: Merlon Wardlow Hendrix (b. 1921, d. 1978), Ella Bird Hendrix Tucker (b. 1922, d. 1986), John Allen Ozbirn, Violet Wages Mitchel. Standing: Mr. Hambrick (principal), Horace Doyle Nash, Lottie Nash Wade, William Alfred Nash (b. 1921, d. 1979), Mary Avis Adair Settle (sponsor).

Rienzi Eagles, 1942. Seated: Mauvelene Gallaher, Doris Liming, Dorothy Johnson. Standing, L-R: Jean Cox, Marie Gallaher, Grace Massingill, Marjorie Perry, Coach Martha Howell, Louise Winfield, Eunice Johnsey, Ruthie Duncan, Bernice Nash and Lottie Nash.

Rienzi High School 1955 Class. Front row, L-R: Edith Mae Moore, Margaret Jane Hearn, Billy Bearden, Shirley Chase Mitchell, Peggie Jo Rorie. Second row, L-R: Virginia Whitley, Harold Morgan, Margaret Mitchell, Travis Williams, Yvonne Malone, Thomas Grant White, Nella Vee Vanderford, Eugene Yarbrough. Third row, L-R: Jerry Coker, Dorothy Jean Hearn, F.L. Pounders, Hautense Benjamin, Roy C. Stacy, Frankie Inmon, Jack Richardson, Agnes Smith.

Rienzi High School, 1965, last graduating class. James H. Moore (principal), Mrs. B.C. Henry (sponsor), Walter Wayne Bullard, Marjorie Kay Wren, Donnie Ray Killough, Charles Melvin Brimingham, Barbara Anne Killough, Bobby Gleen Newborn, Mary Jane Donahue, Roger Dale Jacobs, Martha Jane Palmer (treasurer), Thurman Rudolph Massingill (vice president) Joel Luther Henry (president), Judith Carolyn Goodman (secretary), Bobby Max Calhoun, Jimmy Ray Barnes, Geraldine Grooms, Mable Killough, Rayborn Junior Hendrix, Peggy Ann Felks, Robert Lee Brooks, Lorene Basden.

Scale Street School, late 1920s.

Theo School #2. In 1923 this four-room wood frame structure was built for $2500. In the school term 1929-30 Lottie Brooks was principal and the following 8th grade graduates: Arvid and Bessie Dunn, Harmon Rainey, Truit and Fredra Brooks.

Scale Street School in the late 1950s.

Scale Street School. Mrs. Oneida Lasley, teacher, 1963-64.

Old Union Schoolhouse west of Alcorn County.

Union School. Virginia Moore went to school 1st through 8th grades.

Union School, 1934. Back row: Sally Kate (Mattox) Hall. Corrine Mathis, Mitchell Hodum, Andy Glidewell, Charlene Goforth, Elvie Henderson, Florine Kuykendall, Fay Henderson. Front row: Charlene Lancaster, ? Fryer, Hollis Kuykendall, Mattie Sanders, Dorothy Barnes and ? Rushing.

Union School. Back row: Sally Kate Mattox, ? Yarbert, Buford Lancaster, Corine Mathis, ? Miller, J. R. Lancaster. Second row: ? Shields, Juanita Rencher, Florence Kuykendall, Fay Henderson, Andy Glidewell, Leroy Crowe, ? Yarber, Mable Shaw. Front row: Dimple Rencher, Mottie Sanders, Vivian Shields, Brian Miller, ? Shields, Gene Rushing, Reabon Bridges.

Union School 3rd grade class, 1928. Beecher Lancaster, Olen Miller, Ruby Lancaster, Artye Wilhite, Helen Bennett, Virginia Lancaster, Hester Eaton, Geneva Miller, Elsie Stewart.

Union School Children, 1939.

Union School Reunion

Teachers at Union School, 1939, L-R: Artie Wilhite, Leatha Rencher, Gladys Mathis and Roy Miller. Girl in window is Wilma Rencher.

At Wayside School, which was beside the Old Stage Road (now CR 356) about a mile west of where US 45 now crosses that road, 1915. (1) Robert McCord, (2) Jessie Green, (3) Jennie V. Green, (4) Edward Marecle (?).

Anniversaries

Mary Etta (Lancaster) and Tommy Barnes 50th Wedding Anniversary.

Oswald Clements and Inez Brewer Clements 50th Wedding Anniversary and Howard Clements and Evelyn Smith Clements 25th Wedding Anniversary.

Pat and Lois Johnson Glisson's 50th Wedding Anniversary at their home in Wheeler Grove Community.

Guy Ragan Green (b. July 2, 1897) was the son of Alonzo F. and Kittie (Ragan) Green

Benjamin Henry Hanley and Dora Lynch Hanley's 50th Wedding Anniversary December 1964 with family. Dot, Lee Luther, M.D., Lee Luther Jr. and Hanley Hasseltine; Doris, Harrell Freeman Sr., William and Harrell "Hal" Jr. Jeanes; Dixie, Joseph Edward and Suzannah Criswell.

Rev. A.D. and Mickey Gurley's 50th Wedding Anniversary, November 24, 1968. Pastor of First Pentecostal Church.

50th Wedding Anniversary celebration of R.C. and Sara Hudson, 1989.

Carroll Hudson family 50th Wedding Anniversary celebration, L-R: Lon, Elizabeth McAnally, Joseph and Kay Beavo, Denver and Judy Eshee, Denver Eshee Jr., Emily Eshee, Marie Beavo and Andy Beavo. Center is Sara and Carroll Hudson.

Sam and Virginia Jones' 40th Wedding Anniversary celebration given by their daughter Ginger Jones Holland at the First United Methodist Church, Corinth, MS. Pictured are Ginger Jones Holland, Sam B. Jones and Virginia S. Jones.

Leslie and Virdie Key's 50th Wedding Anniversary celebration.

Bill and Grace Pundt's 50th Wedding Anniversary, May 1995.

50th Wedding Anniversary, 1940-1990. Eveline Elizabeth Nash and Jasper Bonnie Palmer (b. 1919, d. 1996). Standing: Debra Diane Crowe, Martha Jane Gardner, Johnny Odell Palmer, Robert Larry Palmer, Alma Fay Lassiter, Ricky Len Palmer and Ruthie Mae Shadburn. Celebrated at Sardis Primitive Baptist Church.

Albert R. and Mable (Suitor) Settle's 50th Wedding Anniversary celebration in the home of Frank and Bernice Baker, Tupelo, MS.

Cousins together at Mable Settle's anniversary celebration. Front row: Clara (McCord) Bridges and Mable. Back row: Geneva (Marecle) Chadwick, Katherine Suitor and Beatrice (Suitor) Savage (sister).

Charles and Edna Clements Shipman's 50th Wedding Anniversary. Children: Mike and Kristina Shipman; Mark and Trish Shipman. Grandchildren: Christopher, Tad, Bradley, Nicole and Julia.

50th Wedding Anniversary, April 24, 1957 of Sanford Stanley and Clara Sue Smith Rorie. Children, L-R: Staton, James, Lillie Mae, Virgie, Eva, Ollis and J.W.

Edd and Cleo Shipman's 50th Wedding Anniversary. Children, Charles, Virginia, Lee Virl and Geneva.

John H. Taylor and Elzie (Wilbanks) Taylor celebrating their 50th Wedding Anniversary, 1979.

Joe L. Walker and Mary Suitor Walker's 50th Wedding Anniversary in Hinkle Community.

Baptisms

Baptism at Surratt's Pond. For many years Surratt's Pond was the "in" place to be baptized. It was located across from where Lakeview Baptist Church is now on Shiloh Road in Corinth, MS. In preparation for baptism, sticks were placed at intervals to help the people not slip in the muddy bottom of the pond. Usually these baptisms took place in the middle of the afternoon after church services. We think this picture was taken in the 1903s. Lottie Taylor King was baptized here and years later her son, Donald O. King Sr. was also baptized here.

Baptizing at Oliver Maltox Lake. Bro. Joe Crawford, Bill Oxner, Verell Wilhite, Gene Rushing, Reed Kuykendall, Hollis Lancaster, Ernest Moore, Charleen Lancaster, Jewel Robinson Sullivan, Juanita Rencher, August 23, 1940.

Birthdays

Birthday party in 1950 held at the Bon-Air, Liddon's Lake.

Ellen M. Barnes celebrating her 100th birthday April 13, 1985. She was 106 at the time of her death (b. April 13, 1985, d. April 24, 1991).

Birthday party for Juanita Leggett. Back row: Elizabeth Latta, Ernestine Tapp, Jean McCalla, Juanita Leggett, Dorothy Godwin, Ann Holloway, Patsy Driver, Stephanie Leggett. Front row: Bennie Mills, Patricia Smith, Ivory Butler, Ruth Latta.

Aunt Letha Nash's 62nd Birthday, June 11, 1959. Community reunion. First row, L-R: Kenneth Allen Lambert (b. 1947, d. 1997), James Randal Nash, Robert Ray Nash, Jerold Edwin Nash, Millard Filmore Nash Jr. (b. 1946, d. 1985). Second row, L-R: Elgin Alvin "Dick" Nash (b. 1900, d. 1965), Rev. Cleveland C. Rinehart (b. 1888, d. 1966), Earie Roscoe Nash (b. 1918, d. 1993), Sonja Annett Nash Jones, Jasper Bonnie Palmer (b. 1919, d. 1996), Gary Ray Nash, Willard Difford "Wid" Nash, Millard Filmore "Red" Nash (b. 1926, d. 1995), Earie Roscoe Nash (b. 1895, d. 1978), Julian Millard Dowd (b. 1926, d. 1983), Ferrel Wade Lambert, Charlie Larkin Lambert, Ervin Ferrel Lambert (b. 1914, d. 1982), Kenneth Leon "Don" Nash (b. 1943, d. 1982), Leslie Clay "Dess" Nash (b. 1902, d. 1986), Harold Dewain Nash (b. 1951, d. 1990), Cecil Ray Langston, Major Burcham (b. 1909, d. 1994). Third row, L-R: Lottie V. Nash Wade, Marylane Louise Wade Koch, Beulah Mae Vanderford Nash (b. 1903, d. 1999), Eveline Elizabeth Nash Palmer, Ricky Len Palmer, Alma Fay Palmer Lassiter, Opal Flanagan Nash (b. 1920, d. 1994), Lavern Estell Nash Dowd, Steve Lee Nash, Viola Bertha Austin Nash (b. 1928, d. 1985), Ruthie Mae Robinson Shadburn, Dorothy Austin ?, Robert Larry Palmer, Thelma Jean Burcham Langston, Donnie Ray Langston, Carolyn Jean Nash, Martha Jane Palmer Gardner, Debra Diane Palmer Crowe, Mary Glen Nash Rushing, Wanda Ann Lambert Burcham, Gladys Lee Nash Lambert, Mary Susie Bullard Nash, Avis Luconer Nash Burcham Crum, Victoria Elzie "Vicki" Whittemore Rinehart (b. 1892, d. 1968), Letha Elizabeth Vanderford Nash (b. 1897, d. 1983).

Cornith Centennial

Corinth Centennial Celebration, May 1954. GM&O Agency Force shown: L-R: Agent J.C. White, Check Clerk H.M. Hahn, Cashier W.E. Kemp, Assistant Cashier H.L. Archer, Claim Clerk A.H. Taylor, Chief Clerk G.N. Pankey, Rate and Bill Clerk Hoyl Phillips and Miss Virginia Staggs, secretary to agent.

Scene from the 1954 Corinth Centennial Parade.

Scene from the 1954 Corinth Centennial Parade.

Scene from the 1954 Corinth Centennial Parade. Driving the small Nash car pulling the float is Marlin Roaten with his son Kenneth R. Roaten along for the ride.

Una Sanders and Levera Lancaster during the Centennial.

Hubert and Dimple R. Mitchell, Centennial.

1954 Corinth's 100th Anniversary: Lee, Audie and Connie Horton.

Juanita (Rencher) Davis during the Centennial.

1954 Corinth Centennial Celebration. John H. Roaten and wife Lottie V. Hardwick Roaten.

Dock, Virginia and Terri Lynn Oaks during Corinth's Centennial, 1954.

1954 Corinth Centennial Celebration. Ira Ellis Glisson and wife Jewell Vastie Roaten Glisson.

1954 Corinth Centennial Celebration. Back, L-R: James Marlin Roaten and wife Eddra Irene Osborn Roaten. Front: Kenneth R. Roaten and sister Patricia Roaten.

Corinth Centennial Parade, May 1954. On the float are Junior Phillips, Randel Wall, Darrell Woodruff, Leck Counce; girls are Jane Driver, Virginia Vanderford and Virginia Hall.

Scene from the 1954 Corinth Centennial Parade. Dr. Stroupe is driving Mr. Benzie's car.

Parades

"Red Cross" Fund Raising Parade, Waldron Street, April 13, 1918. First gas operated truck owned by Corinth Coca-Cola Bottling Works (Model T). Lady in car looking is Mayor Henry's wife.

Armed Forces Day Parade, May 19, 1954. L-R: R.O. McKewen, Annette Dees, Becky Walker, Macon Lamberth.

Clockwise from upper left: Christine Walden (Grand Marshal) and Josephine Hilburn and scenes from the Rienzi Christmas Parade of 2000.

Reunions

Armstrong Reunion, ca. 1988. L-R: Dora Cleatus Armstrong Woodruff (b. 1924, d. 1988), Archie Lee Armstrong (b. 1902, d. 1994), Mary Ruth Holloway Armstrong, Charlie Glenn Armstrong (b. 1922, d. 1989), Dalton Kelly Williams. Second row: Ila Armstrong Wade (b. 1906, d 1994), Artie Armstrong Lambert (b. 1908, d. 2001), Iness Lavada Armstrong Williams (b. 1915, d. 1997), Dora Clark Wren Armstrong, Nancy Wren Rinehart Rorie.

A group of people from around Biggersville and Hinkle (occasion not known). Seated: unknown, unknown, third and fourth Cleo and Hillie Bridges, fifth and sixth Houston and Sammie Mitchell, seventh and eighth Hubert and Lida Bridges. Second row: unknown, second Will Settle, behind his shoulder is Velma and Roy Suitor, unknown, unknown, seventh and eighth Nina and Harry Lee Biggers, unknown. Back row, unknown, Ruby Epps, Roy Carpenter, unknown, unknown, unknown, unknown, Mauldin Rinehart, unknown. This picture was among Ann Carpenter's but had no names on it. Contact the Genealogical Society in Corinth to help identify others.

Eddie Belle Cox Family in 1944. Front row, L-R: Peggie Jo Rorie, Gene Calvary, Mickey Calvary. Second row, L-R: Jewell Rorie, Geraldine Calvary, Hillie Calvary, "Miss Eddie" Cox, Dewey Stacy, Lona Stacy. Third row, L-R: Ollis Rorie, Ganelle Calvary, Eddie Calvary, Victor Calvary, Jo Ann Calvary, Lucille Calvary, J.B. Calvary, Mary Glenn Cox and Bud Cox.

Hardin Family Reunion

Rorie Family Reunion. Home of Sanford Stanley Rorie, March 29, 1942. Neighbors and friends also attended.

Rorie Family Reunion, 1942. Sanford and Clara Sue Rorie Family: Back row, L-R: James Elwyn Rorie, Ira Lee Rorie, George Milton Gordon, Eddie Clyde Burcham, Eva Arminta Rorie Burcham, J.W. Rorie, Raymond Earl Rorie, Clara Frances Burcham, Sanford Staton Rorie. Center row, L-R: Tillman Burcham, Virgie Aval Rorie Burcham, Nancy Maxine Burcham, Clara Sue Smith Rorie, Sanford Stanley Rorie, Nellie Mae Hamlin Rorie, Reuben Frederick Rorie, Roy Ollis Rorie, Jewell Eddie Calvary Rorie. Front row, L-R: Tillman Carlos Burcham, Orie Leon Burcham, George Wallace Burcham, Betty Luella Burcham, Lillie Mae Rorie, Mary Christine Burcham, Annie Sue Burcham, Olan Clyde Burcham, Cleston Cleveland Burcham, Kenneth Clay Burcham, Peggie Jo Rorie.

Sanford and Clara Sue Rorie Family Reunion 1950. L-R: Gordon, Staton, Lillie Mae, Ollis, James, Clara Sue, Eva, Sanford, Ira, Virgie, Reuben, Raymond. J.W. was the only child missing.

Four brothers, L-R: Eugene Bailey, Sanford Stanley, J.F.W. "Fred" and William Hubbard "Bill" Rorie, 1952 Rorie Reunion.

Family reunion at Hickory Flat Schoolhouse. Seated: Maude Vanderford (b. 1901, d. 1978), Louise Vanderford (b. 1911, d. 1991), Leatha Nash (b. 1897, d. 1988), Mabel Tucker Glidewell (b. 1907, d. 1973), Amye Nash (b. 1901, d. 1983), Beulah Nash (b. 1903, d. 1999), Giffie Nash (b. 1906, d. 2000). Standing: Dave Vanderford (b. 1899, d. 1993), Leonard "Bill" Vanderford (b. 1904, d. 1980), Earie Nash (b. 1895, d. 1978), Ely Glidewell (b. 1891, d. 1986), Archie Nash, Leslie "Dess" Nash (b. 1901, d. 1986), ca. 1965.

Whittemore Reunion, ca. 1970. Seated: Etheleen Little Whittemore (b. 1931, d. 1999), Ruby Duncan Whittemore, Vera Eunice Burcham (b. 1914, d. 1979), Louise Shipman Whittemore Harris, Ruthie Duncan Whittemore. Standing: John Curtis, Cecil, Jodie Terrell (b. 1919, d. 1988), Herman Hardy Whittemore, Roy Burcham (b. 1908, d. 1972), Perry Dalton (b. 1913, d. 1987), Clinnon Whittemore (b. 1917, d. 1992).

Various

Abe Dilworth place at Hinkle on Mitchell Hill Road. Results of the ice storm of 1951.

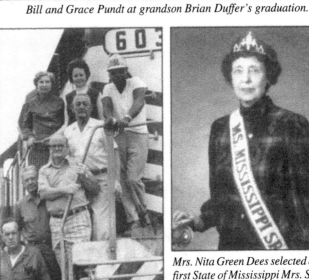

Bill and Grace Pundt at grandson Brian Duffer's graduation.

Mrs. Nita Green Dees selected as the first State of Mississippi Mrs. Senior Mississippi in 1991. She represented the state in National Mrs. Senior America Pageant in Atlantic City, NJ and won one of five top awards, "Special Recognition," which signifies the qualities of an all around person.

Nurses in front of McRae Hospital, Corinth, MS. Ada Alma Maddox Dean in front center, ca. 1925.

Reception at our church August 1971. Jewel Anderson, great-granddaughter of Rev. John H. Byrd. Husband, Rev. A.L. Davis and daughter Eunice Davis.

Recipients of 25 year service pins with the ICG Railroad, Corinth, MS. Top: Virginia S. Jones, Nadine King, W. Walker Jr. Bottom: D.D. Hicks, Irl T. Alexander, H.D. Kemp, R. P. Kinard, September 5, 1974.

This page sponsored by WalMart Supercenter of Corinth, MS

Mrs. J.A. "Nita" Dees Junior Auxiliary 1993 Outstanding Citizen of the Year. Also attending the occasion were grandchildren John and Paula Ferguson and son-in-law and daughter, Harvey and Deanna Ferguson of Hernando, MS.

Doug White with picture of Rienzi in Washington, DC.

Weddings

Sandra Arbagast and Howard A. Suitor on their wedding day November 22, 1973. L-R: Francille Mathis, Howard Suitor, Sandra and Howard, Mildred Suitor, Linda Zimmerman. Back: John Mathis and son Johnny, Greg Zimmerman. Howard Suitor is the son of Elbert N. and Minnie Kate Suitor.

Jennifer Smith Johnson and Allen Johnson on their wedding day.

Rev. Wade Allen Holland and Rev. Virginia Joyce (Ginger) Jones wedding August 29, 1987 at the First United Methodist Church, Corinth, MS.

Nelda MacIntyre's Family, L-R: Carrie Jenkins (granddaughter), Ron Jenkins (son), Katie Jenkins Kovach (granddaughter), Paul Kovach (grandson-in-law) and Susan Jenkins (daughter-in-law).

Sam Booker Jones and Virginia Dell Staggs wedding, April 19, 1959 at the First Methodist Episcopal Church So., Corinth, MS. Also pictured: Rev. Joe T. Humphries, Catherine Purvis (organist) Nelda Wright Woodard (soloist), Walter E. Kemp (usher) Howard H. Lamon (usher).

Stella and Steve Pundt's wedding, September 22, 1986. His is the great-great-grandson of John H. and Nancy Byrd.

Lorie McKee Smith and Bradley K. Smith on their wedding day.

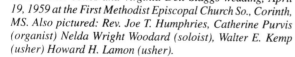

L-R: Ronnie Patrick, Lois (Patrick) Waldrop, Herschel C. Jones, Ellie Mae (Morgan) Jones, Kathy (Jones) McCalister, Joyce (Jones) James, David W. Jones and Lonnie Jones. Taken at the Curlee House on Kathy's wedding day.

Jeff and Melissa Moore Sheirwagen on their wedding day.

Hilda (McCalister) Haley, Betty Sue (McCalister) Rogers, Clara (Potts) McCalister, Jim Edd McCalister, Jimmy H. McCalister, Terry Leon McCalister and Eddie Joe McCalister. Taken at the Curlee House on Jimmy's wedding day.

The wedding of Maxine Wallace and Bynum Wilbanks. Her father and mother, Vance and Eva Wallace; her sister Opal Pace and Ira, her sister Betty and brothers Bobby, Buddy, Billy and Tommy Wallace. Her aunt and uncle Roy and Vera Vanderford, their daughter Virginia and son Charles. His brother Clayton Wilbanks and minister Herbert Summers.

Karen Hughes Smith and Tracy S. Smith on their wedding day.

Julie Jobe Robertson and Brian Scott Shirley on their wedding day December 30, 1995 at the Waldron Street Christian Church. Bride is the daughter of Thomas E. and Betty King Robertson. Groom is the son of Dennis and Vicki Fortson Shirley.

Kelli King Robertson and John Whitney Hughes Tomlinson on their wedding day, August 22, 1998 at the Waldron St. Christian Church. Kelli is the daughter of Thomas E. and Betty King Robertson and John is the son of John Brewer Tomlinson Jr. and Carolyn Richards Tomlinson.

Old Soldiers Reunion

War Between the States Veterans Reunion at the Grove in Kossuth, MS, ca. 1900. First row, L-R: S.A. Dalton, Maj. Glen Sharp, Jim Enochs, Jim Stevens, unknown, unknown, Maj. G.W. Bynum, Pete Pannell, John Savage, unknown, John White, L. Burge Mitchell, Josh Blackwell, unknown, Turner Bynum, Euel McHaffey, Nat Bynum, 19 and 20 unknown, W.M. Scally, John H. Dilworth (directly behind front row man with glasses on), Rufe Settle, Newt Suitor, Dr. L.A. Hill, __ Burnett, John A. Miller, John Wagnon. First row number eight, then go to left again. James Dillington second on front, Dr. Herman third on front.

Civil War Vets Reunion

Camp Pike, WWI.

Confederate Veterans Reunion, Corinth, MS, ca. 1918. Third from left is Christopher Columbus Hearn.

WWI Company. L-R: M.J. Hurd (Buie, OR), S.P. Meda, (CA), Angelo Terrangelo (New York, NY), J.L. Goggin (Rocky Mountain, VA), Jas. R. Couvillon (Plancheville, LA) S.B. Jones (Corinth, MS), Roy Ward (Watkinsville, GA), C. Scruggs (FL), Jno. C. English (Versailles, OH).

On the steps of Corinth Courthouse, L-R: Leroy Gray, Roscoe Turner, John D. Mercier, Les Horn.

Corinth National Guard leaving for Fort Jackson, SC to train for the Korean War.

WWII, front row, L-R: unknown, J. __Oker, Helmerson, Griffin, unknown. Second row, L-R: Wood, South, unknown, Dupont.

A group of servicemen during a drill in Manila in the Philippines during WWII of which Roy Savage was assigned. Their barracks are shown in the background.

Corinth National Guard, 1980. Mike Shipman is carrying the flag.

Arnet Barnes, son of Clifford and Lola (Dixon) Barnes.

Glennie H. "Shorty" Barnes, son of Clifford and Lola (Dixon) Barnes, husband of Maxine (Wallace) Barnes.

Jimmy Barnes, twin son of Melzar and Glorie Barnes, was killed in Vietnam.

Grady Barnes served in the Marines during WWII. He was wounded in action in the Battle of Okinawa and received the Purple Heart. Son of Clifford and Lola (Dixon) Barnes, husband of Doris (Wallace) Barnes.

Melzar Barnes, son of Clifford and Lola (Dixon) Barnes.

James V. Bingham (b. September 19, 1923, d. January 10, 1995) US Army, 1942-64. Picture taken 1942.

Ernest Darris Bowen, Korean War.

James Howard Bowen, WWII.

Delbert Clyde Bowen, 1950.

William Ester Boatman Family, 1943. Seated: Ester Boatman and wife, Luna Johnson Boatman. Top Clifford O., Nelda and James E. "Sonny" Boatman.

Robert W. Brewster served in WWI, taken July 26, 1918.

Boilerman 2/c James H. Briggs, USN, USS Hollister. He received the WWII Victory Medal and Good Conduct Medal, 1945-49.

Bill Wayne Brooks, US Air Force, 1959-62, son of Mrs. Louise Kirkland Brooks and R.C. Brooks.

Billy J. Brooks (b. 1929), Korean War, Co. H., 155th Infantry, Mississippi.

Donald Ray Brooks, US Army, 1964-65, son of Mrs. Louise Kirkland Brooks and R.C. Brooks.

Elisha Allen Brooks (b. 1836, d. 1863) CSA, brother of Perry M. Brooks and buried in Ebenezer Cemetery, Tippah County, MS.

Sgt. Truit A. Brooks (b. 1916, d. 1978) WWII, Army, Korean War, MP Army.

Mike Byrnes Sr., crew member on Confederate ship Merrimac. Mike Byrnes Jr. served in France, WWI.

Home on leave during WWII. Left is Victor Stephen Calvary and on the right is John Hillie Calvary, sons of Mrs. Eddie Belle Scott Calvary Cox and Samuel Stevens Calvary (b. 1877, d. 1920).

Charles E. Chastain in Yokohama, Japan.

T/Sgt. Howard Clement. (Article from the newspaper). "T/Sgt. Clement, Nazi Captive, Is Back Home." Corinth boy, first prisoner of Nazis from Alcorn County, escaped three times only to be retaken; is in fine health now. Back from the horrors of war and the terrors and deprivations of a German prison camp, T/Sgt. Howard Clement, the first Alcorn County man to fall into the hands of the Nazis in WWII and the first such captive in the county to be repatriated from Stalag IIIB prison, arrived in the city last night aboard the Tennessean from Kennedy General Hospital in Memphis. He was accompanied by his wife, who has been with him at the hospital since he arrived there on March 1st.

Paul Clements. (Newspaper article) Paul Clements, 76 of Cleveland, died Sunday, November 26, 2000 at his residence. Funeral services are at 10 a.m. Tuesday at Ray Funeral Home Chapel in Cleveland with the Rev. Danny Powell officiating. Burial will follow at New Cleveland Cemetery under the direction of Ray Funeral Home of Cleveland. Visitation is from 6-8 p.m. today at the funeral home. Mr. Clements was born Feb. 9, 1924 in Corinth to the late William Oswald and Lela Inez Brewer Clements. He served his country in the US Army in WWII. He saw action in Germany and France and was wounded in the Battle of the Bulge and received two Purple Hearts. In 1960 he became the founder and president of "Paul's Mart" in Cleveland. Mr. Clements was preceded in death by two brothers, William Howard Clements and Richard Nelson Clements. He is survived by his wife, Jane Brown Clements of Cleveland; two sisters, Edna Shipman of Corinth and Mildred Suitor of Terri Haute, IN. Pallbearers will be Johnny Sheedy, Hal Clements, Kent White, James Brown, David Schlatter and Brooks Reynolds.

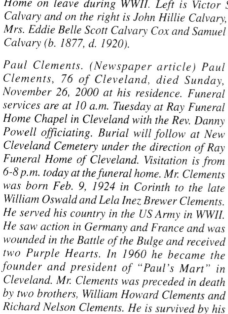

James Edward Cosby served in the US Army during WWII 1943 to January 1946 in the European Theater.

James Randall Cox served in the US Navy Submarine Force between 1969 and 1992. The son of James Rupert Cox, he is pictured receiving a commemorative plaque at his retirement ceremony onboard the USS McKee (AS41) in October 1992.

William Audie Cooley Sr., WWI Germany, Volunteer Company, organized at Corinth, MS. Mustered into service August 12, 1917.

James Rupert Cox served in the US Navy during WWII. and saw action in the Pacific onboard the USS Samuel M. Moore.

Jack Crow

James Albert "Bud" Dees (b. 1915, d. 1984) drafted for active service January 6, 1942 and honorably discharged December 1, 1945. Served full time overseas duty. Husband of Nita Dees, father of Mrs. Harvey (Deanna) Ferguson of Hernando; grandfather of John Allen Ferguson of Corinth and Dr. Paula Ferguson Wilson of Birmingham, AL.

James Dillingham, Co. H, 10 MS CSA.

Mike Dillingham, Co. H, 10 MS CSA.

Earl Driver, US Navy, 1945-47

Douglas Durm, 56th Navy Seabees, WWII, 1942-45.

J.G. Driver, served in China.

Dexter Driver, Army 1942-46.

Bill Essary, US Army, 1973-77.

James Larry Essary, US Army, 1950-53.

Richard Aaron Forman, Served in the Army overseas duty in Germany, taken in 1952/53.

Jackson (b. July 1831, d. November 21, 1917) and Elizabeth Perrin Ginn, Confederate soldier. Parents of Rube, Quirles, Sally and Mary Etta.

PFC Mervin Gatewood served in Germany.

Guy Ragan Green (b. July 2, 1897) son of Alonzo F. and Kittie Ragan Green. He served in the Navy, WWI, 1917-19 and did sea duty on the USS South Carolina.

Guy Ragan Green Jr. (b. March 6, 1925) served in the Army in North Africa and Italy during WWII. He re-entered the military in 1951 and served in Korea with the 31st Infantry as a 2nd Lieutenant in Field Artillery, retiring as a Colonel in 1977.

Issac Martin Green (b. 1833, Bedford County, TN, d. 1897, MS), served in 6th MS Cavalry, Capt. Dunn's Co. G. (Mississippi Rangers) during the Civil War, 1862-63.

Charles Lloyd Griffin and Effie (Pounds) Griffin, ca. 1953. Charles served in the Korean War and was awarded the Bronze Star and Purple Heart.

Ricky Lloyd Griffin, US Army, son of Charles and Effie (Pounds) Griffin.

A friend and T/Sgt. Glen Oneal Griffin. Oneal is the son of Clarence and Fanny (McCrary) Griffin. He served over 15 years in the US Air Force and served in the Korean War.

1st Sgt. Charles Fred Haley (b. March 3, 1952) served in the USAR May 5, 1971 to May 5, 1991. Married to Hilda McCalister Haley (b. August 9, 1952).

Seaman 2/c Frank Charles Haley (b. March 13, 1927, d. September 29, 2001) served from May 15, 1944 to March 30, 1946. Husband of Margaret Morton Haley (b. March 11, 1927).

Pharmacist 2/c Richard Harber, WWII, South Pacific from 1942-45.

Pvt. William C. Harden (b. 1833, TN, d. 1898 MS) served in Co. D, 6th Tennessee US Cavalry, 1862-65.

Col. Lee L. Hasseltine, MD (b. 1907, d. 1973) WWII. Served in the US Army Medical Corps and was a Pearl Harbor survivor, December 7, 1941. After 20 years he retired and belonged to the Retired Officers Association.

Elizabeth Hearn Harwood and James Henry Hill Harwood, late 1942 or early 1943.

David Carl "D.C" and Orfee Little Hearn.

Oner Dee Hearn, WWII.

L-R: Christine Ryder, Rupert Hearn, Gladys Palmer.

Thurman Leo Hendrix (b. 1920, d. 1982) US Navy, WWII and wife Alma Fay Vanderford Hendrix.

Allen Wayne Hendrix, served in the Army 16 years. Great-grandson of William H. and Willie Cox Rorie and grandson of Pat and Virgia Rorie Vanderford, ca. 1985.

R.C. Hivley, National Guard, Co. H, WWII.

Jimmy G. Hurley, retired SM/SGT, US Air Force.

David Jennings, US Army.

Sgt. David Neal Jennings, son of Mr. and Mrs. David Jennings.

Capt. Martina Jones in Hawaii, 1995.

Two buddies and Robert U. Jones.

Pvt. Sam B. Jones at Jacksonville, FL. Finished basic training and is leaving for France March 17, 1918.

Sam Booker Jones (standing) and James Rene Couvillon in France July 4, 1918.

PFC Otha Lee King, 8th Air Force, WWII.

James M. Bill Kirkland, US Army, 1939-62, brother of Mrs. Louis Kirkland Brooks.

James Hollis Kuykendall Sr. (b. August 19, 1923, d. June 13, 1949) US Army, WWII, Co. E, 342nd D Infantry, Black Hawk Reg.

T/Sgt. Reed H. Kuykendall (b. April 15, 1921), US Army, WWII, 306th Bomb, 367th Squadron, 8th Air Force.

William Aaron Kuykendall (b. December 27, 1918, d. October 14, 1982), US Army, WWII, Co. H, 155th Infantry.

J.R. Lancaster (son of Charlie Lancaster) was in Fort Benning, GA.

Roy Leon Lancaster

Robert Lancaster and Hollis Lancaster, sons of Charlie Lancaster.

Tom Lancaster (right) and friend. Tom is the son of Charlie Lancaster.

Tom and Cleo Lancaster, son of Charlie Lancaster.

Nolie Maddox, US Army after WWI. He was in the hospital at Waynesville, NC after being gassed and sent back to the States.

James M. "Jim" Maness (b. 1891, d. 1968) WWI, husband of Adie Mae Woods Maness (b. 1900, d. 1934) and Mary Lee Smith Maness (b. 1895, d. 1951).

SFC Harold Ray Marecle, Co. H, 155th Infantry, 31st Dixie Division, Fort Jackson, SC.

James Harrison Mattox, ca. 1918, WWI.

Raymond T. Mattox, US Army Air Force, WWII, 1942-46.

Mattox Brothers, WWII. Winford Mattox served in the Army 1944-46 and Raymond Mattox served in the Army Air Force 1942-46. The picture was taken in Macon, GA and presented to their parents Jim and Lorena Mattox.

Airman Basic Bobby Wayne Mays, Parks AFB, CA, July 1956.

John Thomas McCrary served in WWII, 1946 in Ireland, where he met his wife.

Billy Joe McNair, US Army 1958 to 1964, served in Germany.

Michael A. McNair joined the US Army in 1982.

Cpl. Joseph Burton "J.B." Meeks, US Army, WWII, August 19, 1942 to October 5, 1945. He served in Normandy, South Africa and Sicily.

PFC Malcolm Moore, Co. F, 314th Infantry, US Army, WWII.

Charlie R. and Sue (McFalls) McNair and their children Terry Lynn (Lloyd) and Robert Steve in 1963 while on duty in France. Charlie joined the US Air Force November 1951 and retired July 1973. During his career he was stationed in Selma, AL; Thule, Greenland; Savannah, Atlanta and Warner Robins, GA; Memphis, TN; France, Hawaii and North Carolina. Most of his duties were in recruiting and recruiting related fields. When he retired he was an administrative superintendent. He married in 1955 and resides in the Wenasoga Community.

Sgt. Wesley Moore, US Army Corps of Engineers, Kossuth, MS. His group followed Gen. Patton and built bridges for them to cross and then blew them up.

James Robert Morton (b. September 25, 1914), US Navy, WWII, in Medic Corps.

Marcus H. Morton (b. April 28, 1918, d. December 20, 1993), US Army, WWII, HQ DET 4833 Service Command Unit.

Wilson McKinney Morton Sr. (b. June 7, 1845, d. April 21, 1909) Co. D, 32nd Infantry MS CSA. Married to Jennie Fitzgerald (b. March 17, 1856, d. January 31, 1953). Children: Lena, Minnie, Mary Belle, Wilson Jr., Douglas, Annie, Martha and Georgia.

Sgt. Jerold Edwin Nash, US Air Force for four years, served in Vietnam. Husband of Pauline Rogers Nash, son of Willard and Susie Bullard Nash. He received a medal for Outstanding Service, ca. 1967.

Cpl. John M. Nash served January 19, 1953 to August 19, 1955 with the Hell on Wheels, 43rd Armored Infantry Division in Bombholder, Germany.

Sons of Earie and Leathie Nash. Robert Roscoe Nash (b. 1918, d. 1993) with Mary Glen Rushing and Wayne Allen Nash. Willard Dilford Nash with Kenneth Leon "Don" Nash (b. 1943, d. 1982).

Frank P. Oaks, WWI.

Dock and Virginia Oaks, 1950.

1951 Korean War, 81MM mortar. From the left is Dillard Rickerson, James Austin and Dock Oaks.

J.C. Osborn served in the Army during WWII.

Jasper Bonnie Palmer, WWII, (b. 1919, d. 1996) son of Jasper Odell and Bessie Cox Palmer, husband of Eveline Nash Palmer.

John T. Phillips in Milton, FL, 1942-45.

First cousins in Basonson, France, October 1944, WWII. L-R: Sanford Potts, Hubert Taylor, Ross Pittman. Hubert was wounded and the others got passes to go see him in the hospital.

Ross Pittman, October 1944 WWII in France.

Thelma Ray Pittman, US Army, son of Albert and Jenny (Dixon) Pittman.

Zachariah Garrett Prince served in the 2nd Alabama Infantry CSA. He made shoes for soldiers during the Civil War and later was a farmer and preacher.

1st Lt. Cecil Philip Ramer, US Army, served in the Pacific Area during WWII.

This is Christine Suitor Reynolds on the left and a friend while serving as a nurse in England.

Christine (Suitor) Reynolds (b. 1918, d. 1998) served as a nurse in an England base hospital during WWII. She met Don Reynolds (b. 1919, d. 1996), a medical technician and was married there. They had two daughters after returning to the States.

2nd Lt. William Max Rhodes (b. 1936, d. 1999), US Marine Corps and wife Joy Dale Wilbanks Rhodes, Quanitco, VA, 1960.

John M. Rhodes earned commission through Army ROTC at Mississippi State University in 1987. Upon completion of Infantry Officer Basic Course and Airborne School at Fort Benning, GA, he served with the 1st Battalion 6th Infantry, 1st Armored Division in Germany and Southwest Asia during the Gulf War. Received honorable discharge from the Army in July 1991. Currently serves with the Mississippi National Guard as a Major with the 155th Armored Brigade. Decorations include Bronze Star Medal, Army Commendation Medals, Combat Infantry Badge, Southwest Asia and Kuwait Liberation Service Ribbon. His wife is the former Debbie Little; children are Suzanne and Nathan.

Lawrence Rider at Great Lakes Naval Base. He served aboard the LST 1005 during WWII.

James Marlin Roaten (left) served in the Army as a munitions expert and fought in the Philippine Liberation of WWII. John H. Roaten (right) served in the US Navy during WWII.

Kenneth Allen Rinehart, US Navy, served June 3, 1999 to June 2001.

Hillie D. Roaten served in the National Guard during the tenure of WWII.

Kenneth R. Roaten, US Air Force, May 1965-June 1971.

Daniel Ray Roaten, US Army National Guard, 1989-95.

Willie B. Roaten served in the U.S. Navy during WWII.

S/SGT. Howard E. Robertson, US Air Force, November 27, 1941 to October 30, 1945.

Aaron Rogers and Russell Odle, good friends and classmates. Russell was in Pearl Harbor Dec. 11, 1940. He was killed in a working accident in Pecos, TX in 1978 and is buried in Savannah, TN.

Sarah Johnson Rogers and Millard Lee Rogers (Navy, WWII), 1944.

Serving in WWII, George Milton Gordon Rorie (b. 1923, d. 1973), son of Sanford Stanley and Clara Sue Smith Rorie.

Serving in WWII, James Elwyn Rorie (b. 1919), son of Sanford Stanley and Clara Sue Smith Rorie.

Serving in WWII, Raymond Earl Rorie (b, 1925), son of Sanford Stanley and Clara Sue Smith Rorie.

Gilbert Rorie (b. 1893, d. 1953) WWI; son of William Hubbard Rorie and Emley Caroline (Rinehart) Rorie and grandson of James Frederick Withers Rorie and Sarah (Cheek) Rorie.

Roy Ollis Rorie (b. 1909, d. 1993) in 1936. Served in Civilian Conservation Corps, son of Sanford Stanley and Clara Sue Smith Rorie.

Serving in the Korean Conflict, Sanford Staton Rorie, son of Sanford Stanley and Clara Sue Smith Rorie.

First Sgt. Ben Roy Savage (b. 1919, d. 1984) was a twin of Johnnie Ray. Received his basic training at Fort Bragg, NC. He was in the Philippines for 14 months as an administrative NCO during WWII.

First Sgt. Johnnie Ray Savage and wife Rozella. He served in the Army in WWII, stationed in Germany for a lengthy period of time. He was a twin to Ben Roy Savage, son of Bob and Len (Mills) Savage.

First Sgt. Roy Savage shown with two of his buddies during WWII in Manila, Philippines.

Clifton B. Sawyer, US Army.

Alex Worth Shadburn (b. December 27, 1892, d. August l, 1969), WWI.

Newton Guy Shadburn (b. July 1, 1891, d. March 18, 1925) WWI, married on October 27, 1922 to Lillie Belle Morgan (b. February 19, 1901, d. July 14, 1966).

PFC Winfred Ely Shadburn (b. May 15, 1924) US Army Air Force.

PFC Charles Shipman, son of Edd and Cleo Shipman, husband of Edna C. Shipman.

Melissa Moore Sheirwagen

Mike Shipman, 1979 at Camp Shelby, MS. Mississippi Army National Guard, 108th/ AC Unit, Corinth.

PFC Charles Shipman, US Army 1946-48. Stationed in Germany in the Horse Patrol for military government.

Grover G. Smith, WWII, served about 30 years.

Joe C. South, WWI.

John Morgan Stewart retired as a Captain from the Mississippi National Guard, November 11, 1961.

William Robert Stewart and Estelle Carter Stewart with daughter Marilyn Lynette Stewart, 1943.

William Robert Stewart served in WWII and the Korean War, now a full-time employee with the Mississippi National Guard.

Harold Strachan

Suitor Brothers: T/Sgt. Albert F. Suitor served 20 months overseas with Gen. George S. Patton's 3rd Armored Division in North Africa and Sicily. He was discharged October 1945 and among his ribbons were Soldiers Medal of Merit. Joseph N. Suitor (center) graduated from Louisville (KY) Presbyterian Seminary in 1946 and preached for 40 years. Coxswain Howard W. Suitor served in the Navy for over three years in the Mediterranean and European Theaters and later in the Pacific. He received many ribbons and was honorably discharged November 1945.

Ray Suitor

William Howard Suitor (b. 1919) served during WWII (1942-45) in the Navy on cargo ships. They carried supplies to Casablanca and Anzio Beach in Italy, etc., also to islands in the Pacific.

Albert Franklin Suitor (b. 1914, d. 1986) served during WWII, 1941-45 in Gen. George S. Patton's 3rd Armored Division in North Africa and Sicily before being injured.

Christine Suitor, daughter of Robert and Kitty Suitor, received her RN degree from Baptist Memorial Hospital in Memphis, TN. She served as a nurse in England during WWII.

William Newton Suitor (b. 1845, Alcorn County, d. 1922) son of William and Emily (Shields) Suitor. He served in the 11th Mississippi Cavalry, Co. B, Hamm's Regiment (1863-65). He married soon after being discharged and became the father of 11 children.

Sumner brothers from left: Auston, US Navy, WWII and Doyle Veston, US Army, WWII sons of J.T. and Minnie Armstrong Sumner.

Sumner brothers from left: Garvis Elton, US Army, WWII, Laudie, US Air Force, WWII and Nolan Curtis sons of J.T. and Minnie Armstrong Sumner.

Brothers and sisters at Wenasoga, MS. Back row, L-R: Willie Surratt and Vernon Surratt. Front row, L-R: Dorothy Surratt Johnson and Velma Surratt Norvell, early 1940s.

CW4 Bobby N. Taylor, administrative officer, receiving the Meritorious Service Medal from MG A.H. Sweeney, US Air Force Command, Fort McPherson, GA, June 30, 1977.

Donald Maurice Taylor, US Air Force (Lackland, San Antonio, TX), Korean War, 1954.

Fillmore Baxter Taylor (b. 1896) served in France in WWI; son of James Major and Mattie Jane Pinkard Taylor.

Harris Neal Taylor, US Army, WWII 1944.

Hubert Taylor, WWII in France, October 1944.

James Major Taylor, US Army, WWII 1941.

Henry "Doc" Tice served in the CSA at Shiloh.

Alexander Allison Walker (b. 1828, NC, d. 1895, MS) served in 32nd Regiment Infantry of Mississippi Volunteers CSA, 1863-64.

Vester "Punkin" Vanderford (b. 1923, d. 1992), Navy WWII. Husband of Jeffie Hendrix Vanderford (b. 1927, d. 1998), son of David (b. 1899, d. 1993) and Maude Maness Vanderford (b. 1901, d. 1970) ca. 1940s.

Jessie W. Walden, US Navy in WWII, 1942-45.

S/SGT. Kenneth C. Walker, Air Force and Sgt. Doris J. Preston Walker, Air Force.

Harold N. Wingo (son of Mrs. Maggie Wingo) served during WWII in the infantry at Pine Camp, NY.

Arlin Yarber, 104th Infantry, Timberwolf Division, 1944-46, served in Germany.

Jerry Yarber, 1st Battalion, 22nd Artillery, Neurnberg, Germany, 1968-70.

Jimmy W. Yarber, Vietnam, 101st Airborne Div., Screaming Eagles. Enlisted 1968 and received an honorable discharged 1970.

John William Yates, WWI.

Wood carvings of natural color woods on display at a Memphis fair in early 1900s. These carvings were made by E.S. Lancaster (seated in front of carvings) and his daughter, Ida Miller near Rienzi, MS. The carvings (completed in 1904) are of Jefferson Davis, President of the Confederacy; Ida Miller, Abraham Lincoln, James Garfield, William McKinley and a portrait of Christ.

Logging crew using oxen. Date and names unknown.

Clemmie Luna Johnson shown here in the parlor of Ramer, Tennessee home, ca. 1914. Luna Boatman operated this switchboard in their home before she married Ester Boatman in 1916. She did this while taking care of the younger children and cooking dinner for all the workers in the field. (She even cared for some neighbor's children whose mother had died.) She was quick to figure out how to get help so she connected the widower with a spinster lady who had an invalid mother. Each thought the other one made the first call. They married and had a child of their own and lived happily ever after. Note the pistol on the right-hand side of the switchboard.

Mark M. Cornelius family making molasses on family farm off Oakland School Road.

Peddlers from the past.

Surrey and buggy used for transportation in the early 1900s. Harve Miller, wife and daughter Ida and Opal Miller; Mrs. E.S. Lancaster, Lizzie Barchman, E.S. Lancaster and Oscar Edwards, Rienzi, MS.

Hubert Ray Robertson (b. 1920, d. 1981) pictured here while working for the Royal Crown Cola Bottling Co. of Corinth, MS in the 1940s.

Unknown "Courters."

Sunshine Laundry employee on Meigg Street. W.O. Wheeler and Harry Steen, owners.

SPONSORS
- Crow Family Veterans -

John Mattox - Confederate Army, Civil War

Ambrose Williams - Union Army, Civil War

D. Crow Jr. - U.S. Army, WWII

J.C. Crow - U.S. Army, WWII

Leroy Crow - U.S. Army, WWII

Ray Crow - U.S. Army, WWII

Billy W. Crow - U.S. Army, Korean War, 1950-1952.

Billy J. Martin - U.S. Air Force, 1956-1960.

Dolphus Crow III - U.S. Army, served in Vietnam.

Ray Crow, Jr. - U.S. Army, Vietnam era.

John S. Martin - U.S. Navy, Submarine Service USS Lewis & Clark, 1980-1985.

Patrick H. Ginn Lt. JG - U.S. Naval Reserve, served with U.S. Marines in Desert Storm, 1996. Son of Kerry and Joy Crow Ginn.

Tanya L. Crow 1st Lt. - U.S. Air Force.

Jamie Spencer - Mississippi National Guard, serving in Bosnia at present.

188

In Memory of
Levin Bryant Hardin (1911-2000) and Erlene Morehead Hardin (1917-1995)

Levin Bryant Hardin was born in the tiny community of Whynot, Mississippi on July 26, 1911, to Hubert Ulmer Hardin (1888-1917) and Virgie Wallace Hardin (1890-1988). Erlene Morehead was born near Vaiden in rural Montgomery County, Mississippi, on July 20, 1917, to William Curtis Morehead (1873-1947) and Lelia Annis Hambrick Morehead (1878- 1967).

Bryant's daddy died of pneumonia in February 1917; his grandfather was murdered in May; and his 18-month-old sister died in August, a few days after playing with a cousin who had died a day or two after they played. Because of these traumatic deaths so close together, Virgie soon went to live with her parents who could help in raising Bryant, age 6, and his sister Thelma, age 4.

After a few months, Virgie went to nearby Meridian to get a job. While there she met a man who was to become her husband. Bryant began his entrepreneurial career at about age 7, at first selling newspapers and then magazines in Meridian, from a cart pulled by a goat.

Bryant and his cart pulled by a goat.

Several years later Bryant's family moved 40 miles north to Philadelphia, where he attended and graduated high school. He continued his selling career for a few years before he enrolled in the Civilian Conservation Corps and was stationed in Dyer, Tennessee, for three years.

Erlene Morehead, the 11th of 12 children, and her family lived near Vaiden, Mississippi, during her childhood years. Some of the older children, who were still living at home when Erlene entered her teen years, worked at the local cotton mill. When it closed, the Moreheads moved to Tupelo in search of work in order to be better able to make a living. Erlene left school after her junior year in high school, going to work at the cotton mill a little over two blocks from their home on south Green Street.

It was while Erlene was working at the cotton mill that she met Bryant Hardin. He was in Tupelo visiting his sister who had recently married a young man from Tupelo.

Bryant Hardin and Erlene Morehead married on January 1, 1939. The young couple lived for the first three years of their married life on south Green Street in Tupelo.

On June 15, 1940, their first daughter, Peggy Brylene, was born. Bryant continued his sales career, working for Pepsi-Cola Bottling Company of Tupelo.

Bryant Hardin introduced Pepsi-Cola to extreme northeast Mississippi in 1943, and soon moved his wife and young daughter to Corinth. They moved first to a duplex on Eighth Street, and later bought the middle house of three identical houses across the street, at 1725 Webster Street, where Bryant and Erlene lived until their deaths.

On May 18, 1946, Erlene gave birth to their second daughter, Betty Dianne, two months premature, but healthy.

Because of health problems, Erlene was never able to hold a job, but remained at home raising their two girls and supporting Bryant in his Pepsi-Cola business.

Bryant continued selling Pepsi-Colas, building the business in a few years from the one truck in the beginning, covering five counties, to three trucks serving all of Alcorn County and part of Tippah and Tishomingo Counties. He became a distributor during this time and operated in this capacity until economic conditions forced him to sell back to the company in 1964. He worked as an employee once again until they let him go in 1966.

A couple of months later Bryant was offered a job with Coca-Cola in Corinth, and he accepted. Soon after he joined Coke, Kenneth Williams began Refreshments, Inc., with the help of Bryant and Bobby Franks. Bryant officially retired from Refreshments, Inc. in 1976, but continued to work part-time until he was 83 years of age.

Bryant, in addition to being a very hard worker and devoted provider for his family, was active in the community. He and Erlene were members of Tate Street Baptist Church for over 50 years, where Bryant served as a deacon for many of those years. He was Associational Training Union director for seven years, was a member of the Senior Adult Choir and the ABCee's.

He was one of the founders of the Corinth Boys' Club, a charter member of the Civitan Club, selling Claxton fruit cakes for over 50 years and being top salesman several of those years. He was a member of the Chamber of Commerce a number of years, and worked with the United Way. He served many years as a race official during the Coca-Cola 10K Classic. He was an avid coin collector and spearheaded the Shiloh Coin Club; was a member of the Corinth Coin Club and the Selmer, Tennessee Coin Club. He operated a coin booth at the original Corinth Flea Market from the day it opened until the day it closed, moving across the street and operating his coin booth there until his death in October 2000.

Erlene was killed in a wreck on September 7, 1995, and Bryant died of a stroke on October 27, 2000. *Sponsored by Brylene Hardin Teague and Betty Hardin Roberts.*

Bryant and Erlene Hardin - 1995.

Thomas Elmo Jobe (1896-1946), son of Thomas Jefferson and Susie Jackson Strickland Jobe is shown here with his wife, Gracie Mae Coke Jobe (1903-1995). She was the daughter of Richard Franklin and Mary Elizabeth Steen Coke. To this union were added three children: Virginia Ruth (pictured at right), Weyman Elmo and Billy Hayes.

Virginia Ruth Jobe and Hubert Ray Robertson, son of Cletus Joseph and Lillie Hill Simpson Robertson on their wedding day, March 22, 1941 in Alcorn County. They were blessed with a daughter, Scottie Ray and a son, Thomas Elmo.

Pictured on back row, standing l-r: Brian Scott Shirley, Thomas E. Robertson and John Whitney Hughes Tomlinson. Middle row, sitting l-r: Julie Robertson Shirley, Betty King Robertson and Kelli Robertson Tomlinson. Children, l-r: Madeline Grace Shirley, Frank Fleming "Hank" Howell Jr. (twin), Thomas Hughes Tomlinson and Holly Lee Howell (twin).

Pictured l-r: Billy Blan Riddell, Scottie Robertson Riddell, Ruth Ellen Riddell (Mrs. Lyle) Tucker and John Christopher Riddell (husband of Judy Whitehurst).

Judkins Family Memorial

The Guy Judkins Family

Guy's Sawyers line was in this area before 1840;
his Meadows line was here by 1867.

At left: John, Jamie, Gale and Guy

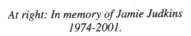

*At right: In memory of Jamie Judkins
1974-2001.*

General Jacob "G.J." King and Myrtle Annie Taylor King are shown here celebrating their 50th wedding anniversary, November 13, 1954.

General Jacob King (1878-1958), son of Solomon Cooper and Nancy Adeline McAfee King, is pictured with his wife, Myrtle Annie Taylor (1884-1966), daughter of James Major and Mattie Jane Pinkard Taylor. This is their wedding day, November 13, 1904 in Alcorn County, Mississippi. To this union were added two children, Mattie Elizabeth (Mrs. Herbert) Williams and Hugh William King.

Hugh William King (1909-1979) with his wife, Mary Lee Lipford King (1916-1999), daughter of Abe and Naomi Plunk Lipford. This picture was taken in 1939.

Pictured above in 1995 are Mary Lee Lipford King (sitting) and children (l-r): Charles Wayne King (husband of Deborah Isbell), Mary Dale King (Mrs. Gerald) Cranford, Sandra Kay King (Mrs. David) Arnold and Betty Lee King (Mrs. Thomas E.) Robertson.

Tribute to
Robert Edward "Bob" (1871-1954) and
Nannie Elizabeth Rorie Nash (1869-1948)

Robert "Bob" had a family business: landowner, farmer, country store and sawmilling (first with steam and later tractor with gas). He blew the whistle at the steam mill at 6:00 a.m. and 12:00 noon. Nannie was a great homemaker, helped doctors with neighbors and delivered babies. *Sponsored by Lottie V. Nash Wade, granddaughter.*

Eddard Tucker, husband of Mabel Nash; father of Harold, Opal and Helen Tucker. Killed in car accident circa 1935.

Circa 1908. First row: Archie Clelland, Laura Mabel and Allie Rufus. Second row: Robert Edward "Bob", Leslie Clay (Dess), Nannie Elizabeth Rorie Nash and Elizabeth Jane Rinehart, mother (1841-1924). Third row: Elgin Alvin "Dick", Earie Roscoe, Cora Lee Nash Howard (1899-1918). Not pictured: Nora May (1904-1906) and Carlie N. (1887-1887).

Seated: Laura Mabel Tucker Glidewell (1907-1973) and Newton Ely Glidewell (1891-1986). Standing: Harold Tucker, Opal Tucker, Helen Tucker, Robert Ely Glidewell (son of Ely Glidewell).

Seated: Avis Burcham, Earie Roscoe (1895-1978), Letha Vanderford Nash (1897-1988) and Lavern Dowd. Standing: Eveline Palmer, Millard Nash (1926-1995), Willard Nash, Gladys Lambert and Robert Roscoe Nash (1918-1993).

Jimmie Loyd (1932-1972), James, Leslie Clay (Dess) (1901-1986) and Giffie Vanderford Nash (1906-2000). Not pictured, Jewel Frances Felks.

Elgin Alvin "Dick" Nash (1900-1965), Beulah Vanderford Nash (1903-1999) and Lottie V. Nash Wade, daughter. Circa 1942.

Left to right: Archie Nash Jr. "Bugg" (1930-2000), Delma Morman, Amye Wood Nash (1901-1983), Archie Clelland Nash, John Nash (front) and Amye holding Doris Collins. Circa 1928.

Allie Rufus (1898-1979) and Susie Sellers Nash (1899-1978). Not pictured: Orbie, Essie and Edward Nash. Second wife, Ruby Payne Nash (1918-1984), Charles, Belle and Preston Nash. Circa 1920.

Tribute to
Mark (1879-1938) and
Neal Samantha Maness Vanderford (1881-1958)

Three generations of sawmillers are shown on this page: Mark, Lillborn and Buddy. Family business: Land owner, cotton gin, sawmill, gristmill, feedmill and farming at Leedy. All children worked in the family business: Aaron, Rufus "Pat", Hershel "Short", Cleston, Winston "Wink", Lillborn "Lib", Beulah Nash, Giffie Nash and Velma Clark.

For all, old and young, Sundays at Grandpa and Grandma's house were special times, pitching washers, playing marbles and card games (high nine and Rook). Christmas morning a great time! Peppermint stick candy, oranges, apples, hoop cheese from plant at Corinth. Grandpa and Grandma - a great blessing to all! *Sponsored by granddaughter, Lottie Nash Wade.*

Lillborn "Lib" Vanderford (1922-1996) and son, Orland "Buddy". Not pictured: Doris Tebo, Linda Layton, Joan Musgrove, Donnie Hodum, Wanda Korba, Gayle Westbrook, Susie Boyles, Lillborn Lynn Vanderford, Craig Vanderford, Phillip Vanderford and Ellen Hodum.

Mark (1879-1938) and Neal Samantha Maness Vanderford (1881-1958).

Seated: Virginia Rorie Vanderford (1910-1998), Rufus "Pat" Vanderford (1908-1991). Standing: Donald Vanderford, Rufus Lee Vanderford, Billy Wayne Vanderford, Beulah Vee Crain, Edward Earl Vanderford, George William Vanderford and Marie Hendrix Burkes.

Cleston "Cless" Vanderford (1912-1984), Verda Esther Burcham Vanderford and Charles Harley, 3 years old, circa 1939.

Seated: Sula Richardson Vanderford (1904-1989) and Aaron Vanderford (1901-1985). Standing: Cletes Melvin, Milton Waldrep, Mae Carter (1925-1986), Ray, Fay Hendrix, Linda Byrd, Brenda Sonnenberg, Elton "Top", Bobby and L.Q. Vanderford. Circa 1980.

Front row: Nelda Dean Woodard, Winston Jasper "Wink" Vanderford (1916-1989), Ella Woodruff Vanderford (1913-1991) and Waynona Davis. Back row: Hazel Vanderford and James Hulon Vanderford. Circa 1986.

Tribute to
Elgin Alvin "Dick" Nash (1900-1965) and
Beulah Mae Vanderford Nash (1903-1999)

Dick and Buelah Nash lived in Hickory Flat Community all their lives. They farmed and he sawmilled. Dick was bailiff two terms and deputy sheriff under sheriffs Bert Coleman, Hillie Coleman and "Little" Bert Coleman. Buelah gardened in summer, quilts in winter and cooked well for family and neighbors. They left us a great example of being a good neighbor. *Sponsored by grandchildren: William Nash Wade, Marylane Louise Wade Koch and Leslie Alvin Wade.*

Buelah Mae Vanderford Nash (1903-1999) and Elgin Alvin "Dick" Nash (1900-1965). Daughter, Lottie V. Nash Wade.

Seated: Jewel Frances Felks, Leslie C. (Dess) Nash (1901-1986), Jimmie Loyd Nash (1932-1972) and Giffie Vanderford Nash (1906-2000). Standing: James Marion Nash, Bertha Stewart Thornton and Robert Ellis Maness.

L-R: Harry Jr. Clark, Mary Helen Clark Genna, Barbara Ann Clark Owens (1943-1999), Robert Lee Clark, Velma Lee Opal "Sis" Vanderford Clark and Leonard Clark.

Hershel "Short" Vanderford (1910-2001), Giffie Hendrix Vanderford (1923-1979) and Harlis Lanie. (Not pictured, Karen Annette.)

Lottie V. Nash Wade, daughter; William Doyle Wade (1924-1993), son-in-law; and Leslie, grandson of Dick and Beulah Vanderford Nash. Circa 1975.

Grandchildren of Dick and Beulah Vanderford Nash: Dr. Leslie Alvin Wade, Dr. William Nash Wade and Marylane Louise Wade Koch. Circa 1998.

Great Grandchildren of Dick and Beulah Vanderford Nash: Meridith Grace Wade Koch, Chelsea Elizabeth Wade and Dylan Armstrong Wade. Circa1998.

In Loving Memory
"The McLains"

Minta McLain 1880-1913

William Guss McLain 1878-1913

At right: Children of Guss and Minta McLain. Front row, l-r: Hubert McLain, Vera (McLain) McKenzie and William Cleaburn "W.C." McLain. Back row, l-r: Cliff McLain and Ector (McLain) White.

At left: Back row, l-r: Mable McLain, Raymond McLain, Everette Howell, Cleaburn McLain, Everette White, Hubert McLain and Cliff McLain. Second row, l-r: Vera (McLain) McKenzie, Geraldine (McLain) Howell, unidentified, Georgia McLain, Ector (McLain) White and Dorothy McLain. Front row, l-r: Jimmy McLain, Gerald McLain, Jane (McLain) Dickerson, Ann (McLain) Castile, Nancy McLain, Bonnie McLain and George McLain.

Georgia B. McLain, 1903-1993 and William Cleaburn "W.C." McLain, founder of McLain's Grocery and Hardware, 1902-1973

Geraldine McLain Howell (only child of Georgia and W.C. McLain)

Everette N. Howell, 1921-1979, husband of Geraldine McLain.

Kathy M. Howell, only child of Everette and Geraldine Howell. Owner of Howell Home Center and part owner of Custom Creations and Factory Outlet.

Minnie Lee Howell (1887-1952) and Marshall Hardeman Howell, founder of Howell Lumber Co., 1883-1950.

Parents and children, front row, l-r: Minnie Howell and Marshall Howell. Back row, l-r: Everette "E.N." Howell, Joan (Howell) Wroten, Frank Howell and Arron Howell.

Front row, l-r: W.C. McLain, Georgia McLain, Valerie Howell, Arron Howell holding Margo McBride, Minnie Howell, Marshall Howell, Frank Howell, Lila Howell and Gene Howell. Second row, l-r: Mitch McBride, Barbara Howell, Frances McBride, Nell Howell, Bobbie Howell, Arthur Wroten Sr., Joan (Howell) Wroten, Geraldine Howell, Everette Howell and Jimmy Howell. Back row, l-r: Dewitt Howell and Bobby Wroten. Children standing in front: Arthur Wroten Jr. and Joan (Wroten) Stewart.

Eight Brothers – All Veterans – Span Three Wars

by Amy Sims, Staff Writer

John Vandiver U.S. Army World War II   *Edd Vandiver U.S. Army World War II*   *Austin Vandiver U.S. Army Korean Conflict*   *Robert Vandiver U.S. Marines World War II*   *Otis Vandiver U.S. Marines World War II*   *James Vandiver U.S. Army World War II*   *Paul Vandiver U.S. Army Vietnam Conflict*   *Marcus Vandiver U.S. Air Force Korean Conflict*

For one Alcorn County family, eight sons equaled eight veterans.

A photograph taken at the May 30, 1959 Vandiver family reunion is probably the most cherished artifact in the possession of Retha White, the sister of five WWII and two Korean War veterans and one veteran who served stateside during the Vietnam War, as it captures all dozen Vandiver children and their parents in a still frame for the history books.

The reunion, held annually on their now 96-year-old mother's birthday, along with Veterans' Day, serve as at least two days of reflection on almost a century of living and four decades of fighting under the shelter of the Vandiver family tree with patriarch, William "Earnie" Vandiver as its root.

In 1918, William, a carpenter, farmer and Alcorn County gravel truck driver by trade, married Roxie Ann. They next celebrated another milestone - the birth of their first-born son, Earnest, in 1919.

As the years went by, Edd was born in 1921, Otis in 1923, Robert in 1925, John in 1927, Leon in 1929, Mark in 1931, Lula in 1934, Lena in 1936, Retha in 1938, Louise in 1941 and Paul in 1944. All were born and reared in Alcorn County around the Strickland area minus Leon, who was the odd man out for six weeks in Dallas, TX before his parents came to their senses and moved back home, according to Retha.

When World War II began, five of the boys, Earnest, Edd, Otis, Robert and John, found themselves enlisted at the same time.

Today, five of the eight brothers remain alive.

During 1945, Otis and Robert, both privates first class in an unusual set of circumstances, served side-by-side in the in 3rd U.S. Marines, sleeping in the same foxhole, working and fighting together in Guam and Iwo Jima.

"We protected each other. We didn't have time to think. The only thing you knew to do was to keep your head down and keep safe," remembered Robert, who recalled a specific incident when he and his brother were pinned down by a Japanese soldier firing at their seven-man squad from atop a cliff.

"Otis stuck his head around the rock to get a better look at a shot, and when he did I saw the dust fly off the rock. I grabbed him and said 'get your head in here,' but I didn't use those words," joked the part-time minister and Sunday School teacher at Locust Grove Baptist Church in New Albany. "The people just wouldn't understand what it was like, even if you tried to tell."

Later on, the two brothers met up with their eldest brother, U.S. Army Staff Sergeant Earnest Vandiver, who to their surprise, had been stationed only eight to 10 miles away from their camp in Guam.

Edd, a corporal in the Army Air Reserve from 1941 to 1945 in Australia and New Guinea, worked as an aircraft mechanic on the front lines, while John served as an industrial painter in the Army in WWII from 1945 to 1947 in Italy and Alaska. In 1951 he re-enlisted in the Air Force and was stationed in Alaska and Illinois.

Fighting back tears Retha recalled the emotions being endured at home when she was only 6 years old, while her brothers were risking their

World War II veteran Robert Vandiver, a former U.S. Marine, displays a flag for Veteran's Day.

lives for the freedom of this country.

"We didn't have a TV then. We only had a battery radio, and every time the National Anthem came on, daddy made us stand up and salute to the flag," she said, describing how vivid her memories were of another flag embroidered with five stars that the Red Cross had presented to the Vandivers to hang in the window in honor of their five brave sons.

"I can remember that momma would always cry when the mail came in," Retha said, explaining that they never knew when they might receive a letter announcing the demise of a Vandiver sibling.

Fortunately that never occurred, but because the mail was censored to prevent leakage of confidential military matters, soldiers used code words and phrases to ease family worry.

She remembers once when her father jumped up, they thought something was wrong. William informed them instead, that one of their brothers had asked how the 'guineas' were, thus revealing to them that he was in New Guinea.

Most of all, she remembered when she and her sisters ran with their arms stretched wide to meet their brothers with duffel bags in tow, finally returning without injury from the "great war."

"It seemed like we would cry forever more," she said.

Then came the Korean conflict, when Leon was a corporal in the Army infantry from 1949 to 1952 loading ammunition into Howitzer guns, while Mark was in charge of commissary supplies in the Air Force from 1951 to 1954, stationed in Japan and San Antonio, Texas.

He, along with youngest brother, Paul, never saw combat.

Paul held a specialist E-4 ranking and was trained as a gunner on 105mm Howitzers and a battery clerk from 1965 to 1967 with the 101st Airborne and the 321st Artillery Division in Fort Campbell, KY. In the summer of 1966, he trained cadets in artillery at West Point Academy. He came up for service in Vietnam four times, but for some reason, never called to serve.

"I believe it was our prayers that kept him out of that awful place," said Retha - a proposition in which her brother firmly agrees.

On Veterans' Day 1999, the surviving Vandiver siblings and their families will settle for a quiet, prayerful observance of the

wars each generation faced and long for the day when they can again attend parades like those held in honor of World War II veterans, as they feel the lack of respect for veterans has diminished over the years.

"They were fighting to protect the best interest of the United States. Veterans of all wars and any man who has served his country needs proper recognition and appreciation. I know they have a vote of thanks from me," exclaimed Paul, whose emotions were obvious as he spoke of friends who died in Vietnam or experienced serious trauma as the result of the brutality and horrors of war. "Wartime is not the same as it was back then. It's high tech, and you're no longer standing eyeball to eyeball with your enemy. We abuse the freedoms my brothers fought for. We do not have proper respect for authorities, and I appreciate the fact that these veterans went out and fought for the freedoms our forefathers gave us."

Robert commented without hesitation, that if he had to do it all over again, he would in a second, believing all his brothers would answer the same.

Presently, Otis is a retired carpenter living in Somerville, TN; Robert and Betty, his wife of almost 53 years, live in New Albany; John is a retired carpenter and painter in Selmer, TN, and Lena Harmon resides in Memphis, TN, while Alcorn County residents include Leon, who retired from Intex Plastics Corp. and his wife Emma; Lula Essary; Retha and her husband Joe and Paul, who retired after working in the Alcorn County School system over 23 years and his wife, Linda.

Earnest, Edd and Mark Vandiver have passed away, along with their sister, Louise Davidson.

Looking over family albums from the Vandiver family include (from lkeft) Robert Vandiver, Paul Vandiver, Retha White and Roberts, wife, Betty. Of the 12 Vandiver children, eight are alive today. The family gets together each Veteran's Day.

Tribute to Herman Truitt Stockton

Tech-Sergeant, 75th Infantry Combat Engineers, 1943-1945.

Herman Truitt Stockton was born February 9, 1921 in Belmont, Mississippi, the youngest of five children, to Grady Holman Stockton and Josie Elizabeth Johnson. Jobs were scarce during the Depression, so when Grady got a job working on the railroad in California he left his young family to travel to Alcorn County to live with Josie's parents on their farm in Glen, Mississippi. During these hard times the values he learned became the credo by which he lived his life-honesty, integrity, independence, decisiveness, determination, perseverance, fair mindedness and hard work.

Truitt attended Glen School graduating as valedictorian in 1938. While there he learned the rudiments of his future vocation with a NYO (National Youth Organization) project by building the gym at school. He continued his training while working with a major construction company on defense projects in Tennessee and Arkansas during the first years of WWII. In 1943, Truitt entered the European Theater of Combat serving in the Army with the 75th Infantry Combat Engineers as a tech-sergeant building pontoon bridges in France and guarding German prisoners. After the war ended in Europe at home on leave in August 1945, awaiting orders for the Pacific Theater, he married his sweetheart, Vernice Jewell Sims of Jacinto, Mississippi. While home, the war ended and Truitt finished his tour of duty at Fort Polk, Louisiana guarding German prisoners.

After the war jobs were not plentiful, but opportunities abounded. Truitt took advantage of his training in construction and the need for low cost housing, and in the spring of 1946 he and Jewell pooled their savings and began building houses. With one employee and an old '35 Chevy he used as a truck, he built his first house on Tennessee Street for $3,250. After 12 years in residential construction Truitt's company, S&S Construction, became a pioneer in commercial construction in this area. S&S Construction built many manufacturing plants, schools and government buildings within a 100 mile radius. Some examples of their work locally are: Tyrone Hydraulics (timber products), ITT (ACT), Dean Truck Line, Century Electric (Caterpillar), additions to Wurlitzer and Southbridge Plastics (Intex), City Hall, Corinth Library, Mississippi Welcome Center and many others. S&S Construction has erected or built additions to most of the schools in our area including Northeast Mississippi Community College - quite an achievement. Northeast honored him with an associate of arts degree for his interest in vocational education and the youth of our area. Other business interests have included General Building Supply, Corinth Ready Mix, CIG, S&J SteelBuilders in Booneville, Harper Square Mall, Ginger's, Dad's and Lad's, Truitt's Restaurant, several motels (former Holiday Inn Executive Inn, Noel and Illinois Motels - two of the first motels built in Corinth, and most recently the Holiday Inn Express). The Illinois motel was built on old Highway 45 north and so named because this highway was the main tourist route between Chicago and Florida. Through the years he has disseminated thousands of pieces of information on Corinth and compiled two books (*War Between the States* and *North and South*) on the Civil War in our area. Tourism has always been important to our town especially during the last 10 years when manufacturing opportunities have diminished. Through his tireless efforts, tourism is now considered one of our major industries.

The economic development and future of our area has been of vital interest to Truitt. To this purpose he has worked with many organizations concerned with the betterment of our community: while a member of the Board of Directors for the Chamber of Commerce (Governmental Affairs and Industrial Recruitment) helped broaden the base of the Chamber from just city to encompass the whole county, hired an industrial recruiter and spear-headed the building of the current Alliance building; worked 12 years on the board of the Yellow Creek Port Authority (chairman 1977-1981) a state organization as a liaison between TVA and local governments of Alcorn, Prentiss and Tishomingo counties - improved forestry in the area by providing trees for reforestation, upgraded area livestock, started 911. Organized the Tenn-Tom Tri-State Industrial Support Group whose purpose was to combine the legislative power of the three state area of Tennessee, Alabama and Mississippi in our connecting corner to bring projects to the betterment of our common area. Alcorn County Planning Support Group - persuaded the businesses along Appalachian Drive, Golden Drive and Harper Road to rename the road from Highway 72 to Highway 45 through the industrial park one name - S. Harper Road. He also spear-headed an effort to oppose storage of nuclear waste at the defunct nuclear plant at Yellow Creek which was successful. He is a 32nd degree Mason and has been a member of Christ United Methodist Church (formerly Trinity Methodist) for 55 years.

However perhaps Truitt's major accomplishment has been the legacy of his family. He and Jewell were blessed with four loving children and five grandchildren: George Richard (deceased); Terry Eugene and sons, Kevin and Jeffrey; Vernice Ladonna "Donna"; Ricky Ray, wife, Ginger Smith and children: Sara Beth, Wesley and Emily Anne.

Through his 81 years Truitt has given tirelessly to his community, friends and family leaving a wonderful legacy which will live for eternity.

With love by the family of Truitt Stockton (Jewell, Terry, Donna and Rick).

Stockton family on Truitt's 80th birthday celebration. L-R: Donna Stockton, Terry Stockton, (his sons) Jeffrey Stockton and Kevin Stockton, Truitt, Jewell, Rick Stockton, (his daughter) Sara Beth Stockton, Ginger Stockton, Rick's wife, Emily Ann Stockton, Wesley Stockton (Rick's other children).

DOWNTOWN CORINTH
LOCATION - CORNER WALDRON AND TAYLOR STREETS
THEN ... IN 1920S
WALDRON HOTEL

NOW ... IN 2002
510 TAYLOR STREET
CORINTH, MS 38834

202

BANCORPSOUTH

To tell the story of BancorpSouth is to tell the story of the banks that joined together to create it. Since the turn of the century more than 30 banks have merged into what ultimately became BancorpSouth banks. The primary story is woven around the history of three of those banks.

The year was 1876. George Armstrong Custer and his men were massacred at Little Big Horn. Alexander Graham Bell spoke the first words over his new invention, the telephone, to his assistant, Mr. Watson, and Raymond Trice and Company, a mercantile operation in Verona, MS, received a perpetual charter to set up a bank in the corner of their store. What would eventually evolve into BancorpSouth was born.

Hand in hand this fledgling bank and its community began a journey toward maturity. Cotton was still king and was the economic backbone of the region.

Ten years later, in 1886, Raymond Trice and Company would move its banking operation to a new city, Tupelo, formed by the crossing of two railroads, and would change its name to Bank of Lee County. Later it would become Bank of Tupelo, and in 1966 it would become Bank of Mississippi.

In August 1886, when Raymond Trice and Company was moving to Tupelo, a group of entrepreneurs in Jackson, TN met in the law offices of Pitts, Hays and Meeks to form Second National Bank. The population of Jackson, TN was ap-

proximately 8,000 at the time. Judge John Pitts became the first president. Even then, the regions around Tupelo, MS and Jackson, TN were vastly similar as they are today. Both areas lived and died, for the most part, on the ebb and flow of the cotton industry, and both were just recovering from the Civil War. Second National Bank would later change its name to Jackson National Bank and then to Volunteer Bank in 1993.

In 1895, over two hundred miles to the south of Tupelo in Hattiesburg, MS, our third bank in this story came to life. Hattiesburg was founded in 1884 by Captain William H. Hardy, a pioneer lumberman and civil engineer who named the fledgling community after his wife Hattie. Eleven years after Hattiesburg's incorporation, Bank of Commerce was chartered. Later it became First National Bank of Hattiesburg then First Mississippi National Bank when it expanded to Biloxi and Jackson, MS.

The three banks not only shared a common destiny, they shared a common philosophy. Each bank's philosophy was one of participating in and supporting the economic growth of its markets.

The three banks weathered the depression and supported the war efforts during World Wars I and II. But, growth was not significant among any of them during that period, and neither was the economic growth of the areas they served. However, after World War II, each of the banks began to grow, building its own major banking system through acquisitions, mergers and internal growth.

From here the story takes a different twist, to one of attitude, cooperation and a willingness to dream big: how Northeast Mississippi and Tupelo created a business environment that would become the headquarters of a large multi-state, multi-bank holding company ... BancorpSouth.

Decisions made by the leaders of Bank of Mississippi in cooperation with the business leaders of North Mississippi altered forever the future of this moderately successful financial institution. As World War II wound to a close, it was clear that unique employment challenges faced the area. How could the economy satisfy the job needs of two groups - the many women who had joined the work force during the war, as well as the men who were returning from the war?

In Northeast Mississippi, manufacturing plants, such as those in the garment industry, were built, but for the most part, they employed women. As the farm economy weakened, jobs were desperately needed, especially by displaced men. Local business leaders in Northeast Mississippi wanted the right kind of industrial development. They planned for economic growth to be spread across a wide economic base, throughout the region.

An alliance of financial institutions in and around Northeast Mississippi joined forces with the community development foundations to build an economic base, and Bank of Mississippi played a major role by providing financing to match the pace of growth for businesses, utilities, education and individuals in towns throughout the area. Over the following decades the economy of Northeast Mississippi was boosted by the influx of national companies.

The formula for success in the region was one of cooperation. The banks worked together cooperatively in pursuit of the common goal of a greater economic pie. As they worked hard to make the pie bigger, everyone prospered.

Main Office - 601 Fillmore

The attitude of growth through cooperation that permeated the economic development efforts of the area became an integral thread throughout Bank of Mississippi. That attitude is one of commitment built on goal oriented teamwork.

It is important to understand the philosophy and culture fostered at Bank of Mississippi during this time because from that culture and philosophy of hard work, cooperation and enthusiasm came the management of BancorpSouth.

In 1976, Bank of Mississippi entered its second century of service and announced construction plans for its seven-story contemporary administrative headquarters building, now the home of BancorpSouth administrative offices. When making the dedication of the new headquarters, J.C. Whitehead who was then chairman, said, "This contemporary architecture echoes the progressive and optimistic vision that characterizes this company."

The year 1976 saw the Bank of Mississippi's entry into the Corinth, MS market with Bank of Mississippi acquiring certain assets of the First American National Bank's Corinth branch. With its main office at 601 Fillmore in historic downtown Corinth, the bank increased its service in 1980 by opening a second full-service banking office at the busy Harper Road intersection with U.S. Highway 72. In 1990 a free standing automated teller machine was placed at 3108 E. Shiloh Road to add banking convenience in the Corinth market.

Historically, statewide banking had been prohibited in Mississippi. Bank service areas were limited to 100 miles from its headquarters. However in 1986, banking laws were changed to allow statewide banking, and Bank of Mississippi was ready. A key figure in this significant new direction was Aubrey Patterson, who had been named president in 1983. His leadership guided Bank of Mississippi into statewide banking. Finally, Bank of Mississippi had grown into its name, serving communities from the Tennessee line to the Gulf of Mexico.

Bank of Mississippi, through its merger with First Mississippi National Bank, became Mississippi's first statewide bank in 1987, immediately upon the approval of the statewide banking law. It followed the same strategy into Tennessee shortly after the Federal Interstate banking law was passed in 1992, and entry into Alabama came in 1998 with the merger with Highland Bank in Birmingham.

It became obvious too that Bank of Mississippi had outgrown its name and became BancorpSouth system wide in 1999.

A true watershed event occurred with the advent of the new millennium with the merger with First United Bancshares and entry into Arkansas, Louisiana and Texas, making BancorpSouth the largest Mississippi-based banking company.

But the history is rich in more than geographic expansion. The banking law changes of the nineties provided new product and service opportunities - Insurance, Brokerage and more.

The BancorpSouth way in Corinth and bank-wide is one of providing its clients with every financial service they need and not a single one they don't need.

Whatever financial goals customers aspire to, they can achieve through BancorpSouth's wide variety of products and services, state-of-the-art technology, a growing network of commercial locations and financial experts who truly realize the backbone of the Company's success is personal service with sound advice.

The message is simple. BancorpSouth. Get there from here.

BancorpSouth in Corinth Presidents
William G. Hardin Jr.   1976 - 1980
Terry M. Cartwright   1980 - present

Current Officers
Terry M. Cartwright   President
C. Ellis Rhett III   Vice President
Debra Gallaher   Assistant Vice President
Greg Kiddy   Assistant Vice President

Past General Administrative Board Members
Hugh W. King (deceased)
William L. Sharp (deceased)
John Stanley III (deceased)

Current General Administrative Board Member
H.L. "Sandy" Williams, Jr.
Past Local Advisory Board Member
E. Joseph Curlee (deceased)

Local Advisory Bank Directors
C. Richard Dobbins
Dr. John D. Dodd
Jimmy B. Fisher
Mark Gardner
Sammy Kemp
Phillip M. Little
Doris Baker, Director Emeritus
James R. Dillingham, Director Emeritus
James E. "Buck" Marsh, Director Emeritus

Highway 72 Branch Office (front entrance).

Highway 72 Branch Office (rear entrance).

Main Office - 601 Fillmore

Directors - Left to Right: Jimmy Fisher; Dr. John D. Dodd; Mark Gardner; C. Richard Dobbins; H.L. "Sandy" Williams Jr., BancorpSouth General Administrative Board; Doris Baker, Director Emeritus; Phillip Little; James E. "Buck" Marsh, Director Emeritus; Sammy Kemp; and James R. Dillingham, Director Emeritus.

Officers, Left to Right: Terry M. Cartwright, President; C. Ellis Rhett III, Vice President; Debra Gallaher, Assistant Vice President; and Greg Kiddy, Assistant Vice President.

Main Office Employees: 1st Row: Terry M. Cartwright, Debra Gallaher, Gale Rickman, Sondra Swallow, Debbie Adams, Angie Rickman and Annette Warren. 2nd Row: Greg Kiddy, Judy S. Jeter, Janet Johnson, Gerald Jones, Jan Allen and Rita Tate. 3rd Row: Judy R. Taylor, Ellis Rhett, Stacey Floyd, Lori Counce and Megan Smith.

Highway 72 Branch Employees: Debra Gallaher, Lynnette Ferguson, Alisha McCarter, Amanda Meeks, Lisa Maddox, Rebekah Curtis, Sue Phillips and Lori Moore.

BERRY'S TRADING POST

Frank Berry Sr. was the founder of Berry Motors in the 1940s. Mr. Berry was an inventor with numerous patents.

Frank Berry Sr. married Beverly Cozette Spencer Nov. 24, 1935. They had two children, Frank Berry II and Vicki Elise Berry Kitchens.

Frank Berry II married Jane Driver in 1970. In 1971 he opened his gun store, Berry's Trading Post.

J.G. "Punch" Driver married Susie Rose Joslin in 1940. They had three children: Maggie Jane Driver Berry (pictured), Jessie Faye Driver Barr and Joel Glenn Driver.

Jane and Frank Berry II

Frank and Jane Berry have one daughter, Dolyna Rose "Dolly" and one granddaughter, Britton Beverly, age 2.

Frank and Jane Berry opened the Cherry Tree Jewelry in 1980.

BIGGERS ACE HARDWARE STORE

Submitted by
Jo Anne Biggers Brooks

Left to right: Mrs. A.J. Biggers, Frank Biggers, Mr. and Mrs. J.D. Biggers Sr., Elizabeth Biggers, Annie Lou Biggers in front of their home at Biggersville, 1899.

Mr. and Mrs. J.D. Biggers Sr. She was the former Annie Morrison. 1935.

The Biggers Brothers, left to right: Raymond Biggers, Roy Biggers, Preston Biggers, J.D. Biggers Jr., Harry Lee Biggers and Neal Biggers, 1951.

The Biggers Sisters, left to right: Mary Biggers Hyland, Elizabeth Biggers, Janice Biggers and Annie Lou Biggers Taylor, 1973.

SAMUEL D. BRAMLITT HOUSE

The Historic Samuel D. Bramlitt House
-A-
Victorian Bed and Breakfast

National Register - "Small-town Victorian Mansion"

Located in the Historic Civil War Town of
Corinth, MS
1125 Cruise St.
Corinth, MS 38834

Phone: (662) 396-4979
Email: Sthughes1@vol.com

Host: Wilson and Sharmaine Hughes

Come and experience the many attractions and activities that Corinth has to offer. From antiquing, Civil War museum, fine local dining, golfing, horseback riding and many more. Or just sit on one of our four verandas and enjoy the soft summer breezes and the sweet fragrance of magnolias and roses from our garden.

Packages available for anniversaries, honeymoons or private dining. Arrange for a picnic basket for two and/or use of our two bikes for travel on the historical bike tour.

Located 84 miles east of Memphis and 124 miles west of Huntsville off of Hwy. 72 and Cass St.

For the business traveler:
Fax machine and Internet access available.
"Enjoy old world southern hospitality and have new world technology available."

Wilson

The Bramlitt House is located in the Historic District of Downtown Corinth. Built in 1892, it is one of the city's finest examples of Queen Anne architecture. The house is set inside a replica of the original white picket fence, and is surrounded by beautiful landscaped gardens.

As with many old southern homes, the Bramlitt House has a rich and colorful history. It is filled with many period antiques and original fixtures from the post Civil War era. After an extensive restoration in 1995 the home was featured in the winter issue of Country Victorian Magazine.

The present owners, Wilson and Sharmaine Hughes, purchased the home in December 2001 after vacationing in Corinth a few weeks earlier. It was love at first sight for the couple that had dreamed of owning a Victorian period bed and breakfast.

There are four luxurious guest rooms, each named after a previous owner of the house. All are furnished with antiques and have central air and heat. Prices range from $65.00-$95.00 per night.

A full breakfast is served daily in the formal dining room on an early 1900s mahogany Duncan-Phyfe table with rose-backed chairs. The room is adorned with a bronze chandelier.

Public rooms include a formal parlor, library and dining room each ornamented with the original hand carved mantles.

COMMERCE NATIONAL BANK

Commerce National Bank's first location.

Commerce National Bank new facility January 28, 2002.

Commerce National Bank, Corinth's only independent and locally owned banking institution, opened for business on January 19, 1999 with $4,000,000 in capital. Located at 301 South Cass Street, the traditional full service bank employed a staff of 11 people to offer a wide variety of lending and deposit products and services to its customers.

At the time of opening, Hull Davis served as the bank's chief executive officer and chairman of the board. President and chief operating officer was Bobby Roberts and Rusty Sharp served as chief financial officer. The board of directors included Hull Davis, Bobby Roberts, Hardwick Kay, Randall Long, David

Staff of Commerce National Bank, seated left to right: Lisa McCollum, Linda Rogers, Rita Shaw, Judy Layton and Barbara Franks. Standing, left to right: Margaret Dobes, Cathy Marsh, Hull Davis, Bobby Roberts, Sarah Reynolds, Rusty Sharp, Lynn Short, Lanny Monroe, Sandra Odom, Jennie Garrett and Jimmy Caldwell.

Palmer, John Stanley, Joe Vann and Lynn Davis Anderholm. Completing the bank's original staff were Judy Layton, Linda Rogers, Jennie Garrett, Lisa McCollum, Sandra Odom, Sarah Reynolds, Cathy Marsh and Rita Strickland. The bank began with 54 local stock holders.

At the time of charter, Davis cited the reason for seeking the new charter, "The bank's organizers believed that Corinth needed a locally owned bank fully focused on directing al of its energy and resources toward meeting the financial needs of the local community. We rely on delivering very personal service."

Commerce National Bank closed out its first year of operation with $25,400,000 in total assets. As a result of the first year's growth, the bank outgrew its facility and purchased a building into which it relocated and reopened for business on November 20, 2000. The new office at 306 South Cass Street offered an opportunity for continued growth and the bank provided its customers with additional services including a mortgage loan department, safe deposit boxes, a second drive-through teller window and an on site ATM machine.

By the end of December 2001, Commerce National's assets had grown to $44,093,000 and the bank posted 5,879 accounts.

In January of 2002, as the bank enters it fourth year of operation, the original staff of eleven has grown to sixteen. New staff members include Lynn Short, vice president and mortgage loan officer; Lanny Monroe, executive vice president for investments and loans; Jimmy Caldwell, vice president and loan officer; Barbara Franks; and Margaret Dobes.

Commerce National Bank attributes its success to its dedicated officers, staff and directors; the loyal support of stockholders; and the confidence and positive response of the community.

According to president Bobby Roberts, "As the bank's customer base continues to grow, we forecast a bright future. We pledge to continue to serve Corinth and the surrounding area with integrity and pride and will provide quality personal service to all of our customers."

Coca-Cola Bottling Works

Coca-Cola

A.K. WEAVER, MANAGER

BOTTLERS OF HIGH GRADE
SODA WATER & *Coca-Cola*

Corinth, Miss.

A.K. Weaver

Our story begins in 1905, when Avon Kenneth Weaver bought an interest in Corinth Bottling Works, a small soda water plant owned by Mr. C.C. Clark. At that time, Coca-Cola was produced in Jackson, TN and was shipped to Corinth by rail. Mr. Weaver and Mr. Clark were intent on a franchise to bottle Coca-Cola and while waiting on the Coca-Cola Company to grant the franchise in Corinth, they were granted a license for Coca-Cola in New Albany, MS. Mr. Clark moved there to begin that operation in 1906.

It was April 30, 1907, that Coca-Cola Bottling Works of Corinth was formed and a license was granted by Coca-Cola Bottling Co. (Thomas), Inc.

Early equipment was simple. Bottles were washed and filled by hand and were capped with a foot-powered machine.

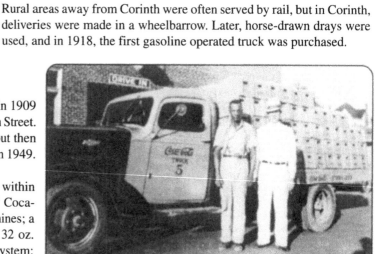

VERY EARLY BOTTLING ROOM - Waldron Street, right to left: Luke Caldwell, J. Simpson, Kenneth Weaver Jr. and L. Doyle.

EARLY HOME OF COCA-COLA BOTTLING WORKS: 401 Waldron Street (Pre-1925).

The first operation consisted of four people and in the first year, 1,186 gallons of syrup were used.

Rural areas away from Corinth were often served by rail, but in Corinth, deliveries were made in a wheelbarrow. Later, horse-drawn drays were used, and in 1918, the first gasoline operated truck was purchased.

The first years saw many changes and several moves. In 1909 Coca-Cola moved to its very own building at 403 Waldron Street. The operation expanded several times at this location but then moved to its current location at 601 Washington Street in 1949.

Coca-Cola Bottling Works has pioneered many things within the soft drink industry. Some of these are "King Size" Coca-Cola; premix cup dispensing; multi-drink vending machines; a 28 oz. non returnable bottle with a resealable closure; 32 oz. returnables; Tab, Sprite, and Fresca; an advance-sales system; Tel-Sell; and bulk delivery of cases. More recently, there was the 2 liter bottle and the contour 20 oz. plastic bottle.

1936 - Russell Smith and Tommy Goddard - Cruise Street.

In 1962, the field of food vending was entered. This operation is now Refreshments, Inc. and operates facilities in Corinth, Tupelo and Jackson, TN.

Tupelo - 1977

1969

Acquisitions include Dr. Pepper Bottling Co. of Corinth in 1969; Tupelo Coca-Cola Bottling Works in 1977; Coca-Cola of Lexington, TN in 1985; and Mrs. Sullivan's Pies in 1993. Nothing about the history of Coca-Cola Bottling Works could be more outstanding than the many people who have contributed to its success.

Lexington, TN - 1985

401 Waldron Street - Mid 1940s.

601 Washington Street - 1949.

This includes loyal consumers, retail customers, members of management, salespeople and workers at every level of employment. Each is a part of the legacy of Coca-Cola Bottling Works.

Coca-Cola Bottling Works Staff - 2001

Coca-Cola Bottling Works continues to be owned and operated by the descendants of Avon Kenneth Weaver and members of the fourth generation of the family are in management positions. It is with pride in the past, an unfailing trust in its employees and customers, and overwhelming optimism for the future, that Corinth Coca-Cola eagerly looks forward to its 100th Anniversary in 2007.

Descendants of A.K. Weaver in management positions: H.L. "Sandy" Williams Jr., Kenneth W. Williams, Ken Williams and H. Lee Williams III.

Corinth Coca-Cola Bottling Works - 601 Washington Street - 2002.

The Corinthian Funeral Home, 506 Kilpatrick St. Corinth, Mississippi is owned by Ricky Holland, Elbert Holland and Gerald Hammond.

Opening in May 1992 in a small office space with plans to provide the people of Corinth and Alcorn County with funeral and insurance needs. Now after 10 years in business and a much larger building, it has grown and built a reputation of great service at a reasonable price. The Corinthian Funeral Home has a goal of making a time of loss less stressful for families. The Corinthian Funeral Home is a full service funeral home; offering everything from traditional services to cremations.

Corinthian Funeral Home

GENERAL'S QUARTER'S BED & BREAKFAST INN
924 Fillmore Street
Corinth, MS 38834

The earliest picture of the home available is this postcard of Fillmore Street from 1909.

This beautiful home was originally built as St. Jude's Episcopal Church in 1872. When the parishioners were unable to make the payments on the construction loan the bank foreclosed on the property and sold it. It was converted into a home and early records indicate that the Bynum family were the first to live there. Over the years many owners have found a warm and gentle way of life here. Some have even made a living for themselves by providing accommodations for weary travelers.

Fillmore Street was busy Highway 45 which ran from Chicago to the Gulf of Mexico. In 1942 Mr. and Mrs. Cecil Philip Ramer opened their home to traveling tourists, becoming the first tourist home in the area. Mr. Ramer died in 1942 and Mrs. Inez Ramer continued running the tourist home until she died in 1969. She is pictured here in front of her home with her grandchildren. The Ramers' son, C.P. Ramer Jr., and their granddaughters, Rebecca Northcutt and Marianne Rogers, still reside in Corinth.

In 1994, Charlotte Stephenson Brandt and Luke Doehner purchased the property. They relocated to Corinth from Baltimore, Maryland to make their dream of owning a bed and breakfast come true. Both had worked for the Marriott, Corporation in Bethesda, Maryland and met there in 1990. Charlotte was born in Lancaster County, Pennsylvania and Luke in Syracuse, New York. After 18 months of renovation and restoration they felt the house was ready for a wedding. They were married here in July of 1995. Since that time many couples have found this a beautiful site to begin their lives together. Mr. and Mrs. Luke Doehner now operate The Generals' Quarters Bed and Breakfast Inn at 924 Fillmore Street as an award winning Bed and Breakfast.

KING MANUFACTURING COMPANY, INC.

King Manufacturing Company, Inc., as we know it today, began as a very different business. Hugh William King started a woodworking business in 1946 making doors, windows, church pews and woodworkings as was needed by area residents. His business was a 16 feet by 30 feet building located on what is today Highway 145 North. The present business evolved in a unique way. Mr. King invented a safety device in 1948, called the King E-Z Safety Feed. It is used to prevent injuries while feeding lumber and other materials through a saw. When he found that he could not buy a certain part he just invented, patented and manufactured it himself. As the manufacturing business grew, the woodworking business was phased out. Mr. King moved from his first building to a foundry at the end of Fifth Street, then to the old Corinth Hotel building that once stood on Wick Street across from the Depot. The last move was made in 1956 to the present location on Fulton Drive in the Industrial Park.

Hugh William King (October 10, 1909-July 14, 1979)

On September 30, 1963, King Manufacturing Company, was incorporated as a metal fabricating business. In addition to still making the E-Z Safety Feed we also manufacture a wide variety of parts ranging from highly precision automatic machine products to large metal stampings on up to 200 ton punch presses. On July 14, 1979, Hugh King died suddenly from a heart attack. The business was then in the hands of his family members: his wife, Mary Lee Lipford King became CEO; son, Charles Wayne King, president; daughter, Dale King Cranford, secretary; and daughter, Sandra King Arnold, treasurer.

On November 1, 1984, Thomas E. and wife, Betty King Robertson (daughter of Hugh King) purchased the company from the other family members and they continue to operate it today along with Dale King Cranford. We are presently located in three buildings with a total of 140,000 square feet ranging from 100 to 200 employees. We are still a one family operation and strive to live by Mr. King's quote, "Growth comes from service. When we quote a job, we do it for that price and deliver it on time." That motto has worked for us in the past and continues to hold true today. We are proud of the legacy started by a man with determination and foresight and carried on by his family.

Hugh W. King shown here working on one of his inventions.

This is the newest addition to King Manufacturing Company, Inc. It was added in 2001 to the second existing building located across the street from the original building that was built in the Industrial Park in 1956.

Pictured above from left to right are: Thomas E. Robertson, owner and CEO; Frank Howell, president; and Brian Shirley, vice-president.

Plant #3 located on Harper Road in the Industrial Park. This is where the headsets for telephones are made for CORTELCO.

THE CORINTH ROBBERY
128 Years Ago
by Bill Wagoner - Courtesy of Rankin Printery

A little after noon on December 7, 1874, four grizzled hard cases took lunch at a boarding house in Corinth. The strangers had been dropping into town off and on for the past three weeks. They claimed to be drovers working cattle into Texas and were on their way home to Kentucky, they said.

The quartet rode fine animals and they wanted to rest over a spell before heading north. Considerable gold was exhibited by the men and they made trips to the Tishomingo Savings Bank on a pretense to exchange gold for currency. It would be easier to carry currency on the long trip, they said. No exchanges were ever made.

The men paid their fare at the boarding house and asked for grub put up for traveling. The sacks of food were laced to their saddles with strips of leather. Few people were made suspicious by their heavy armament: Colt's revolvers and heavy caliber Winchester rifles.

It was a Monday approaching 1:30 p.m. when they went to the bank again. There was a discussion and again no exchange of money. In reality they were casing the bank and made the last trip to relieve the town of some of its assets. At the bank three dismounted and one remained outside, he held the horses. The three approached bank president A.H. Taylor. One pulled the shades and locked the door. They demanded money and were refused by Taylor.

Here stories are conflicting. Taylor allegedly told T.R. Sanders later that he replied to them, "I'd rather be in hell with my back broke than to be in Corinth without these people's money." The leader, a slender man with sandy beard and blue eyes replied: "I can put you there damn

fast." Taylor said the man struck him across the eyebrow with a long barreled Colt revolver, the skin dropping down over the eye. Newspaper reports say Taylor was struck with a knife.

The horse holder sat cock-a-leg on the horse outside. He fired indiscriminately at anyone. After sending a ball past a man's ear he killed the dog beside him then went back to his cigar. Meanwhile, blood ran freely from the banker's wound while the trio inside cleaned out the safe. The booty was $5,000 in currency, $2,500 in diamonds and 12 gold watches. A black depositor was detained while the proceedings went on.

Within 15 minutes the job had been done. Folklore has it that one of the robbers held up a seamless sack and exclaimed to no one in particular: "Here goes your Corinth bank." Another story relates that a chicken's head was shot off by one of the robbers while at full gallop.

Isaac Bolton was on the street that day in Corinth and saw the robbers. The Bank was located north of the courthouse and out of the immediate business district of the day. A posse was summoned by the sheriff and pursuit taken in less than an hour. The robbers headed toward Tennessee and no apprehension took place.

Robbers Identified

Memphis authorities were contacted immediately and descriptions of the robbers given. It was soon determined that a band of robbers using the same methods had hit a bank in Russellville, Kentucky; St. Genevieve, Missouri; Columbia, Kentucky; and Scranton, Iowa.

Three cashiers had been killed for refusing to open safes.

It took little effort to surmise that the tall heavy set fellow with the red complexion was Cole Younger; the tall spare man with the Kentucky accent was Frank James and the lean one with the sandy beard was Jesse James (this is not conclusive and is only supposition based on knowledge of these men). The third one could have been one of several men. Some authorities contend that the robbery was done by Cole Younger and not Jesse James.

The robbers allegedly had spent some time in the Western part of McNairy County posing as cattle buyers. Frequent trips were made to Corinth and about the countryside as they cased out the escape routes. On the Locke farm they camped. A favorite past time was to ride around a large beech tree firing a circle of bullets into the tree. The rings remained well into the 20th century. This was an act learned while the Younger boys and the James brothers were associated with Wm. Quantrill and rode in his Missouri based Civil War guerrillas.

In Chester County, Tennessee four horsemen rode up to a small boy swinging on a gate. The leader, a man on a fine horse with a silver studded saddle, flipped the boy a gold dollar and asked him to open the gate. He identified himself as Jesse James. Henry Bell Lewis' family kept the gold dollar until 1952 when Henderson blew away.

The robbery took place in the brick building that later housed the Rankin Printery in Corinth. Several reenactments of the robbery have occurred down through the years, including the centennial celebration of the town in 1954.

RAY KING ROOFING

Five sons of John Harve King. Seated l-r: Albert Sidney Johnson King, grandfather of Jourdan Ray King; Charlie P. King, Benjamin Franklin King. Standing l-r: Jefferson Davis King and Edmond Beauregard King.

LESLEY'S CARPETS
2500 South Harper Road

Lesley's Carpets originated in 1992, formerly Bill's Carpets. Lesley Raines purchased it in February 1992. It was located in the Village Square Shopping Center on Highway 72 East in Corinth.

In 1995 Lesley purchased Chamblee's Discount Carpets from Marvin Chamblee at 2150 Billingsly Road at the intersection of Highway 72 and Harper Road.

In 1999 Lesley sold their location to the Spectra Corporation and built their new store at 2500 South Harper Road across from Wal-Mart. They moved into that location in May of 2000.

LOWE'S COMPANIES, INC.

In 1921, L.S. Lowe opened a hardware store in North Wilkesboro, North Carolina. He operated it until his death in 1940. The store was passed into the hands of his children, Ruth and Jim Lowe. Shortly thereafter, Ruth sold her interest to Jim and married H. Carl Buchan.

While Lowe and Buchan were serving in the military, an accident caused Buchan to return home. Lowe contacted Buchan and offered him an equal partnership if he would manage the hardware store while he was away.

Lowe returned home in 1946 and with Buchan developed the hardware store into a thriving business.

Buchan and Lowe developed the concept of purchasing large quantities of products from the manufacturer and selling directly to the customer, thus eliminating the wholesaler and lowering prices. This enabled them to open the first branch store in Sparta, North Carolina in 1949.

In 1952, Carl Buchan traded his interest in a car dealership and a cattle farm to Jim Lowe for the hardware business. Buchan opened his third location in Asheville, North Carolina the same year.

In 1956, Buchan introduced the Lowe's Companies Profit Sharing Plan and Trust allowing employees partial ownership in the company.

In 1960, Buchan unexpectedly died, however, the Profit Sharing Plan and Trust purchased the remainder of the company from his estate.

In 1961, Lowe's Companies, Inc. was created as a publicly traded company. The Profit Sharing Plan and Trust emerged into today's Employee Stock Ownership Plan (ESOP) which still allows employees to share in the growth and prosperity of the company. Even though Lowe's is a publicly traded company, our employees own about 25% of the company.

After becoming a publicly traded company in 1961, Lowe's Companies, Inc. has had 11 stock splits, with the most current being a 2 for 1 split in 2001.

We currently have 700 + stores in 42 states.

With 2001 sales of $22.1 billion, Lowe's Companies, Inc. is the world's second largest home improvement retailer. Headquartered in North Wilkesboro, North Carolina, Lowe's is the 14th largest retailer in the U.S. and the 30th largest retailer worldwide.

With a wide variety of services, more than 40,000 home improvement items and a Special Order program that features over 400,000 items, Lowe's Companies, Inc. employs 105,000+ employees to serve more than six million do-it-yourself retail and commercial business customers each week.

Lowe's Companies, Inc. is a Fortune 200 Company, has been listed three times as one of the "100 Best Companies to work for in America", also rated in *Fortune* magazine as "One of America's Most Admired Companies."

Lowe's Companies, Inc. sports sponsorships include, Lowe's Racing, Lowe's Motor Speedway, Carolina Panthers and Utah Jazz.

Lowe's of Corinth, Mississippi #091 opened on June 27, 1996 at 1800 South Parkway.

Many of our original employees that were hired here in 1996 have gone on to be promoted in other locations within our company. With 100+ employees currently, we still employ 24 originals at this location. Lowe's is a great place to work and is truly a place of excitement, opportunity and ownership.

Our company has enabled us to do a lot of things for our community, like participating in United Way, American Red Cross and Muscular Dystrophy (Shamrock) fundraising efforts. We are active in the community by sponsoring sports activities, offering kids clinic building workshops and the Lowe's Heroes Program that is focused on safety in and around the home.

We, here at Lowe's of Corinth #091, are proud to be part of this community.

Phillip Blanchard, store manager; Tom Roberts, assistant store manager; John South, assistant store manager; Eddie Ozbirn, assistant store manager; and Jeff Rinehart, assistant store manager.

Martha's Menu Restaurant
702 Cruise Street

Martha and Greg Cherem moved back to Corinth on February 2, 1992, and purchased the building at 612 Cruise Street and established "Martha's Menu" Restaurant. The business expanded quickly and a larger building was needed, so we bought the current location at 702 Cruise Street on October 25, 1999.

We completely renovated the downstairs, enlarged the kitchen and installed restrooms and closed the former restaurant at 612 Cruise. We moved March 20, 2000 with the help of some of our customers. Our future plans are to add apartments upstairs.

Our current building has a great deal of history. It was built in 1911 by Tom Holman. The location of our present kitchen was a livery stable for mules and horses.

Later Mr. Dolmer Barnhill Horn bought the building and added two more floors. He divided the upstairs into 51 rooms. They rented for 30 to 40 cents per night. The office and kitchen were the only heated rooms, so coal had to be hauled upstairs in buckets. The coal was piled on the street. The 51 rooms had only one bathroom, consisting of one toilet, one sink and tub. Mr. Horn also had a mule and wagon that went around selling ice for 10, 25 and 50 cents.

According to a newspaper article dated September 20, 1928, "What has been the past few years the "Horn Feed Store," on Cruise Street will change its name to the Corinth Feed Store, and D.B. Horn, the former owner, is taking a vacation from business activities. He sold his business this week to E.A. Farris, Aubrey Farris and Jim Hanley and the two latter will have charge of the business."

R.L. Smith bought the building in 1932. He renovated the downstairs and put in a general store. People came from surrounding counties and Tennessee. He sold tobacco products, snuff, Osh-Kosh overalls and Red Ball boots. In one part of the store he sold staple groceries (not needing refrigeration). On the walls hung mule collars and harnesses. He also sold all kinds of farming equipment. People would buy hoop cheese and crackers or a Moon Pie and RC Cola and eat by a big pot-belly stove in the back of the store. Mr. Smith added Purina Feeds to his stock. He redid the outside of the building in red and white checker board. At that time he owned a 1939 GMC truck and used it to deliver feed. The feed store was located in the second part of the building (the current location of the kitchen). You could purchase baby chickens and at one time he had two hogs.

The building was later inherited by his son, W.H. Smith. At his death it was inherited by Charles W. Smith and his sister, Carolyn Colton. They rented it to Tommy Curry to be used as a furniture store. When Mr. Curry moved out, the building was rented to Bro. Merle Spearman for a church. He stayed several years. Afterwards the building was a "This-n-That" shop.

Most of this was told to Martha Cherem in an interview with Mr. Charles "Bill" Smith. The upstairs has quite a history also. Several people have told of their family renting rooms and staying for awhile. I hope we can keep this building alive for a long time.

Special thanks to Bill for sharing this information with us.

MAGNOLIA REGIONAL HEALTH CENTER

Magnolia Hospital about 1966

Magnolia Hospital, founded in 1965, represents a commitment to providing the quality, quantity and diversity of health care services area residents want and need.

Magnolia Hospital began as a consolidation of the 68-bed Community Hospital and the 30-bed Corinth Hospital. It is jointly owned by the city of Corinth and Alcorn County.

The original facility housed space for 116 patient beds. Due to the community needs for additional services, the hospital was expanded in the 1980s so that now it provides for 164 patient beds. In addition, the Emergency Room and Labor & Delivery/Postpartum Unit were redesigned and expanded in 1994 to accommodate an increasing community population.

Renamed in the 1990s to Magnolia Regional Health Center, the new name reflects the many services offered to the community. With an ever-increasing medical staff, the community is served by many physicians with a wide range of practice specialties. Currently, we have 52 active physicians on staff. Some of the services include cardiology, internal medicine, gastroenterology, invasive cardiology, ophthalmology, orthopedic surgery, neurology, pediatrics, obstetrics and gynecology, oral and maxillofacial surgery, otolaryngology, urology and general surgery.

Late in the 1990s, the institution expanded to add additional ambulance services and greater outpatient services by relocating some of the programs to a large outpatient facility on Harper Road. Included in this facility are the Medistat Clinic which is open daily, a branch of EMS, Rehabilitative services, Home Health, Corporate Health and a community medical resource library.

Magnolia Regional Health Center is proud to be of service to the citizens of Corinth, Alcorn County and the surrounding area of northeast Mississippi.

Magnolia Regional Health Center 2001

Current Administrator

Dianne Boatman

Former Administrators

Gary J. Bland

Rhon Butterfield

Fletcher Crawford

Doug Garner

Claud L. Lollar

Verl Wood

Winston C. Whitfield

221

On Location, Inc.
Professional Photography Studio

1206 North Parkway became the home of On Location Photography March 1, 2001. We are proud of our spacious studio as well as our scenic gardens and babbling brook. We are excited about the future as we continue to expand our outdoor areas to better serve our clients. We invite everyone to come by and visit!

Our studio has been home to many. E.L. Long purchased the land in 1945. The home was never lived in by the Longs. Frank Berry purchased the unfinished home in 1949, completed the building and enjoyed raising his family here. In 1970 Michael Turner purchased the home and sold it to Samuel Lizer in 1972. William G. Hardin Jr. purchased the home in 1978 and sold it back to the Berry family in 1981. The home was sold to William Vanstory in 1986 by Frank Berry Jr. Michael Lovett, the youth director at Tate Baptist Church purchased the home in 1998. A move to the Memphis area meant selling the home. We have enjoyed hearing stories and "tales" of past activities that have taken place in the home and on the property.

Even though we are only five years young, we look forward to becoming part of Corinth's history. As you look through this book you will see how important the photographs are. They tell stories and record history. We hope that our portraits will be treasured by family members for many, many years.

Thank you for asking us to be a part of the history of Corinth.

Sue Elam

Owner/photographer

THE PEOPLES BANK AND TRUST COMPANY

The Peoples Bank and Trust Company opened its doors March 1, 1904 in Tupelo, Mississippi. There existed a need of farmers and businessmen alike for a bank that was intended to belong to "the people," a bank free from political and social alliances and one that truly served everyone in the small communities of Northeast Mississippi. Although banking has changed dramatically since that date, the directors, officers and staff have been dedicated to delivering products and services with a pride for excellence. Since that time, the bank only closed for a brief three-year period during the depression of the 1930s. It reopened its doors in 1933 and proceeded to repay every dollar to every depositor, an unheard of practice for that era.

The Corinth Branch pictured above was acquired in 1984. This bank was owned by local shareholders who began Alcorn Bank & Trust in 1977 in response to the strong economic growth in Alcorn and surrounding counties.

Today The Peoples Bank and Trust Company, with assets of $1.2 Billion operates forty-one branches throughout North Mississippi. It has been recognized repeatedly as one of America's safest banks based on its outstanding performance. The bank is dedicated to providing quality financial services to customers with personal attention to each, while providing optimum returns to shareholders.

Today, as in the past, The Peoples Bank and Trust Company is committed to remaining financially sound and to being good citizens in the communities in which we live and serve.

PAULA HUTCHENS

PHONE: (662) 287-4426
PHONE: (662) 287-4427
FAX: (662) 286-9561
TOLL FREE: 1-866-295-1905

the Rankin Printery

Printing & Office Products Since 1905

DUKE HUTCHENS

POST OFFICE BOX 386
603 FILLMORE STREET
CORINTH, MS 38835-0386
E-MAIL: rankin@avsia.com

The Rankin Printery was founded in May of 1905 in Corinth, Mississippi. With 97 years experience in the printing and office products trade, we can help make your office run smoothly. Rankin Printery has grown to be recognized in the printing industry as one of the premier printers in the North Mississippi area. As the ever increasing need for quality and reliability has evolved, Rankin has risen to meet the challenge to better serve our clientele and the community. Fast production time, competitive pricing, high quality and free delivery to your office are just a few of the reasons why you should give us a chance to earn your business.

Let us help you build your business! It's our job to keep your office—and your day running smoothly. Our high standards of excellence ensures that the finished job will reflect well on your company. Our friendly staff is here to help make your buying experience a rewarding and pleasant journey.

From typesetting through to delivery. Rankin personally manages your order. We treat every job like it is the most important job—after all that's what it is to you!

TULL BROTHER'S INC.

In 1962, Ray and Sam Tull started a partnership which is now known as Tull Brothers Incorporated. The two brothers made the decision to open this company after serving their apprenticeship as glaziers with Binswanger Glass Company of Memphis, which at that time served glass needs all over the Mid South. Among the jobs Ray and Sam performed as employees of Binswanger Glass, prior to starting their own business, were installations for First United Methodist Church, National Bank of Commerce branch office on Shiloh Road, the Wurlitzer building, Intex and other numerous storefront renovations. As you can see, Ray and Sam spent a good amount of time working in Corinth

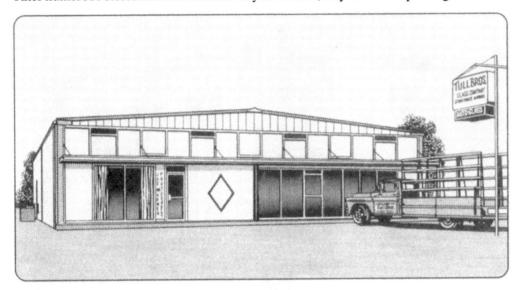

on various occasions for Binswanger Glass, therefore they came to the conclusion that Corinth would be a good place to start a glass business of their own. Another reason they chose Corinth is so that they could be closer to "home." Ray and Sam spent their childhood just north of Corinth between Selmer, Tennessee and Bethel Springs, Tennessee.

Tull Brothers was first located in the Moses Building at the corner of Highway 72 and Highway 45, which was eventually outgrown. Within a year they had rented a 40 x 60 metal building located at 205 Highway 45 South (Tate Street). The next year they purchased a piece of property located on Highway 72 East and built a 60 x 80 building. They rented a section of the building to Joe McKewen Studio. After a few years, Tull Brothers' business had expanded to the point that they needed the whole building. In the late 1970s, they bought more property and built an 80 x 80 addition onto the existing building.

Tull Brothers has consistently grown though the years. The business now occupies over 50,000 square feet of offices and warehouse in Corinth. There is also an office in Jackson, Tennessee, Tull Brothers of Tennessee Incorporated, that occupies 12,000 square feet. The company employs 43 full time employees in the Corinth office and 18 full time employees in the Jackson, Tennessee office. This equaling a combined payroll of over $2,100,000 annually.

In 1992 after 30 years as partners, Ray and Sam decided that Tull Brothers would be better served if one partner bought the other's stock. This decision was based on the fact that there was now another generation of Tulls. Sam had three sons and Ray had two. Ray and Sam concluded that Sam would buy Ray's part of the stock. This seemed to be in the best interest of all parties involved, due to the fact that all three of Sam's sons were located in Corinth, as well as the fact that Sam was the younger of the two brothers involved in the partnership.

There are now eight Tulls involved in the business. The officers of Tull Brothers Incorporated include: Sam F. Tull Sr., CEO; Fred L. Tull, president; Sam F. Tull Jr., vice president; and Michael K. Tull, vice president.

Thanks to the good relations between partners and all the family support along with dedicated employees, Tull Brothers Incorporated is currently recognized as one of the leading construction related companies in the Tri State Area.

SOUTHBANK

On May 4, 1990, a group of Alabama businessmen organized as SOUTHBank, a Federal Savings Bank, purchased substantially all of the assets and liabilities of Fidelity Federal Savings Bank, whose home office was located at 303 North Madison, Corinth, Mississippi. Other branches were also located in Iuka, Belmont, Booneville, Oxford and Jackson, Mississippi. Fidelity Federal was chartered in 1957 as a federal mutual savings and loan association, and operated as a traditional thrift institution until conversion to a stock form of organization in 1984. On April 6, 1989, Fidelity Federal was placed under the management of Resolution Trust Corporation, an agency organized by the federal government to bail out the troubled savings and loan industry during the late 1980s and early 1990s. The RTC placed the assets and liabilities of Fidelity Federal out for bids with qualified investors, and SOUTHBank was the successful bidder.

SOUTHBank initially operated from the principal office of Fidelity Federal at 303 North Madison Street, but in February 1991, purchased the vacated Post Office building in downtown Corinth at 515 Fillmore Street. The renovations of this historic building was completed in September 1993, and now is the home office for SOUTHBank. This building is an outstanding facility in the heart of downtown Corinth, in close proximity to the other financial institutions of this community.

Construction of this U.S. Post Office building began in 1912. It was used continuously by the U.S. Postal Service as the main post office for Corinth until 1987, when this historic building was vacated for a new modern handicapped equipped facility located five blocks east of the original location. Fire gutted the building in 1924, when downtown Corinth was almost leveled by fire. Initially, the lobby of this Post Office building had Paladian windows and cathedral ceilings. In 1929, the exterior door facing Fillmore Street was relocated to the center of that side of the building, and second floor offices were added inside the building, along with a marble staircase. Over the years, the Paladian windows and cathedral ceilings in the lobby were replaced with flat ceilings and wrought iron which remain part of the building today. This building was placed on the National Register of Historic Places on January 29, 1992.

Presently, SOUTHBank has offices in Mississippi (Corinth and Oxford), Arkansas (Blytheville, Manila and Osceola), Alabama (Huntsville and Madison), North Carolina (Cary, Durham and Raleigh), Tennessee (Selmer) and Florida (West Palm Beach). SOUTHBank is owned by Commonwealth Savingshares, a holding company, whose sole and only stockholder is Danny L. Wiginton, a Belmont, Mississippi native. The current staff at the Corinth branches include the following officers: Gerald McLemore, president of Mississippi and Tennessee Offices; Ron Herrington, city president; Margie Franks, senior vice president; Pat Jacobs, senior vice president/mortgage loans; Brian McCullen, senior vice president/lending; Peggy Gurley, vice president/teller supervisor; Sheron Tennyson, assistant vice president/branch manager; Jan Hurley, vice president/marketing; and the following employees: Donna Taylor, Pam Scott, Peggy Moore, Judy Wilbanks, Lee Ann Howie, Sandy Murray, Leigh Ann Hammock, Ronda Cagle, Dawn Smith, Teresa Benick, Sherry Doyle and Leslie Ann Wright.

The Board of Directors for SOUTHBank consist of Danny L. Wiginton, Chairman of the Board; William C. Hussey; Lon Taylor III; Gerald R. McLemore; Harry Brock III; Dr. Marshall Schreeder and Christopher Wiginton. Advisory Board Members for the Corinth area at the present are: William C. Hussey; Lon Taylor III; Gerald R. McLemore; William T. Dalton Jr.; Dr. Bernard Shipp and Jeff Gardner.

At the end of 2001, SOUTHBank in Corinth had deposits in excess of $77 million with offices at 515 Fillmore Street and 2222 South Harper Road. SOUTHBank's success is directly attributable to its slogan, "Distinctively Personalized Banking ... With A Touch of Southern Hospitality".

First Baptist Church Of Corinth

First Baptist Church has served as an influence for good and a beacon of Christian hope with almost 150 years of ministry, supporting missions endeavors not only in Corinth, but also around the world. Many members have entered church-related vocations, and others have engaged in mission projects worldwide. Local churches started as missions of FBC are Kendrick, South Corinth and Tate.

First Baptist Church was organized in the summer of 1855, when Rev. Mark Perrin Lowrey, founder of Blue Mountain College, and about a dozen other believers met under an oak tree at the northeast corner of Franklin and Childs Streets. On September 19, 1856, the newly formed church joined the old Chickasaw Baptist Association. The Rev. Lowrey served as the first pastor of the 19-member congregation.

"The meeting under the oak."

In 1857, Reverend A.H. Booth became pastor. He and a few other members purchased a lot located on the southeast corner of Franklin and Childs Streets where the first house of worship was erected. This one-room frame church was destroyed by Federal troops during the Civil War. The 60 members were without a meeting place for 12 years. A $6,000 petition for retribution was submitted to the U.S. Congress on August 13, 1894, and on March 4, 1915, Congress appropriated $800 to satisfy the petition.

The first meeting house - 1857-1862.

During 1874 a single story one-room white frame building with bell tower and steeple was constructed on two lots on the southeast corner of Fillmore and Childs. The large bell in the bell tower also hung in the first church. The building faced Fillmore Street and contained two large doors–one for the men and the other for the women. During 1887 controversies over prohibition caused a church split and the Second Baptist Church was formed. Those favoring local option continued to worship at this building. A reconciliation of the two churches was achieved in October 1889 and the rejoined congregation met together again in this building. The church was known as the Corinth Missionary Baptist Church.

Building two, Fillmore and Childs - 1874-1894.

During 1894 the frame building was sold and torn down so that a larger brick building could be built on the same site at Fillmore and Childs. During the period of construction, worship services were on the second floor of Ray's Shoe Store, a building located at the southeast corner of Waldron and Franklin Streets. The new building was occupied in mid-1895 and consisted of an auditorium and several Sunday School rooms. Some of this structure is still visible at this site. During the building dedication service the church voted to send the bell that hung in the previous two churches to the Rev. E.Z. Simmons, a missionary to China, who was from Kossuth Baptist Church.

Building three, Fillmore and Childs - 1895-1951.

On February 26, 1942, a building fund was initiated by an anonymous gift of $1250. The W.T. Adams property at Main and Fillmore was purchased to become the site for the fourth building. The remainder of that half block was also acquired to provide ample space for the structure. On February 16, 1950, a large crowd gathered for the groundbreaking ceremony, and on July 3, 1951, the cornerstone for the facility was laid. The congregation occupied the new sanctuary on August 5, 1951, with Rev. D.L. Hill, pastor and Dr. T.W. Young, former pastor, conducting the first service. Upon completion the total cost of the building and furnishings was approximately $500,000. Rev. Hill retired in 1964 after 19 years as pastor. He was succeeded by Rev. P.A. "Red" Michael who served until 1969. The church membership had grown to over 1200 by 1970, when Rev. John M. Causey began the first of his 15 years of dedicated service. During this time the church's position in the community continued to grow and solidify. The educational space, church offices and library were extensively remodeled in 1976.

Building four, Main and Fillmore - 1951.

"The Rubel House"

In 1904 Mr. Abe Rubel, a prominent merchant in the city, built this stately home facing Jackson Street, on the block bordered by Jackson, Main, Polk and Second Streets. In 1970 the church purchased the home from the Rubel family. It has been used for many wedding receptions and parties and is currently being used by the youth organizations of the church.

In 1986 Rev. Dennis H. Smith became the pastor of FBC. "Brother Dennis," as he is known by most, guided the church through a major renovation in 1988. The sanctuary was updated with new carpet and colors, a remodeled choir and pulpit area, and 10 beautiful stained glass windows that were designed specifically for FBC. Each window intertwines key images to portray a portion of Biblical history, beginning with Creation in the first window and ending with the resurrected Christ in the 10th. The beginning of the 21st century saw FBC involved in adding space for preschool and children's areas, a large multi-function fellowship hall, new office and library space, as well as remodeling some existing areas to accommodate a growing congregation. First Baptist Church is a place where people find guidance for daily living; a place of life and activity, where there is a sense of family and belonging; a place to discover a living, loving God.

2002 addition

The mission of First Baptist Church is to bring people to a rich and meaningful relationship with God through Jesus Christ and to be an extension of His love in ministry to others.

FIRST UNITED METHODIST CHURCH

DEDICATION
**To Our Members ... Past, Present and Future;
In memory of those who once labored ...
In appreciation to those who now serve ...
In anticipation of an even greater future ...
And to the Glory of our God.**

History of the Church

Methodists in this section of North Mississippi were on the Tishomingo Circuit from 1837 until 1857 Corinth was made a Station Church and in that year the church members bought, for one thousand dollars, a lot on which to build their first house of worship. The lot comprised the north half of city block 125, located east of Court Square. This lot was the site of Methodist churches for 102 years - from 1858-1960.

Three church buildings were erected on it. The first one, completed in 1858, was a two story frame structure. During the war it was used as a stable and was greatly abused.

This building was destroyed by fire in 1868. Immediately another frame church was erected and was used until 1891, at which time the first brick building was contracted for. It was completed in 1892.

In 1895 this first brick building was remodeled. A large wing was added on the south, memorial windows were placed on three sides of the building, a pipe organ was purchased and a furnace was installed. This church was ready for occupancy in 1906.

During the ministry of the Reverend W.C. Newman, a movement was made to start raising funds for a more adequate building. Funds for this purpose came in slowly and it was about 20 years before dreams of a spacious edifice materialized. While the Reverend J.T. Humphries was pastor (1952-1959) plans were set up, a large portion of money needed was raised and work was begun on the present church in 1958. This magnificent structure is located on the northwest corner of Fillmore and Bunch streets and was completed in 1960. The Reverend Roy Grissom was the minister at that time.

HISTORY OF SALEM CHRISTIAN CHURCH
(1873 to 1998)

In 1871 and 1872 Bro. Mancel Kendrick of the Kendrick Community held a series of meetings each year in a brush arbor located approximately 300 yards north of the church's present location. These meetings resulted in several conversions so that by 1873 Bro. Mancel decided the Christian membership was enough to establish a church, to be known as Salem Christian Church.

In 1873 Bro. Kendrick proposed that if the Christian members of the community built a church, he would preach free of charge. This task was undertaken by T.F. Hinton and F. Hullgan who cut poplar logs and then had to wait for Clear Creek to overflow allowing the logs to float down to Bob Morrison's water sawmill. The church was built facing south 100 yards north of the present church on land donated by T.F. Hinton. The land was also to be used as a cemetery.

After the church was built, Bro. Kendrick traveled by horseback on Saturday afternoon from Kendrick to the Salem Community and held services Saturday night, Sunday and Sunday night, then returning home Monday morning. The first elders of the church were R.F. Bob Morrison, I.J. Nelms and T.F.T. Jobe. The first deacons were T.F. Hinton and F. Hullgan. For a number of years the church building was also used as a schoolhouse for the Salem community.

In 1926, the present church was built, using the poplar wood from the old church as weatherboarding. George Anderson, John T. Martin and John H. Hinton were on the building committee. The first minister to preach in the present building was Bro. S.P. Copeland.

Down through the years, the present building has been bricked and expanded with Sunday school rooms, restrooms, fellowship hall and other improvements added.

The first church group of Salem Christian Church, 1888

Salem Christian Church before remodeling – 1958

Rev. S.P. Copeland, preached the first sermon in the present church building – Salem Christian Church, 1923-1931

Salem Christian Church. L-R: John H. Hinton, Dale Darwin, R.T. Darwin, May 1957

Side View of Salem Christian – 1958

Lady church group at Salem Christian Church, 1961

Salem Christian Church

Historical background by: Elder John H. Hinton. Revised and updated 1998 by: Denis Dutka, Minister, Salem Christian Church.

WALDRON STREET CHRISTIAN CHURCH

The Waldron Street Christian Church building is located in downtown Corinth at the corner of Taylor and Waldron Streets. The property on which the present building stands was deeded to the church on July 1, 1858.

The first church erected on this property was a two-story brick building. When Corinth was occupied by the Union troops, during the War Between the States and after the fall of Shiloh, the original building was destroyed. Union solders took bricks from this building and used them to build ovens in which to bake bread for the Union Army.

In 1868-1870 the second building was built with money given by Mrs. Nancy H. Kendrick and friends from Jefferson, Kentucky. This structure was a white one-story frame building. The heat was provided by two large wood stoves and light was by kerosene lamps. There was a belfry and on Sunday the chimes of the bell issued a call to worship. With the passage of time, signs of deterioration began to show on the little white church. Plans were started in 1911 for a new building. The federal government issued $800.00 to compensate for the building that had been destroyed during the war. With that money and numerous donations, the present building (shown below) was built. It is a two-story brick structure and was completed at the end of 1912.

By 1952 the congregation had grown until additional space was badly needed. The work on a fellowship hall, additional classrooms and the redecoration of the building was started. This project was completed in August of 1953. Below is a picture inside the sanctuary as it looked in December 1974.

In 1988 the congregation purchased the McPeter's building directly behind our building. It has been a much needed addition adding extra classrooms, a kitchen

Waldron Street Christian Church, 1974

area and a fellowship room as well as a small chapel. We feel that the Lord has indeed blessed Waldron Street Christian Church in allowing the same gospel to be preached in the same location since 1858. In an ever changing world, we should take comfort in the knowledge that our Lord and His gospel remain the same - yesterday, today and forever.

ALCORN COUNTY

OUR RESOURCES ARE YOUR OPPORTUNITIES

Alcorn County is an active industrial county with plentiful resources and opportunities. Among the industries in Alcorn County are some of the nation's finest: Kimberly Clark, Caterpillar, Quebecor World Color, just to name a few. Our city and county schools rank among the nation's best and Northeast Mississippi Community College is superior in two-year colleges. Alcorn County is blessed with four-lane highway systems, a state of the art airport, recreation, health care facilities and rich in Civil War history. Alcorn County is truly a great place to live!

Front row, l-r: Travis Drewery-Supervisor District 5; Ely Mitchell-Supervisor District 3; Lamar Fields-Supervisor District 1. Back row, l-r: Bobby Mitchell-Supervisor District 4; Wendell Trapp-Board Attorney; Danny Crotts-Supervisor District 2; Larry McCollum-Chancery Clerk; Paul Rhodes-Purchase Clerk.

The Historic Curlee House Museum

Top photo: "The Veranda House" during the Civil War. Above: The Historic Curlee House Museum, circa 1990.

Listed on the National Register of Historic Places, the Curlee House is a significant example of domestic Greek Revival architecture (rivaling any in the state, according to the Mississippi Department of Archives and History). Featuring 16-foot ceilings with elaborate plaster moldings, the home was completed in the spring of 1857 for a cost of less than $10,000. It was built by surveyor Hamilton Mask, who had cofounded the town of Corinth a few years earlier with his brother-in-law, Houston Mitchell.

In March of 1860, Mr. Mask sold the property to Burnett Wilkerson, who, in October of that same year, sold it to William Simongton. Mr. Simongton owned it up until and throughout the Civil War, although the Simongton family evacuated the home early in the war and never returned to live there.

During the Civil War, the house served as headquarters for both Confederate and Union generals. Order #8, authorizing the attack which became the Battle of Shiloh, was drafted in the bedchamber of Confederate General Braxton Bragg. And from the Confederate evacuation of Corinth until late 1864, Union generals, including Henry W. Halleck and Granville Dodge, resided there.

In the fall of 1875, the Curlee House—which had been temporarily occupied by the Corinth Female College—was purchased for $2,000 by William Payton Curlee and his wife, Mary Boone Curlee. Mrs. Curlee, a descendant of Daniel Boone, was the daughter of Francis Marion Boone, the founder of Booneville, and the granddaughter of Ruben Boone, recorded as the first white settler of the Mississippi Territory.

After Mr. Curlee's death in the yellow fever epidemic of 1878, Mrs. Curlee sold the property for $2,200 to the Leroy Montgomery Huggins family. Leroy Huggins and his wife raised a large family in the home, constructing two rear additions around 1885 to accommodate the growing household. (Today, the original structure, which was known as "the Veranda House", remains unaltered. The rear additions, including a kitchen adjoining the back porch, were remodeled in the 1930s.)

It was also during the Huggins' ownership that the block the Curlee House occupied was subdivided. Leander Huggins, Leroy's brother, built a home on the northeast corner facing Jackson Street, two rooms of which remain in existence as a guest cottage. The Huggins brothers had moved to Corinth from Gravel Hill, Tennessee, and operated a grocery store in what is now the four hundred block of Cruise Street. The northwest corner of the Huggins' property was sold and the house constructed there, known as the Young-Ray home, stood until the 1960s.

In 1921, Shelby Hammond Curlee, oldest son of William Payton and Mary Boone Curlee—and founder of the Curlee Clothing Company, located in St. Louis, Missouri—bought the house back from the Huggins heirs for his Corinth home. His sister, Eleanor Katherine Curlee, resided in the house until her death in December of 1944. At that time, the property was given to the city of Corinth to be used as a museum or library, and today, the home serves as "The Historic Curlee House Museum."

THE NORTHEAST MISSISSIPPI MUSEUM

The Northeast Mississippi Museum has been an icon of local history for the Corinth and Alcorn County, Mississippi, area ever since it was founded in 1979. The Museum's first location was in the back of the Curlee House. Exhibits were mounted in vacant buildings throughout the downtown area, and natural history classes were offered to the young folks. Several interesting fund raisers, the Chinese New Year Dinner and American Indian Pow Wows, became trademark favorites for the community.

The Museum grew in leaps and bounds, but unfortunately in the early 1980s, it outgrew the budget and had to go dormant for a couple of years. The Museum's saving grace was community volunteers who decided not to give up hope. They worked to get the Museum reborn and found a permanent home in 1986, courtesy of the city of Corinth, at 204 East Fourth Street in the former

Boy Scout Hut/National Guard Building on the edge of Corinth's Historic District. Here it has been housed for the last 16 years and has hosted thousands of visitors and accumulated a treasury of local collections and artifacts. However, the Museum will once again be on the move in the near future. The Museum's Board of Trustees, working with the Alcorn County Board of Supervisors, came up with a plan to relocate the Museum in Corinth's historic Depot building. With the help of community minded citizens, a grant was awarded to restore the Depot and make it an appropriate place for a museum. The move should take place sometime in 2004.

At its present location, the Museum welcomes guests year around and seven days a week (except for Mondays during the winter). Hours are Monday through Saturday - 10:00 a.m. until 5:00 p.m. and Sundays from 11:00 a.m. until 5:00 p.m. Between six to eight thousand visitors view the Museum annually, and its target audience is local citizens, school groups, tourists, and anyone else who expresses interest. At times the rugged outer facade deceives out-of-town guests, but as they browse our collection and are given special attention by the docents, they are pleasantly surprised and eager to learn more about Corinth's fascinating history.

Moreover, the Museum offers many interesting collections ranging from Paleozoic fossils, American Civil War artifacts, to household objects. Not only does the Museum own a magnitude of items, but it also has on its premises a

magnificent photograph collection and research library. While most of the Museum's collection is on permanent display (due to lack of proper storage), the staff strives to have rotating exhibits on a quarterly basis. In such instances, items of local interest are showcased as well as some special traveling exhibits when space permits.

The Museum looks forward to a bright future. With the community's support, it can continue to grow and add to its collection. As a growing organization, the Museum is always looking for volunteer help or new members. Being a volunteer is easy. One may come by the Museum and provide information about what days or occasions that would be most convenient. Obtaining a membership to the Museum is also a simple process, and there are several benefits of being a member: a quarterly newsletter, special invitation to exhibits and events; free admission to the Museum; and a chance to serve on the Museum Board. For more information on volunteering or becoming a member, write to or call us at Post Office Box 993, Corinth, Mississippi 38835 or 662-287-3120. We are always open to questions, suggestions and exhibit ideas.

CORINTH ROTARY CLUB
Founded, November 23, 1936

Front row, l-r: Richard Milam, Jenny Hibbard and Hull Davis. Standing, l-r: Billy Davis and Dick Wood.

A desire to help his fellow man led Paul Harris, a Chicago attorney, to found the first Rotary Club in 1905. Since that time, Rotary International has spread to the far corners of the globe and serves mankind in 160 countries. This work is done through the hands of some 1.2 million business and professional, men and women working through some 30,000 Rotary Clubs.

In 1936, the Rotary Club of Corinth was founded. Three Rotarians: Erst Long Sr. of Ripley; Dr. J.P. Kirkland and Arthur Rogers of New Albany; came to Corinth in April of that year to meet with local businessmen at the Waldron Hotel. The mission was to share the vision of Rotary. While progress was made, more work was to be done before the Corinth Club would be founded. In the fall of 1936, with more determination than ever, Erst Long Sr. and Arthur Rogers returned to Corinth and with the help of Jameson C. Jones, Paul T. Jones and Hugh E. Ray, the wheels to form the Rotary Club of Corinth were put in motion. Over the next couple of months, with the help of other like-minded individuals, much was done to share the vision and finally on November 23, 1936, the Corinth Rotary Club was organized.

The Corinth Rotary Club has thrived through the years and as of this date, we have 90 members. The commitment to our community is evident by the projects and causes we have undertaken through the years. Today our primary focus is on education. To this end, we honor students and teachers with our Star Student and Star Teacher programs. Leadership for the future is critical and to help young people prepare, we sponsor Interact Clubs, the purpose of which is to help demonstrate the importance of commitment to community at an early age. To further prepare young people for the future, we also send numerous high school students each year to leadership camps, the purpose of which is to teach them how to solve common problems through cooperative efforts.

As the Corinth Club closes in on 75 years of service to our community, we are alive and well and still driven by the same vision that founded the club so many years ago, "Service Above Self."

Carl and Lucy Hearn with first child Annie Mae. Circa 1925.

Charley Moore and wife, Tishie Erma Bennett Moore and daughter Lorena. 1905.

Clarence Eugene Lamberth rode into Corinth to serve on jury duty probably late 1920s.
Mr. Lamberth always took his Civic duties seriously.

Seated: James Abner and Arminta Rebecca Waldrup Smith and

L-R: Maude, Della (Maddox) Maness, Clyde

The Corinth House located on Fillmore St. close to the railroad tracks.

L-R: Mary Lee, John Bynum, Clara Sue, Mattie and Reuben.

Front row from left: James Franklin Miller, Clarence G. Miller and Elizabeth (Rogers) Miller. Back row from left: Virgie G. Miller, Maud (Miller) Rushing, Russel B. Miller and Virnell (Miller) Dickson.

, Floyd and Augustus Maness. Circa 1910.

Haley Johnson Faircloth and his wife, Mary Elizabeth Jones Faircloth of Kossuth, MS. He served in the civil War and was a Justice of the Peace in Alcorn County.

Printed in the USA
CPSIA information can be obtained
at www.ICGtesting.com
JSHW060051150824
68134JS00032B/2709